The Future of Europe

The "Future of Europe" series consists of monographs and edited volumes analyzing topical European issues from the perspective of each EU Member State and neighboring countries, helping to understand the different aspects of the future of the European project. It aims at combining two goals: high quality research-based and/or informed contributions stimulating pan-European national and European, academic and non-academic discussions around the "Future of Europe", involving preferably leading academic scholars and practitioners.

The series provides an authoritative library on the Future of the European Union ranging, amongst others, from general conceptual texts to assessments of countries, regions, key institutions and actors, policies and policy processes. Books in the series represent up-to-date sought-after sources of information and analysis reflecting the most up-to-date research and assessments of aspects related to the Future of Europe. Particular attention is paid to accessibility and clear presentation for a wide audience of students, practitioners and interested general readers.

Aleksandar Stojkov • Thierry Warin
Editors

Western Balkans and the Future of Europe

Between an Enlargement and a Commitment Fatigue

Springer

Editors
Aleksandar Stojkov
Iustinianus Primus Faculty of Law
Saints Cyril and Methodius University
Skopje, North Macedonia

Thierry Warin
International Business
HEC Montréal
Montréal, QC, Canada

ISSN 2731-3379 ISSN 2731-3387 (electronic)
The Future of Europe
ISBN 978-3-031-86464-3 ISBN 978-3-031-86465-0 (eBook)
https://doi.org/10.1007/978-3-031-86465-0

This Springer imprint is published by the registered company Springer Nature Switzerland AG
The registered company address is: Gewerbestrasse 11, 6330 Cham, Switzerland

Preface

Have the present boundaries of the European Union (EU) fulfilled the dream of a united Europe? Or maybe previous European generations have dreamed too big? Was Brexit compelling proof that European integration has gone too far? Will the EU be able to simultaneously strengthen cohesion among its member states (deepening of the European integration) and embrace new member states (EU enlargement)? In the case of future enlargement(s), how long will the Western Balkan countries stay in the European waiting room? What will be the implications for the Eastern Partnership countries such as Moldova, Ukraine, and Georgia?

The EU enlargement policy toward the Western Balkans has been characterized by a complex interplay of strategic aspirations and internal hesitations. Initially, the EU's commitment to integrating the Western Balkans was underscored by the 2003 Thessaloniki Summit, which affirmed the region's European perspective. However, over time, this commitment has encountered challenges, leading to what scholars term "enlargement fatigue." This phenomenon reflects a waning enthusiasm within the EU for further expansion, influenced by concerns over institutional capacity, economic disparities, and political readiness of prospective members.

The protracted accession processes have, in turn, fostered "commitment fatigue" among Western Balkan countries. This reciprocal disillusionment has impeded the momentum of reforms essential for EU integration. The EU's ambivalence has been further complicated by internal crises and shifting geopolitical dynamics, notably the 2022 Russian invasion of Ukraine, which has refocused the EU's enlargement priorities. This shift has, at times, relegated the Western Balkans' accession prospects, exacerbating regional frustrations.

Recent analyses suggest that the EU's enlargement strategy requires recalibration to address both internal skepticism and external challenges. Enhancing the credibility of the enlargement process is pivotal, necessitating consistent political engagement and tangible progress benchmarks. Moreover, the EU must reconcile its strategic interests with the aspirations of Western Balkan nations, ensuring that enlargement fatigue does not undermine the transformative potential of EU integration for the region.

The future of Europe depends not only on internal European affairs but also on the potential to embrace new members into the European family of nations. The discussions on the future of Europe and the EU would be incomplete without exploring the relations between the EU and the Western Balkans. The EU is an immediate neighbor and the most significant geopolitical and economic force in the Western Balkans. It has been considered a "democratizing agent" with strong transformative power for the new member states. Many painful structural and institutional reforms in the EU candidate and potential candidate countries have been pursued "for the sake of" their EU accession.

One of the main questions tackled in this edited volume is whether the EU enlargement fatigue has resulted in broken promises leading to a "commitment fatigue" among the EU candidate countries from the Western Balkans. On one hand, there is a pro-enlargement camp among European leaders underscoring that "each enlargement made the Union better, made a Union of ideas, solidarity, innovation, and diversity. We know that the EU is important to the Western Balkans, and the Balkans are equally important to the EU. Together we can dream and build our European future for a better world." (Speech by President Charles Michel at the Bled Strategic Forum, August 28th, 2023). However, the enthusiasm of Brussels' high-level public officials does not seem to be entirely shared by large numbers of European citizens as well as national leaders. One of the most vocal representatives of this wait-and-see camp is the French President, Emmanuel Macron, who announced that future enlargement must wait for internal reforms within the Union. "The risk is to think we can enlarge without reform. I can testify that it is hard enough for Europe to advance on sensitive topics with 27 members. With 32 or 35 members, it won't be any easier" (Macron: EU Should Consider "Multi-Speed Europe" to Cope with Enlargement, 2023).

In contrast to the cautious perspectives within the EU regarding future enlargements, citizens of EU candidate countries remain strongly supportive of EU accession. However, a widespread misconception persists, viewing the EU primarily as a vast Automated Teller Machine. Expecting unconditional European solidarity and the provision of generous structural and cohesion funds solely for the purpose of an enlarged Europe represents a misguided approach. This perspective fails to acknowledge the complex and multifaceted nature of European integration, where mutual obligations and reciprocal benefits are paramount. The assumption that mere expansion justifies substantial financial support disregards the necessity for candidate countries to demonstrate adherence to the principles and values of the European Union, including the rule of law, democratic governance, and economic stability.

Furthermore, the expectation of unconditional aid does not consider the economic realities and constraints faced by the current member states. The allocation of structural and cohesion funds is a strategic process aimed at fostering regional development, reducing disparities, and enhancing overall cohesion within the Union. Therefore, any approach that overlooks these fundamental objectives risks undermining the long-term sustainability and solidarity of the European project.

In light of these considerations, it is imperative to adopt a more nuanced approach that balances the aspirations of enlargement with the practicalities of equitable resource distribution and mutual commitment to the Union's core values. This would ensure that the process of integration is both fair and beneficial for all parties involved, fostering a stronger and more cohesive Europe. The future of the European

Union will depend on its ability to manage internal cohesion while extending its reach to new member states, ensuring that the ideals of unity and diversity are upheld.

The main arguments for an enlarged Europe revolve around economic growth, political stability, and the promotion of shared values. Economically, enlargement can lead to the creation of a larger single market, which fosters increased trade, investment, and economic opportunities for both existing and new member states. The integration of new members can stimulate economic growth by allowing for the free movement of goods, services, capital, and labor, thus enhancing productivity and innovation across the continent. By incorporating emerging economies from Central and Eastern Europe, the EU can also address regional disparities, promote balanced development, and harness the potential of a diverse and dynamic workforce.

Politically, enlargement strengthens the EU's position as a global actor by extending its influence and fostering stability in neighboring regions. The accession process requires candidate countries to implement significant reforms, which often lead to the consolidation of democratic institutions, the rule of law, and respect for human rights. This transformative power of EU membership can help stabilize post-socialist and transitional countries, reducing the risk of conflict and fostering regional peace and security. Furthermore, a larger EU can more effectively address global challenges such as climate change, migration, and geopolitical tensions, presenting a unified front in international diplomacy.

Another compelling argument for enlargement is the reinforcement of the EU's founding values of freedom, democracy, equality, and solidarity. By embracing new members, the EU demonstrates its commitment to these principles, promoting them beyond its current borders. Enlargement also enhances cultural diversity within the Union, enriching the social fabric of Europe and fostering mutual understanding and cooperation among different cultures and societies. This cultural exchange can lead to a more inclusive and cohesive European identity, where shared values and common goals unite a diverse population.

Moreover, the integration of new member states can lead to greater solidarity and cohesion within the EU. By providing structural and cohesion funds to less developed regions, the EU can reduce economic disparities and promote social inclusion, ensuring that the benefits of integration are widely shared. This not only strengthens the internal cohesion of the Union but also builds solidarity among member states and fosters a sense of collective responsibility and mutual support.

Skopje, North Macedonia
Montréal, QC, Canada
December 6, 2024

Aleksandar Stojkov
Thierry Warin

Contents

United Europe: Boundaries and Challenges 1
Aleksandar Stojkov and Thierry Warin

The European Integration and Western Balkans: What Now? 75
Ivica Bocevski

The European Integration of the Western Balkans and Its Impact on the EU as a Geopolitical Entity 83
Aleksandar Spasov

Stagnation in Western Balkans' Security Regionalization: The Problem of Competing Regional Cultures of Anarchy 99
Ana Bojinović Fenko and Marko Kovačević

The Future Relations Between the European Union and Albania 117
Erjon Luçi

The Future Relations Between the European Union and Kosovo 131
Gazmend Qorraj

Bosnia and Herzegovina on the Way to the European Union: Past, Present, and Future 141
Snježana Brkić

The Path of North Macedonia to the European Union Is the Only Way Forward 165
Fatmir Besimi

Montenegro 2.0: The European Vision of Montenegro 179
Ivan Jovetić, Ivana Vojinović, Milica Vukotić, and Sandra Tinaj

The Future of Serbia's Relations with the European Union 199
Stevan Gajić

European Integration Prospects for Western Balkans 213
Thierry Warin and Aleksandar Stojkov

List of Figures

United Europe: Boundaries and Challenges

Fig. 1 The geographical position of the Western Balkans and Eastern Partnership countries in Europe. 4
Fig. 2 Negative consequences of the integration of CEE countries into the EU. Q: Regarding the consequences of the integration of Central and Eastern European countries into the EU, would you agree or disagree with the following statements? Base: All respondents, % EU27. 7
Fig. 3 Positive consequences of the integration of CEE countries into the EU. 7
Fig. 4 Percentage of respondents in favour of a new EU enlargement? (January/February 2023, Eurobarometer). 20
Fig. 5 Initial conditions vs. growth performance in Europe (1990–2023, 1990 = 100). Notes: [1] GDP per capita is expressed in Purchasing Power Parity terms and in 2017 constant international dollars. [2] Due to missing observations, the initial data only for Bosnia and Herzegovina refers to 1996, for Serbia 1997, and for Kosovo 2000. 28
Fig. 6 Income convergence in Europe (2010–2023). *Country's GDP* per capita *as a share of GDP* per capita *of EU-27 (current prices, in purchasing power parity terms)*. Note: [1] Gross domestic product per capita, current prices, Purchasing power parity; international dollars. [2] The values for 2023 are estimates. 30
Fig. 7 Unconditional convergence within Europe. Note: The implied rate of convergence is calculated by using the formula ($\lambda_u = -\log(1 + \beta_u)/n$), using statistically significant coefficients (β_u) of cross-country regressions on annual data for the entire period (n).. 36
Fig. 8 Institutional gaps in emerging Europe (1996–2021, EU14 average = 100). Note: EU 14 refers to the unweighted average for EU-15 minus the United Kingdom. 39
Fig. 9 An illustration of a three-region partition. 44

Fig. 10 Pruned regression trees of growth drivers in new EU member states (1990–2007). 45
Fig. 11 Pruned regression trees of growth drivers in new EU member states (2008–2022). 46
Fig. 12 Pruned regression trees of growth drivers in EU candidate countries (1990–2007). 47
Fig. 13 Pruned regression trees of growth drivers in EU candidate countries (2008–2022). 48
Fig. 14 Trade integration of Western Balkans with EU-27 (2013–2022). Share of international trade of WB6 with EU-27 in their total international trade (2013–2022, in percent). 54
Fig. 15 Trade balances of WB6 countries with respect to EU-27, in million EUR (2013–2022). 55
Fig. 16 Share of EU direct investment positions in total inward FDI stocks of Western Balkan countries (2013–2022, in percent). Notes: [1] Aggregate data for EU investments in Kosovo has a lot of missing observations. [2] EU direct investment positions, flows, and income, by countries (BPM6) [bop_fdi6_geo__custom_11943169]. 59

The Future Relations Betweenthe European Union and Albania

Fig. 1 Albania's exports to the European Union, 2010–2022 (In billions of euros and in percent of total exports).. 123
Fig. 2 Albania's exports to Central European Free Trade Agreement (CEFTA) countries, 2010–2022 (In percent of country's GDP). . . . 123
Fig. 3 Albania's exports to Central European Free Trade Agreement (CEFTA) countries, 2010–2022 (In billions of euros and in percent of total exports). 124

Bosnia and Herzegovina on the Way to the European Union: Past, Present, and Future

Fig. 1 Bosnia and Herzegovina's exports to and imports from the EU (2003–2022). 144
Fig. 2 FDI stock in BiH, by main investor countries (in million EUR, 1994–2022). 145
Fig. 3 The financial package of growth plan for Western Balkans for Bosnia and Herzegovina. 147
Fig. 4 The EC's assessment of preparedness for Western Balkans (2019). 152
Fig. 5 GDP per capita of EU27 and EU potential candidate and candidate countries in 2023 (purchasing power parity; 2017 international dollar). 159

Montenegro 2.0: The European Vision of Montenegro

Fig. 1 Overview of political stability in Montenegro, 2006–2021. 183
Fig. 2 Alternative models of environmental economic development in Montenegro. 190

European Integration Prospects for Western Balkans

Fig. 1 Illustration of a Three-Dimensional Development Model for an EU candidate country. 217

List of Tables

Stagnation in Western Balkans' Security Regionalization: The Problem of Competing Regional Cultures of Anarchy

Table 1 Conceptualization of levels of regionness 103
Table 2 Regional cultures of anarchy in level of regionness 106
Table 3 Elements of cohesiveness in Western Balkans' security regionalization 110

The Future Relations Between the European Union and Kosovo

Table 1 Absorption Capacity of Kosovo............................ 137
Table 2 EU institutional and absorption capacity challenges............ 138

Bosnia and Herzegovina on the Way to the European Union: Past, Present, and Future

Table 1 EU shares in exports and imports of BiH (in selected years) 144
Table 2 The status of WB Countries on their way to the EU 153
Table 3 From application until achieving EU candidate status........... 154
Table 4 Levels of assessment for BiH (2023)........................ 157

The Path of North Macedonia to the European Union Is the Only Way Forward

Table 1 Volume indices of GDP per capita (EU27 = 100) 167

Montenegro 2.0: The European Vision of Montenegro

Table 1 Ranking of political stability in Montenegro.................. 183
Table 2 Economic Freedom in Montenegro by Heritage Foundation...... 184

Contributors

Fatmir Besimi South East European University, Tetovo, North Macedonia

Ivica Bocevski Center for Research and Policy Making, Skopje, North Macedonia

Snježana Brkić School of Economics and Business, University of Sarajevo, Sarajevo, Bosnia and Herzegovina

Ana Bojinović Fenko Faculty of Social Sciences, University of Ljubljana, Ljubljana, Slovenia

Stevan Gajić Institute of European Studies, Belgrade, Serbia

Ivan Jovetić University of Donja Gorica, Podgorica, Montenegro

Marko Kovačević Faculty of Political Science, University of Belgrade, Belgrade, Serbia

Erjon Luçi Independent Researcher, Tirana, Albania

Gazmend Qorraj University of Prishtina, Prishtina, Kosovo

Uninettuno University, Rome, Italy

Aleksandar Spasov Legal Theory and Legal Philosophy at Ss. Cyril and Methodius University, Iustinianus Primus Faculty of Law, Skopje, North Macedonia

Aleksandar Stojkov Ss. Cyril and Methodius University in Skopje, Skopje, North Macedonia

Sandra Tinaj University of Donja Gorica, Podgorica, Montenegro

Ivana Vojinović University of Donja Gorica, Podgorica, Montenegro

Milica Vukotić University of Donja Gorica, Podgorica, Montenegro

Thierry Warin HEC Montréal, Montréal, QC, Canada

List of Abbreviations

CBAM	Carbon Border Adjustment Mechanism
CEE	Central and Eastern Europe
CEFTA	Central European Free Trade Agreement
CRM	Common Regional Market
EGD	European Green Deal
EU	European Union
FDI	Foreign Direct Investment
GAWB	Green Agenda for the Western Balkans
IEP	Institutional Evaluation Program
IMF	International Monetary Fund
IoT	Internet of Things
ML	Machine Learning
MLAs	Machine Learning Algorithms
PISA	Programme for International Student Assessment
RSS	Residual Sum of Squares
SAA	Stabilization and Association Agreement
SEE	South East Europe
SEE	South Eastern Europe
SMEs	Small and Medium-size Enterprises
STEM	Science, Technology, Engineering, and Mathematics
TEU	Treaty on European Union
WB6	Six countries from Western Balkans
WGI	Worldwide Governance Indicators

United Europe: Boundaries and Challenges

Aleksandar Stojkov and Thierry Warin

Abstract

This work investigates the rapidly changing dynamics of European integration, highlighting some difficulties and opportunities linked to the process of EU enlargement. It serves to provide the historical background that has led to the development of the EU, focusing on major events such as the 2004–2007 Eastern enlargement, and explores the interplay among geography, politics, and economics in shaping the boundaries of the EU. It examines the twin challenges of enlargement fatigue in EU member states and commitment fatigue in candidate countries, specifically in the Western Balkans, while assessing critically economic implications of income convergence and growth dynamics, along with governance gaps in the post-communist economies. It also assesses the transformative power of European integration to deliver stability, prosperity, and cohesion to candidate countries while emphasizing that there are persistent and emerging challenges, such as democratic backsliding and geopolitical tensions. Guided by innovative methodological approaches, the paper concludes with policy recommendations for navigating future enlargement while safeguarding and reinforcing the foundational principles of solidarity and democracy that underpin the EU.

A. Stojkov (✉)
Ss. Cyril and Methodius University in Skopje, Skopje, North Macedonia
e-mail: a.stojkov@pf.ukim.edu.mk

T. Warin (✉)
HEC Montréal, Montréal, QC, Canada
e-mail: thierry.warin@hec.ca

A. Stojkov, T. Warin (eds.), *Western Balkans and the Future of Europe*, The Future of Europe, https://doi.org/10.1007/978-3-031-86465-0_1

Keywords
EU enlargement process · Western Balkans · Enlargement fatigue · Commitment fatigue · Euroscepticism · Geopolitical dynamics

1 Introduction

1.1 Overview of European Integration

The European integration process is a monumental achievement for post-war Europe, a region historically characterized by conflict and shifting borders. This study examines how the European Union (EU) continues to serve as a formula for peace and economic prosperity, despite challenges such as Brexit, enlargement fatigue, and geopolitical instability. We start exploring how European integration has evolved, focusing on its geographical and political dimensions, with particular attention to post-socialist economies in Central, Eastern, and Southeastern Europe.

Contemplating the future of Europe inevitably requires a definition of Europe, as there are numerous interpretations of what Europe is. Despite the fall of the Berlin Wall in 1989, conservative political analysts still use the terms "old" and "new" Europe, by describing post-socialist economies in Central and Eastern Europe as "new" or "emerging" Europe and parts of Western Europe as "old" Europe. We follow the pro-integration rhetoric in the spirit of the powerful message delivered by the U.S. President Barack Obama that "[…] there is no old Europe or new Europe. There is only a united Europe" (Der Spiegel 2009).

The vision of European integration started with the establishment of the European Community for Coal and Steel as well as the European Economic Community and Euratom Treaties, signed in 1951 and 1957, respectively. Another important milestone in the history of European integration was the establishment of the European Union by the Treaty of Maastricht (or Treaty on European Union—TEU) coming into force on 1 November 1993. The EU has emerged not only as an economic union, but also as a democratic multitiered political system promoting common values in a large part of the European continent. The EU itself aims to promote fundamental European values, such as freedom, democracy, and equality; respect for human dignity, human rights, and the rule of law; and solidarity and protection for all (Smith 2019).

Despite the strong blow by Brexit, the EU continues to be *the* formula for economic prosperity and peace. "The European project is a unique experiment that's proven to be the most successful guarantor of peace, stability, economic growth, and social prosperity on the Continent" ("It's Time to Get European Enlargement Back on Track" 2022). The integration of diverse economies and cultures under a common political framework has not been without challenges, but it remains a testament to the power of collaborative governance and shared aspirations (Börzel and Risse 2009).

1.2 Objectives and Scope

This volume aims to address two key objectives: (1) to evaluate whether the geographical and political boundaries of a united Europe have been established for the foreseeable future, and (2) to investigate the prospects of a "European" future for the six countries of the Western Balkans, comprising five EU candidate countries—Albania, Bosnia and Herzegovina, Montenegro, North Macedonia, and Serbia—and one potential candidate, Kosovo. These considerations are equally pertinent to the Eastern European Partner countries, including Armenia, Azerbaijan, Belarus, Georgia, the Republic of Moldova, and Ukraine. Ultimately, the decisions of European leaders and the broader European community will determine whether these regions become integral participants in the European integration process or remain at its margins (Papadimitriou and Phinnemore 2008).

The EU's enlargement strategy has often been characterized by a complex interplay of geopolitical, economic, and cultural factors. As Sedelmeier (2014) notes, the EU's ability to export stability and democracy hinges on its attractiveness and the credibility of its commitment to enlargement. However, the process is fraught with challenges, including institutional readiness, economic disparities, and political will both within the EU and in candidate countries (Grabbe 2006).

Box 1 Description of the key terms for non-European readers

Europe is a diverse continent, consisting of 50 countries and cultures, 225 indigenous languages spoken, and 747 million inhabitants spanning over a territory of 10.2 million km^2 (3,938,000 square miles (Encyclopaedia Britannica 2023)). From a geographical perspective, Europe consists of Northern, Western, Eastern, and Southern Europe.[1] Geographically speaking, the eastern part of the Russian Federation is also part of Europe.

The *European Union* (hereinafter: EU or EU-27) is a political and economic union established with the aim of promoting peace, stability, and economic cooperation among its member countries. EU-27 covers an area of over 4.23 million km^2 (1.6 million sq mi) and is home of estimated 448 million

(continued)

[1] The list of geographic regions presents the composition of geographical regions used by the Statistics Division of the United Nations: Northern Europe (Åland Islands, Denmark, Estonia, Faroe Islands, Finland, Guernsey, Iceland, Ireland, Isle of Man, Jersey, Latvia, Lithuania, Norway, Svalbard and Jan Mayen Islands, Sweden, United Kingdom of Great Britain, and Northern Ireland), Western Europe (Austria, Belgium, France, Germany, Liechtenstein, Luxembourg, Monaco, Netherlands, and Switzerland), Eastern Europe (Belarus, Bulgaria, Czechia, Hungary, Poland, Republic of Moldova, Romania, Russian Federation, Slovakia, and Ukraine), and Southern Europe (Albania, Andorra, Bosnia and Herzegovina, Croatia, Gibraltar, Greece, Holy See, Italy, Malta, Montenegro, North Macedonia, Portugal, San Marino, Serbia, Slovenia, and Spain).

inhabitants (source: Eurostat). It consists of 27 member states (often referred to as EU-27): Austria, Belgium, Bulgaria, Croatia, Republic of Cyprus, Czech Republic, Denmark, Estonia, Finland, France, Germany, Greece, Hungary, Ireland, Italy, Latvia, Lithuania, Luxembourg, Malta, Netherlands, Poland, Portugal, Romania, Slovakia, Slovenia, Spain, and Sweden. The EU is one of the most ambitious undertakings of political, economic, institutional, and cultural integration on the European continent.

The Western Balkans (commonly abbreviated as WB6) refers to a region in Southeastern Europe comprising six former socialist countries: Albania, Bosnia and Herzegovina, Kosovo, Montenegro, North Macedonia, and Serbia (Fig. 1). This geopolitically important region is known for its diverse cultures and very complex history with military conflicts. Most importantly, except for Kosovo, the other Western Balkan countries are EU candidate countries at a different level of approximation of their institutional and administrative capacities with the EU-27. Kosovo has the status of a potential candidate country.

The historical context of European integration is crucial for understanding contemporary debates. Initiated in the aftermath of World War II, the integration process was motivated by a collective determination to prevent future conflicts and promote economic cooperation. The establishment of the European Coal and Steel Community in 1951, followed by subsequent treaties, provided the cornerstone for what would eventually evolve into a distinctive political and economic union. This

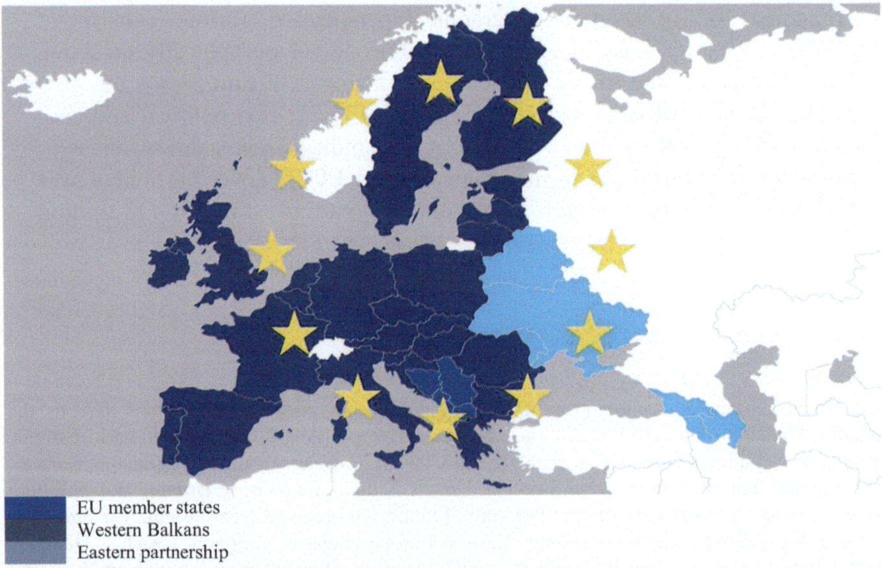

Fig. 1 The geographical position of the Western Balkans and Eastern Partnership countries in Europe. Source: Warsaw Institute (2020)

history serves not merely as a backdrop but as evidence of the EU's ability to convert historical rivalries into productive partnerships (Moravcsik 1998).

Furthermore, the concept of European identity has developed in parallel with the integration process. The EU has actively worked to cultivate a shared sense of identity among its diverse member states by implementing policies that encourage cultural exchange, multilingualism, and the promotion of common values. This effort is exemplified by initiatives such as the Erasmus programme, which has enabled educational exchanges for millions of students across Europe. The success of such programmes highlights the critical role of fostering a sense of belonging and unity among Europeans, a fundamental factor for ensuring the EU's long-term sustainability (Shore 2000).

2 Historical Context

2.1 Evolution of European Integration

The successful European integration project initiated by six Western European countries motivated other countries to join the family of European nations. Until the end of 2023, seven enlargement rounds have taken place. The first round of enlargement welcomed Denmark, the United Kingdom, and Ireland in 1973. "Without Greece, there can be no European Union, as it is the cradle of democracy", highlighted the former German President Christian Wulff (Ellis 2023). Greece joined the European Community in 1981. The country has been eligible to join the Union since its military regime was overthrown and democracy was restored in 1974.

Five years later, Portugal and Spain joined the EU in 1986. The fourth EU enlargement embraced Austria, Finland, and Sweden in 1995. It is fair to underscore that the cross-country income differences as well as cultural differences between the existing and the new EU member states were not large.

The EU's enlargement towards Central and Eastern Europe was the largest expansion so far. In May 2004, the EU welcomed ten new member states: the Czech Republic, Estonia, Hungary, Latvia, Lithuania, Poland, Slovakia, Slovenia as well as two small island nations: Cyprus and Malta. From today's perspective, this marked the peak of Euro-enthusiasm on the continent.

The first enlargement round of 1973 was significant not only because of the increase in member states but also due to the geopolitical and economic implications. Denmark, the United Kingdom, and Ireland's accession represented a strategic expansion of the EU's influence in Northern Europe. The United Kingdom's membership, in particular, brought considerable economic weight and a global perspective to the Union, although it would later become a source of contention leading to Brexit in 2016 (Young 2017).

Greece's accession to the EU in 1981 symbolized a reaffirmation of the Union's commitment to democracy and political stability. This milestone followed the collapse of the military junta and the restoration of democratic governance in Greece, reflecting the EU's broader mission of advancing democratic principles and fostering stability across Europe (Featherstone 2005). Concurrently, Greece underwent significant economic transformations, motivated by the necessity of aligning with EU standards and regulations.

The 1986 enlargement, which included Spain and Portugal, further extended the EU's reach into Southern Europe. Both countries had recently emerged from authoritarian regimes and were in the process of consolidating their democratic institutions. Their accession underscored the EU's role in supporting political transitions and economic modernization. The integration of these nations helped to stabilize the Iberian Peninsula and contributed to regional development through structural funds and cohesion policies (Moravcsik and Vachudova 2003).

The 1995 enlargement brought Austria, Finland, and Sweden into the EU, marking the Union's expansion into the Nordic region. These countries were characterized by their advanced economies and strong welfare systems. Their accession highlighted the attractiveness of the EU as a club of prosperous democracies and reinforced the Union's commitment to social welfare and economic stability (Baldwin et al. 1997).

The most significant enlargement occurred in 2004, with ten countries joining the EU. This round of enlargement was driven by the desire to stabilize post-communist countries and integrate them into the European economic and political framework. The accession of these Central and Eastern European countries was seen as a step towards overcoming the historical divisions of the Cold War and promoting stability and prosperity in the region (Schimmelfennig 2001). This enlargement round also posed substantial challenges, including the need for extensive institutional reforms and the harmonization of economic policies to meet EU standards.

2.2 The 2004–2007 Eastern Enlargement

Eurobarometer (2009) conducted a study of public opinion in the EU, 20 years after the fall of the iron curtain. The main negative consequences of the 2004–2007 enlargements underscored by at least half or more of the EU respondents were: (1) made the enlarged EU more difficult to manage (66%); (2) contributed to job losses in their country (56%); (3) caused problems because of the divergent cultural traditions of the new Member States (54%); and (4) led to an increased feeling of insecurity (50%) in the European Union as a whole (Fig. 2). In a nutshell, the difficult management of the Union, endangered national economic interests, and significant cultural differences were cited as the most important obstacles in the EU integration process.

Figure 3 highlights respondents' perspectives on the perceived negative consequences of integrating Central and Eastern European countries into the EU. A majority believe that integration has made the EU more difficult to manage (65%) and contributed to job losses in their own countries (56%). Furthermore, over half (54%) perceive cultural differences among EU countries as a source of problems. Opinions are more divided regarding feelings of insecurity, with 50% agreeing and

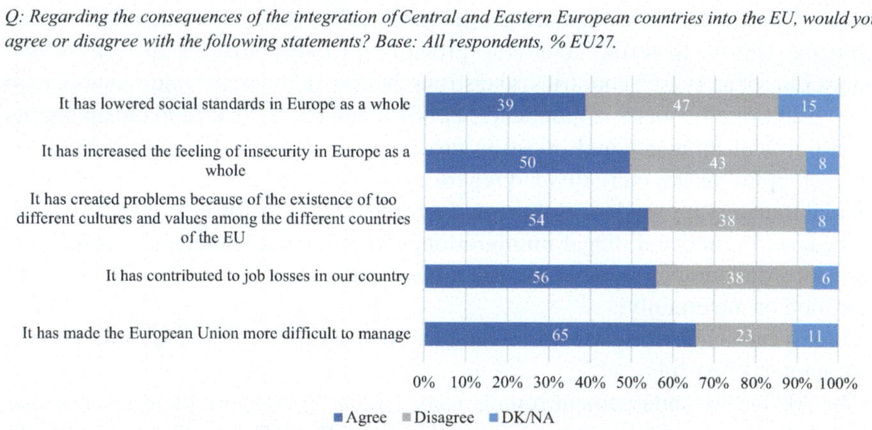

Fig. 2 Negative consequences of the integration of CEE countries into the EU. Q: Regarding the consequences of the integration of Central and Eastern European countries into the EU, would you agree or disagree with the following statements? Base: All respondents, % EU27. Source: Eurobarometer (2009, p. 30)

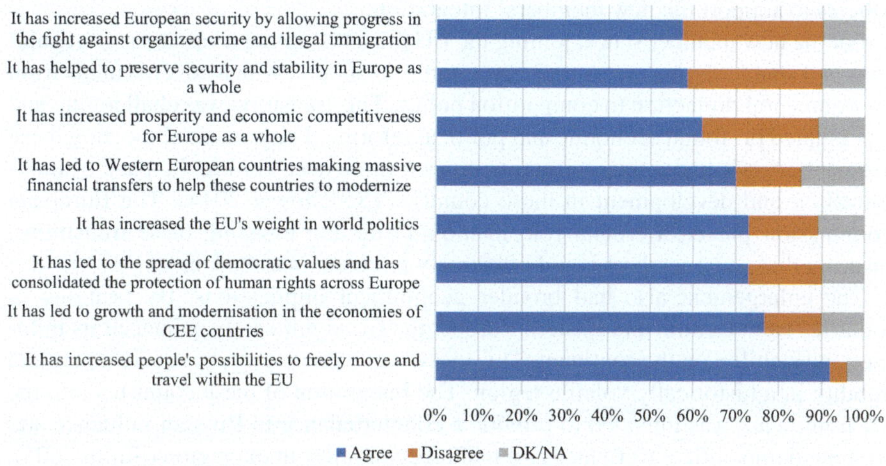

Fig. 3 Positive consequences of the integration of CEE countries into the EU. Source: Eurobarometer (2009, p. 20)

43% disagreeing, and on whether integration has lowered social standards, with 39% agreeing and 47% disagreeing. These findings suggest that while concerns about the challenges and impacts of integration are prevalent, there is no dominant consensus on most issues, reflecting a nuanced mix of apprehension and acceptance among respondents.

Figure 3 illustrates public opinion on the EU's impact across various domains. The data reveals that a majority of respondents perceive the EU as having a positive influence, particularly in expanding opportunities for free movement and travel within the Union, fostering economic growth and modernization in Central and Eastern European (CEE) countries, and strengthening democratic values and human rights. Additionally, many respondents acknowledge the EU's role in enhancing its global political influence and boosting prosperity and economic competitiveness. However, opinions are more divided regarding the EU's effectiveness in facilitating financial transfers for modernization and increasing security through efforts to combat organized crime and illegal immigration. Overall, these findings suggest a predominantly favourable view of the EU's contributions, albeit with some areas of contention or uncertainty.

Three years later, Bulgaria and Romania were admitted in the Union. Finally, Croatia joined first July 2013.

The 2004–2007 enlargement rounds were critical in bridging the economic and political divide that had persisted since the Cold War. This expansion not only extended the EU's geographical boundaries but also its cultural and economic diversity. The integration of these new member states required significant adjustments both within the EU and the acceding countries. The EU had to ensure that its institutions and policies could accommodate the increased diversity and complexity. This was a period marked by substantial reforms in the EU's structural and cohesion policies to support the new members' integration.

For the new member states, joining the EU meant adopting a vast array of regulations and standards, known as the acquis communautaire, which covered areas from environmental protection to competition policy. This transition was challenging and necessitated profound economic and political reforms. The process of meeting these stringent criteria had a transformative impact, often accelerating the pace of modernization and development in these countries (Sedelmeier 2014). The European Commission played a crucial role in monitoring and assisting these transitions, ensuring that new members could effectively integrate into the Union.

The enlargement also had broader geopolitical implications. By bringing in countries from Central and Eastern Europe, the EU significantly enhanced its influence and stability on the continent. This move was seen as a way to secure peace and stability in a historically volatile region. The integration of these countries into the EU framework was intended to provide a counterbalance to Russian influence and promote democratic governance and market economies in the region (Smith 2003). However, the rapid pace of enlargement also led to debates within the EU about the Union's capacity to absorb new members and the impact on its governance and coherence.

2.3 From Thessaloniki (2003) to Bratislava (2023): Paroles, Paroles?

Although not a widely cited document, one of the first important signals to the region of Western Balkans was sent by the EU via the *Final Declaration from*

Zagreb Summit on November 24, 2000 (Vinci 2000). The EU leadership highlighted that:

> The way is now open to all the countries of the region to move closer to the European Union as part of the stabilisation and association process. The European Union confirms its wish to contribute to the consolidation of democracy and to give its resolute support to the process of reconciliation and cooperation between the countries concerned. It reaffirms the European perspective of the countries participating in the stabilisation and association process and their status as potential candidates for membership in accordance with the Feira conclusions.[2]

The EU was much more explicit in terms of the enlargement perspective for Western Balkans on the EU-Western Balkans Summit that took place in Thessaloniki (Greece) on 21 June 2003. The heads of states or governments of EU member states, the President of the European Commission, and the President of the European Parliament expressed once again their unequivocal support to the European perspective of the Western Balkan countries. The intentions were distilled in *The Thessaloniki Agenda for the Western Balkans: Moving towards European Integration*, which was considered a new important step in the favoured relationship between the EU and the Western Balkans.

In the meantime, there has been some success in terms of speeding up income convergence and obtaining candidate statuses. But also, the past two decades witnessed enlargement fatigue and focus on internal problems in the Union and commitment fatigue in Western Balkans, as evidenced by the low pace of reforms and sometimes democratic backsliding. The Western Balkans is sitting in the European waiting room (Belloni and Brunazzo 2017) for a foreseeable future and without a clear timetable. The last EU enlargement was more than a decade ago, when Croatia joined the Union in July 2013.

The war in Ukraine reignited the debate on further EU enlargements. Amid the enthusiasm for enlargement, President of the European Council, Charles Michel, boldly emphasized during his speech at the Bled Strategic Forum in Slovenia on 28th August 2023:

To be stronger and safer, the EU needs to reinforce our bonds and become more powerful. That's why it is now time to tackle the challenge of enlargement. Both for us in the EU and for our future member states. Yes, I believe this is how we should now call the countries with confirmed EU perspective, future member states. [...] To be credible, I believe we must talk about timing and homework. And I have a proposal. As we prepare the EU's next strategic agenda, we must set ourselves a clear goal. I believe we must be ready—on both sides—to enlarge by 2030. (Speech by President Charles Michel at the Bled Strategic Forum, 2023).

One day later, a radically different (corrective) tone and message was sent by the cabinet of the President of the European Commission, Ursula von der Leyen. The Commission's deputy spokesperson at a daily press briefing promptly clarified: "We

---

[2] https://www.consilium.europa.eu/uedocs/cms_data/docs/pressdata/en/er/declang4.doc.html

are not focused on a date but focused on working very closely with candidate countries to get ready for joining the European Union" (Politico 2021).

This cacophony of European leadership's intentions appears to provide further evidence in favour of the so-called Kissinger issue, when the former U.S. Secretary of State Henry Kissinger wittily concluded: "Who do I call if I want to call Europe?" (Economides 2020).

The Thessaloniki Agenda was a significant milestone in the EU's relationship with the Western Balkans, signalling a clear and committed path towards EU membership for these countries. However, the subsequent two decades have been characterized by fluctuating levels of engagement and commitment from both sides. On one hand, the EU has faced internal challenges, including the Eurozone crisis, Brexit, and rising populism, which have diverted attention from enlargement (Taggart and Szczerbiak 2013). On the other hand, the Western Balkan countries have struggled with political instability, corruption, and weak governance, which have slowed their progress towards meeting EU accession criteria (Elbasani 2013).

Moreover, the geopolitical landscape has also influenced the dynamics of EU enlargement. The increasing influence of remote external players, such as Russia and China, in the Western Balkans has added a layer of complexity to the EU's enlargement strategy. Both countries have sought to expand their influence in the region through economic investments and political alliances, challenging the EU's position and complicating the accession process (Bechev 2011). This has made the EU's commitment to the region more critical, as failure to integrate these countries could lead to a shift in their strategic orientation away from the EU.

Despite these challenges, there are reasons for cautious optimism. The renewed focus on enlargement articulated by leaders like Charles Michel suggests that the EU recognizes the strategic importance of the Western Balkans. The proposed 2030 enlargement target, if pursued with genuine commitment and adequate support, could provide a much-needed impetus for reforms in the candidate countries. Ensuring a clear, credible, and consistent pathway to membership will be crucial for maintaining the momentum of the European integration process and addressing the scepticism and disillusionment that have built up over the years (Papadimitriou and Phinnemore 2004).

3 Challenges in European Enlargement

According to O'Brennan (2014), the EU's engagement with the Western Balkans was inconsistent and unsatisfactory. He argues that the enlargement process was on "life support", folllowing a "flat line" trajectory of "frozen negotiating chapters" and characterized by a mutural mistrust. Despite the promise made by the European Commission on the Thessaloniki Summit in 2003, the EU integration of Western Balkans remains increasingly uncertain. As shown in past national elections in the EU, the primary cause for this appears to be the "enlargement fatigue" among its member states.

But this enlargement fatigue might have led to a "commitment fatigue" of the nations on the other side of the European Union border, as evidenced by the reduced enthusiasm for reforms and rising Euro scepticism among the candidate countries. In this edited volume, we present a political economy-based framework, combined with a data science-based empirical approach, followed by a series of case studies about the Western Balkan countries and their "commitment fatigue". We study the rising scepticism and persistent doubt over the process' conclusion. Finally, we offer our assessment of whether the future of Europe could hold another wave of enlargement.

3.1 The Enlargement Fatigue

The concept of enlargement fatigue, drawn from various bodies of literature, suggests that Europeans are somewhat exhausted by the continuous expansion of the EU. This sentiment has significant implications for the pace and magnitude of future expansions. Understanding this issue is crucial, especially in light of recent events such as Brexit and the Russian invasion of Ukraine. These instances have not only reshaped the geopolitical landscape of Europe but also influenced the attitudes and perspectives of Europeans towards enlargement, highlighting the need for extensive study.

Brexit, in particular, has served as a stark reminder of the complexities and potential drawbacks of European integration. The decision of the United Kingdom to leave the EU has raised questions about the sustainability and desirability of further expansion. It has exposed underlying issues related to national sovereignty, economic disparities, and cultural differences within the Union. The Brexit vote was, in many ways, a reaction against perceived overreach by EU institutions and a desire to reclaim national control over various policy areas. This sentiment resonates with enlargement fatigue, as it underscores a growing wariness among EU citizens about the continuous addition of new member states and the potential challenges that come with it.

Similarly, the Russian invasion of Ukraine has highlighted the strategic importance of EU enlargement, particularly in Eastern Europe. While the conflict has galvanized support for the integration of countries like Ukraine, Moldova, and Georgia into the EU as a means of enhancing regional stability and security, it has also exposed the limits of European solidarity and the practical challenges of incorporating new members during times of geopolitical tension. The war has emphasized the need for a careful and strategic approach to enlargement, balancing the aspirations of candidate countries with the readiness and capacity of the EU to absorb new members.

Another clear indication of enlargement fatigue is the moderate support for enlargement among EU citizens, as measured by occasional Eurobarometer surveys. The Eurobarometer (2023) indicates that 53% of respondents were in favour of future enlargement, with considerable cross-country deviation. For example, support for enlargement is relatively low in Austria (29%), reflecting concerns about economic competition and cultural integration, while it is significantly higher in Latvia (77%), possibly due to historical and geopolitical factors that make EU expansion appear more beneficial.

This variation in public opinion highlights the complex and multifaceted nature of enlargement fatigue. It is influenced by a range of factors, including economic conditions, political climate, historical experiences, and geographic proximity to candidate countries. For instance, countries in Eastern Europe, which are closer to potential new members and may share historical and cultural ties, tend to be more supportive of enlargement. In contrast, countries in Western Europe, which are further removed from these regions and may face more immediate economic and social challenges, are more likely to exhibit fatigue.

Enlargement fatigue is a significant phenomenon that reflects broader concerns and challenges associated with the continuous expansion of the EU. While events like Brexit and the Russian invasion of Ukraine have underscored the strategic importance of enlargement, they have also highlighted the complexities and potential drawbacks of this process. Understanding and addressing enlargement fatigue is crucial for the future of the EU, as it navigates the delicate balance between integrating new members and maintaining cohesion and stability within the existing Union. The Eurobarometer surveys provide valuable insights into public sentiment, revealing a need for careful consideration of the diverse perspectives and concerns of EU citizens as the Union contemplates future expansions.

There are numerous reasons behind the enlargement fatigue.

Feelings of Insecurity Concerns about immigration are also regularly cited as a significant reason against future EU enlargements. Immigration can bring about cultural and social changes within communities, leading to feelings of insecurity among some EU citizens who may perceive these changes as threatening to their cultural identity or way of life. This apprehension is often rooted in the fear of cultural dilution and the potential for social discord as new populations integrate into existing communities.

However, this argument is not entirely valid, as it overlooks the common values and shared views that exist between the citizens of the EU and those in candidate and potential candidate countries. Many of these countries, particularly in the Western Balkans, have a deep historical and cultural connection with Europe. Their populations often embrace democratic principles, human rights, and the rule of law, aligning closely with the core values of the EU. Moreover, these societies have demonstrated a strong desire to integrate with the EU, recognizing the benefits of being part of a larger, more stable political and economic union.

Further, empirical evidence suggests that immigration can have positive economic and social effects. Immigrants can fill labour market gaps, contribute to economic growth, and bring cultural diversity that enriches societies. Studies have shown that immigrants often complement the native workforce rather than compete with it, helping to address demographic challenges such as ageing populations and labour shortages in certain sectors (Dustmann and Frattini 2014). The influx of skilled workers and entrepreneurs from candidate countries can also stimulate innovation and economic dynamism within the EU.

Additionally, the EU's framework for managing immigration and integration is designed to mitigate potential negative impacts and promote social cohesion. Policies aimed at supporting integration, combating discrimination, and fostering intercultural dialogue help ensure that immigration contributes positively to society. The European Commission's Action Plan on Integration and Inclusion (2021–2027) emphasizes the importance of inclusive education, employment, health, and housing policies to facilitate the successful integration of immigrants.

The perception of immigration as a threat is often amplified by political rhetoric and media portrayal rather than grounded in objective reality. Public discourse can sometimes exaggerate the challenges associated with immigration, overlooking the substantial benefits and the capacity of societies to adapt and thrive in diverse environments. It is essential for policymakers and leaders to address these fears through informed dialogue, emphasizing the shared values and mutual benefits of enlargement and integration.

While concerns about immigration are frequently mentioned as reasons against EU enlargement, these concerns are often based on misconceptions and fears rather than facts. The common values shared by EU citizens and those in candidate countries, combined with the potential economic and social benefits of immigration, present a compelling case for continued enlargement. Effective integration policies and positive public discourse can help mitigate fears and highlight the advantages of a diverse and inclusive European Union.

The feeling of insecurity is also one of the driving forces of *rising populism*. The anti-immigration sentiment often intersects with populism, as populist leaders exploit fears about immigration to mobilize support among their followers. Populist rhetoric frequently frames immigrants as a threat to national identity, security, and economic stability, creating an "us versus them" narrative that resonates with segments of the population feeling left behind by globalization and rapid social change. This approach leverages the identity threat argument, which posits that immigration challenges the cultural and social fabric of the nation, leading to a perceived erosion of traditional values and norms.

Right-wing political parties are particularly adept at capitalizing on these concerns. They often highlight issues related to globalization and multiculturalism, portraying them as sources of economic insecurity and cultural dilution. The narrative that immigrants take jobs away from native citizens, strain public services, and undermine social cohesion is a common theme in their political messaging. This strategy not only garners support from those directly affected by economic changes but also appeals to broader segments of society who fear the loss of cultural homogeneity.

The identity threat argument is powerful because it taps into deep-seated anxieties about change and the unknown. When societies face rapid demographic shifts due to immigration, individuals who identify strongly with their national or cultural heritage may feel that their way of life is under siege. This sentiment can be exacerbated by media coverage that sensationalizes crimes or conflicts involving immigrants, reinforcing negative stereotypes and fears.

However, this argument overlooks the potential for positive outcomes from immigration and the capacity of societies to adapt to diversity. Research indicates that multiculturalism can enrich societies by bringing different perspectives, skills, and innovations (Alesina and La Ferrara 2005). Countries with diverse populations often experience dynamic cultural and economic environments that drive growth and creativity. Moreover, policies that promote integration and inclusivity can help mitigate the challenges of immigration, fostering social cohesion and mutual respect among different cultural groups.

It is also important to recognize that the concerns about immigration are not uniformly distributed across all segments of society. Younger generations, urban populations, and those with higher levels of education tend to be more open to diversity and immigration. These groups are more likely to see the benefits of a multicultural society and are less susceptible to populist and right-wing narratives. Therefore, addressing the identity threat argument requires a multifaceted approach that includes promoting positive narratives about immigration, implementing effective integration policies, and fostering inclusive communities.

Ultimately, the anti-immigration sentiment driven by populism and right-wing politics reflects broader anxieties about change and identity in an interconnected world. While these concerns cannot be dismissed outright, they must be countered with evidence-based policies and positive engagement that highlight the benefits of diversity and the shared values that unite societies. By doing so, the European Union can continue to pursue its enlargement goals while addressing the legitimate concerns of its citizens and fostering a more inclusive and resilient community (e.g. Economides et al. 2024). Interestingly, Taydas and Kentmen-Cin (2017) find that religious attachment plays a limited role in shaping the public opposition towards new enlightenments.

Deepening Instead of Enlarging Deepening the European Union (EU) involves strengthening integration among existing member states through enhanced policy coordination, institutional reforms, and increased harmonization of regulations. This process aims to create a more cohesive and efficient Union, capable of addressing internal and external challenges more effectively. On the other hand, enlargement refers to the expansion of the EU by admitting new member states. Both deepening and enlargement are critical for the development and evolution of the EU, yet there is an ongoing debate among politicians, academics, and public figures about the priority of deepening over future enlargements.

Proponents of deepening argue that the EU needs to solidify its internal structures and processes before taking on new members. They believe that a more integrated and harmonized EU will be better positioned to support new members effectively. This perspective emphasizes the importance of addressing existing challenges within the Union, such as economic disparities, political fragmentation, and the need for a more robust and unified foreign policy. Strengthening the EU internally can ensure that the Union is resilient and capable of sustaining further expansion without compromising its core values and objectives (Schimmelfennig, 2014).

One of the key arguments for deepening is the need to address economic disparities among member states. The Eurozone crisis exposed significant economic vulnerabilities within the EU, highlighting the necessity for stronger economic governance and fiscal coordination. By deepening integration in areas such as banking union, fiscal policy, and economic convergence, the EU can create a more stable and resilient economic environment. This, in turn, would provide a stronger foundation for future enlargements, ensuring that new members can integrate smoothly into a well-functioning economic system (Baldwin and Wyplosz 2015).

Another argument for prioritizing deepening is the enhancement of political cohesion and unity within the EU. The rise of populist and nationalist movements in several member states has challenged the principles of solidarity and cooperation that underpin the Union. Strengthening political integration and fostering a sense of European identity can help counter these divisive trends. Initiatives such as enhancing the role of the European Parliament, increasing transparency and accountability in decision-making processes, and promoting civic engagement at the EU level are crucial for building a more united and democratic Union. A politically cohesive EU will be better equipped to welcome new members and integrate them into its political framework (Risse 2010).

Furthermore, deepening integration in the area of foreign and security policy is essential for the EU to play a more effective role on the global stage. The EU's ability to act as a coherent and influential actor in international affairs has often been hampered by divergent national interests and a lack of unified strategy. By deepening integration in this area, the EU can develop a more robust and coordinated foreign policy, enhancing its capacity to address global challenges and promote stability in its neighbourhood. This would not only benefit existing member states but also create a more attractive and supportive environment for potential new members (Smith 2003).

Despite the compelling arguments for deepening, the process of enlargement also holds significant benefits for the EU. Enlargement can enhance the EU's geopolitical influence, promote stability and prosperity in neighbouring regions, and foster cultural diversity and exchange. Admitting new members who share the EU's values and aspirations can strengthen the Union's global standing and contribute to its long-term development. Therefore, it is essential to strike a balance between deepening and enlargement, ensuring that the EU is both internally robust and open to welcoming new members (Lavenex and Schimmelfennig 2009; Wunsch and Olszewska 2022).

Large EU Is Becoming Difficult to Manage Managing a diversity of 27 or more EU member states can be challenging, especially when it comes to decision-making processes and policy implementation that must accommodate the varying interests and priorities of each member state. It is difficult to comprehend what the optimal size of the European Union is and what the capacity to absorb new member states is (Bourguignon et al. 2022).

As the EU expands, the risk of decision-making gridlock increases, as seen in the challenges faced by the European Council and the Council of the European Union, where unanimous decisions are often required on critical issues.

The bureaucratic structure of the EU, including its institutions, agencies, and regulatory bodies, adds another layer of complexity to the enlargement process. These entities are designed to ensure the smooth functioning of the Union, but their effectiveness can be hampered by the increased administrative burdens that come with accommodating new member states. Each enlargement round necessitates adjustments to the EU's administrative framework to integrate new members, which can strain existing resources and slow down decision-making processes.

Streamlining and coordinating the EU's structures is a formidable task that becomes more challenging as- the Union grows. The European Commission, which acts as the executive arm of the EU, plays a crucial role in this regard. However, expanding its responsibilities to manage a larger and more diverse Union can lead to inefficiencies and delays. Efforts to enhance the Commission's capacity to handle these tasks must be balanced with the need to avoid creating an overly centralized bureaucracy that could stifle member states' autonomy.

The European Parliament, representing the EU's citizens, also faces difficulties in maintaining effective representation and legislative efficiency as the number of member states increases. Ensuring that all member states have adequate representation while preventing the parliament from becoming unwieldy is a delicate balance. The proportional representation system must be continually adjusted to reflect the growing and changing membership, which can lead to contentious negotiations and political friction.

Moreover, the regulatory framework of the EU must be robust enough to accommodate the diverse economic landscapes of new member states. Harmonizing regulations across a larger Union requires substantial coordination and compromise, often leading to delays in the implementation of key policies. This regulatory complexity can create barriers to effective governance and economic integration, as seen in the varying degrees of compliance with EU directives across member states.

The expansion of the European Union, while beneficial in many respects, introduces significant challenges in terms of managing diversity and maintaining efficiency in decision-making and policy implementation. The EU must carefully consider its capacity to integrate new member states without compromising its core values and operational effectiveness. By addressing these challenges through institutional reforms and enhanced coordination mechanisms, the EU can continue to grow and evolve while maintaining its foundational principles and ensuring the stability and prosperity of its member states.

Job Losses Due to the EU Enlargement Job insecurity could be a potential driving force behind the anti-enlargement sentiment in some EU countries. One of the central arguments is that European companies may seek to take advantage of the lower labour costs in newly admitted EU countries by outsourcing or offshoring production or services. This can result in job losses in higher-wage countries as businesses relocate operations to lower-cost locations. The fear is that this shift could lead to significant economic displacement and increased unemployment in existing EU member states, exacerbating social and economic inequalities within the Union.

However, this argument does not fully account for the existing economic dynamics between the EU and the Western Balkans. There is already a high degree of trade liberalization and capital account liberalization with the Western Balkans, enabled by the Stabilization and Association Agreements (SSAs). These agreements have progressively integrated the Western Balkan economies with the EU, allowing for the free movement of goods, services, and capital. As a result, European capital could move freely towards the Western Balkan countries well before their formal entry into the EU. This pre-existing economic relationship suggests that much of the potential outsourcing and offshoring might have already occurred, diminishing the likelihood of a significant new wave of job losses post-enlargement.

Furthermore, empirical studies have shown that the economic impact of EU enlargement tends to be positive overall. New member states often undergo substantial reforms to meet EU standards, which led to improved governance and economic policies. This alignment boosts their economic performance, which in turn contributes to the EU's overall economic health. Enlargement expands the single market, facilitating trade and investment flows, and creating new opportunities for businesses across the Union. Increased market size allows for greater economies of scale, benefiting businesses and consumers alike. Additionally, newer members often possess competitive advantages in certain sectors, such as agriculture or manufacturing, which can complement the economic profiles of existing members, leading to more dynamic intra-EU trade relations and a more competitive economy on a global scale (Dabrowski and Myachenkova 2018).

Moreover, the economic benefits of enlargement are not limited to trade and investment. The integration of new member states also brings about structural and institutional reforms within the EU, leading to more efficient and effective governance. The challenges of integrating diverse economies and systems can foster greater flexibility and resilience in the EU's institutions, preparing them for future challenges. This adaptation process can lead to innovative approaches in governance, from policymaking to administration, ultimately strengthening the Union as a whole.

While concerns about job insecurity and economic displacement are valid, they do not fully capture the complex realities of EU enlargement. The existing economic integration between the EU and the Western Balkans, facilitated by the SSAs, has already allowed for significant economic interaction and adjustment. The broader economic benefits of enlargement, including improved governance, expanded market size, and increased competitiveness, are likely to outweigh the potential negative impacts. Therefore, the anti-enlargement sentiment driven by job insecurity concerns should be viewed within the broader context of the overall positive economic effects of EU enlargement.

Slow Macroeconomic Convergence EU enlargement traditionally involves the admission of countries with significantly lower levels of economic development compared to the incumbent member states. This disparity can potentially exacerbate existing economic inequalities within the EU, posing challenges to the Union's efforts towards achieving greater macroeconomic convergence among its member states. However, historical evidence and academic research suggest that, contrary to this concern, many countries have successfully achieved real convergence with respect to the "old" EU member states.

One of the primary concerns with EU enlargement is that the inclusion of less economically developed countries can strain the Union's resources and widen economic disparities. New member states often require substantial investment in infrastructure, education, and healthcare to bring their standards up to the EU average. This need for investment can divert resources from other pressing issues within the Union and lead to tensions among member states. Additionally, the economic disparities can result in imbalances in labour markets, with workers from newer, less developed member states migrating to more prosperous ones in search of better opportunities. This migration can lead to social and political tensions in host countries and brain drain in the countries of origin.

Despite these concerns, evidence suggests that many countries have successfully used EU membership as a catalyst for economic growth and convergence. Franks et al. (2018) and Campos et al. (2019) provide compelling evidence that new member states have made significant progress in achieving real convergence with older member states. For instance, Franks et al. (2018) highlight that the process of EU accession involves rigorous economic and institutional reforms, which can spur growth and development. These reforms often include measures to improve governance, enhance the business environment, and increase competitiveness, all of which contribute to economic convergence.

Campos et al. (2019) further illustrate that the economic benefits of EU membership extend beyond initial reforms. They argue that the integration into the EU's single market provides new member states with access to larger markets, increased investment opportunities, and the transfer of technology and knowledge. These factors collectively contribute to sustained economic growth and convergence. For example, countries like Poland and the Baltic States have experienced significant economic growth since joining the EU, narrowing the gap with older member states.

Moreover, the Cohesion Policy of the EU, which allocates funds to reduce regional disparities, has played a crucial role in supporting convergence. This policy provides financial assistance to less developed regions within member states, helping to improve infrastructure, education, and healthcare. The funds are targeted at projects that promote sustainable development and competitiveness, thereby fostering economic convergence. The success of this policy can be seen in the substantial improvements in the quality of life and economic performance in regions that have received significant EU funding.

The process of economic convergence is not without its challenges. The initial stages of integration can be difficult, with new member states needing to implement extensive reforms and adapt to the competitive pressures of the single market. However, the long-term benefits of EU membership, including access to markets, investment, and institutional support, can outweigh these challenges. The experience of previous enlargements suggests that with the right policies and support, new member states can achieve significant economic progress.

Democratic Backsliding The disappointment stemming from democratic backsliding in some new EU member states has fueled scepticism regarding the transformational role of EU integration. The European Commission, for instance, has initiated infringement proceedings against countries where there are concerns about the rule of law. Additionally, the European Parliament has been vocal in condemning such actions and advocating for measures to address democratic backsliding. Instances of democratic backsliding in some new EU member states, such as Hungary, have also reduced the support for further EU expansion. For example, there has been noticeable deterioration in areas like the rule of law, corruption, and economic governance.

This trend points to a significant challenge: while several countries may have met the criteria for EU accession when they joined, changes often leaned towards cosmetics, with a greater emphasis on the volume rather than the quality of legislation passed. For instance, Croatia, despite passing an average of three laws per day during the period between 2008 and 2010, has since faced criticism for its failure to uphold the rule of law and for pervasive systemic corruption. Such situations highlight that the mere transposition of EU legislation into national law is not sufficient—it must be accompanied by effective implementation and enforcement, along with a genuine commitment to uphold EU values and standards.

The scepticism about the EU's transformational capacity is not entirely unfounded (Fig. 4). While the accession process involves stringent checks and balances, including the Copenhagen criteria that demand stable institutions guaranteeing democracy, the rule of law, human rights, and respect for and protection of minorities, post-accession compliance has been inconsistent. Hungary, under Prime Minister Viktor Orbán, has been a case in point, with significant backsliding on democratic norms and an increase in authoritarian practices since its accession in 2004. This has led to a series of confrontations with EU institutions, including multiple infringement procedures and the invocation of Article 7, which could lead to the suspension of certain rights of a member state, including voting rights.

The case of Poland also underscores the complexities of ensuring compliance with EU norms post-accession. Poland has faced criticism and legal action from the EU for its judicial reforms, which have been perceived as undermining judicial

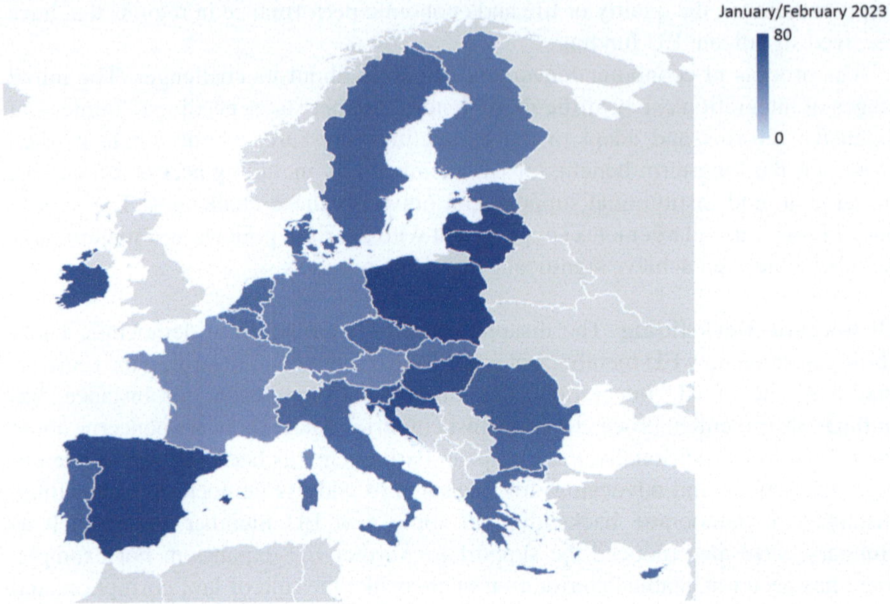

Fig. 4 Percentage of respondents in favour of a new EU enlargement? (January/February 2023, Eurobarometer). Source: Editors' design based on data from the Eurobarometer (2023)

independence and the rule of law. These instances of backsliding have raised concerns about the EU's ability to enforce its values uniformly and effectively across all member states, thereby undermining the credibility of its enlargement policy.

Moreover, these democratic deficits have broader implications for the EU's global standing and internal cohesion. The EU's claim to be a normative power—promoting democracy, human rights, and the rule of law globally—is weakened when it struggles to enforce these standards within its own borders. This internal inconsistency can be exploited by external actors, such as Russia and China, who seek to undermine the EU's influence and promote alternative models of governance.

To address these challenges, the EU needs to strengthen its mechanisms for ensuring compliance with its fundamental values both pre- and post-accession. This could involve more rigorous monitoring and enforcement mechanisms, greater use of conditionality in disbursing EU funds, and stronger support for civil society and independent media in member states. Additionally, the EU could consider reforming its decision-making processes to prevent backsliding countries from blocking collective action, thereby enhancing its ability to uphold its values and standards.

3.2 Commitment Fatigue: For How Long in The European Waiting Room?

Western Balkan countries have witnessed varying progress in EU integration and demonstrated volatile commitment to the EU agenda. There are many reasons behind what we label it as slow reform pace or *commitment fatigue*.

Strong reform-opposing coalitions. There are segments of business and political elites that strongly oppose the EU accession. They prefer ambiguous laws, no public oversight, reduced transparency and accountability, and generally, an environment that does not align with the governance structures and institutional capabilities within the Union. The vested interests of these business and political "elites" encourage them to create reform-opposing coalitions and support Euroscepticism.

Meddling by other international players. The prolonged EU integration of Western Balkans has created a manoeuvre space for other global players to meddle in domestic affairs. These players have their own interests and agendas that are not entirely consistent with the EU aspirations of the Western Balkans.

Unfulfilled promises by the EU towards Western Balkans. The EU was strongly supportive to the enlargement perspective for Western Balkans on the EU-Western Balkans Summit that took place in Thessaloniki (Greece) on 21 June 2003. The heads of states or governments of EU member states, the President of the European Commission, and the President of the European Parliament expressed their unequivocal support to the European perspective of the Western Balkan countries. The intentions were distilled in *The Thessaloniki Agenda for the Western Balkans: Moving towards European Integration*, which was considered a new important step in the favoured relationship between the EU and the Western Balkans. 21 years after, there has been some success in terms of speeding up income convergence and obtaining candidate statuses. The argument of "unfulfilled promises" is also of questionable nature, as the promises were not unconditional. The entry requirements for the EU strongly depend on the country's progress in fulfilment of the Copenhagen criteria.

Low pre-accession assistance (compared to the cohesion policy funds). The EU pre-accession funds are small compared to the EU funds allocated for Cohesion Policy.

In 2021–2027, EU funds allocated to the Cohesion Policy amount to EUR 392 billion. The Cohesion Fund provides support to EU Member States with a Gross National Income per capita below 90% of the EU-27 average. This Fund aims to support the economically less developed Member States, the ultimate goal of which is economic and social cohesion of the EU. The Cohesion Fund will be used for providing financial contributions in the fields of environment and trans-European networks in the area of transport infrastructure. In the period 2021–2027, the Cohesion Fund concerns Bulgaria, the Czech Republic, Estonia, Greece, Croatia, Cyprus, Latvia, Lithuania, Hungary, Malta, Poland, Portugal, Romania, Slovakia, and Slovenia or around 128 million inhabitants of the Union. In the period 2021–2027, EUR 392 million was made available thereto via this Fund, or as per the rough estimates, approximately EUR 3000 per capita in these countries (with a total population of 128 million inhabitants).

During the same period, Pre-Accession Fund—IPA III (2021–2027) is made available to the candidates or the potential candidate countries, amounting to total of EUR 14.2 billion. The purpose of this Fund, based on the principle of solidarity, is to support the candidate countries in implementing the political, institutional, legal, administrative, social, and economic reforms, being required so as to get harmonized with the rules, standards, policies, and practices of the European Union, all to the end of further ensuring its stability, security, and prosperity. As per the approximate estimates, under IPA III, around EUR 140 per capita are provided for the citizens of Albania, Bosnia and Herzegovina, Kosovo, North Macedonia, Montenegro, Serbia, and Turkey (with a total population of 103 million inhabitants).

To sum up, the difference between the status as an EU candidate country and a member state thereof, is EUR 2868 per capita, i.e. 21.8 times more resources in favour of the new EU member states (=3006/138 = 21.8). Such a large support provides stronger financial support for faster convergence of the new EU member states. As presented in Fig. 1, this makes the real convergence of Western Balkans a much more difficult task. In wartimes of geopolitical tensions, the EU must also devote not only development finance, but also resources for addressing the security needs of the applicant countries (Karjalainen 2023).

Large-scale emigration is a peculiar form of EU integration. The opponents of the EU enlargement often cite the EU expansion at the individual level. The liberal policies towards immigration of some EU member states—such as Germany—have allowed many working-age individuals and their families to emigrate. Citizens from Western Balkans desiring to labour and reside within the EU are presently permitted to do so. Hence, those who are in favour of the EU accession can experience the benefits of the EU integration by simply emigrating. The proponents of this argument forget that large-scale emigration has a devastating and profound demographic, socio-economic, and cultural implications for the EU candidate countries.

In conclusion, despite the enlargement and commitment fatigue, there are numerous potential benefits and rationale for continuing the enlargement process. The EU accession is a merit-based process, conditioned by a country's progress in transposing the EU's body of law (*acquis communautaire*) and in achieving agreed benchmarks for implementation of society-wide policy and institutional reforms. Even if all EU conditions are fully met, membership status may not be granted. Country's EU accession also depends on overcoming—and ultimately, overturning—the present modest public support for further enlargement of the Union.

It seems that the radically reshaped geopolitical and geoeconomic context is re-energizing the enthusiasm for another round of EU enlargement. The European Union and its member states are reconsidering the strategic importance of the Western Balkan region. In turn, the Western Balkan countries are more aware of the benefits of EU integration. Their prospective EU membership holds strong transformative power that can be used to implement development-friendly reforms in a more systematic and vigorous way.

4 Economic Implications of European Integration

European integration has brought significant economic benefits to its members, particularly through access to the single market. For new and prospective members, the promise of economic growth, increased trade, and investment opportunities is a powerful incentive. However, these benefits come with costs, such as the need for structural reforms and compliance with EU regulations.

Income convergence, or the reduction of income disparities between member states, has been a central goal of the EU. While some countries, particularly in Central and Eastern Europe, have made significant progress in catching up with their Western counterparts, others, such as the Western Balkans, continue to lag behind. The challenge for the EU is to ensure that integration promotes not only economic growth but also social and political stability.

European economic integration can serve as a potential driver of growth for new and future EU members through various mechanisms. These mechanisms include:

Access to the single market: Membership in the EU grants new members access to the vast single market, which presents opportunities for increased trade, enhanced competition, and overall economic growth. Access to a larger consumer base and the removal of trade barriers can stimulate economic activity and attract foreign direct investment.

Adoption of EU Standards: Joining the EU necessitates the adoption of EU standards and regulations across different governance areas. Compliance with these standards promotes good governance practices, reduces corruption, and encourages efficient business operations. These factors contribute to a favourable business environment, attracting investment and driving economic growth.

Cohesion Policy: The EU implements policies and provides funds to reduce regional economic and social disparities. New members can benefit from these policies, which support infrastructure development, education, research and development, and other areas that foster economic growth. Even during the candidacy stage, countries can receive financial support through the Instrument for Pre-Accession (IPA III) funds.

Monetary Stability: Fulfilling the Maastricht criteria and adopting the euro can provide new EU members with monetary stability. The common currency eliminates exchange rate uncertainties and transaction costs, which promotes trade and investment within the eurozone. However, euro adoption entails meeting strict fiscal and monetary criteria and carries obligations and challenges.

Increased Labour Mobility: European integration enables labour mobility, allowing workers to move to regions with better job opportunities and higher wages. This facilitates the balancing of labour markets and contributes to increased economic productivity. Additionally, access to education in European universities at relatively lower costs compared to non-EU countries benefits the younger generation and enhances human capital development.

Political Stability: European integration fosters political stability, security, and resilience, all of which are vital for sustainable economic growth. The EU's foundation on democratic principles, the rule of law, and respect for human rights promotes stability among member states. New members are required to adhere to these principles, further strengthening political stability and supporting economic development.

While European integration has the potential to drive economic growth, convergence, and overall development in new and future EU members, it is important to acknowledge that these benefits are not guaranteed and may vary across countries. The distribution of benefits may not be equal, and it can take time for the positive effects of integration to materialize.

Furthermore, EU membership comes with significant costs and challenges. Countries seeking to join the EU may need to implement difficult and politically sensitive structural reforms to align with EU standards and regulations. They may also face increased competitive pressures, the obligation to contribute to the EU budget, and the potential for large-scale emigration as labour markets open up. These challenges can pose obstacles to growth and development.

Hence, the overall impact of European integration on economic growth is contingent upon a multitude of factors, encompassing the distinct circumstances and characteristics of each post-communist economy and the efficacy with which they navigate the integration process. Consequently, it is imperative for countries to diligently weigh the costs and benefits associated with EU membership, while formulating strategies to optimize the advantages and address the challenges that ensue.

To further understand the complexities and dynamics of European economic integration, it is essential to examine the historical context and empirical evidence from previous enlargements. The integration of Central and Eastern European countries into the EU, which began in earnest in the early 2000s, provides valuable insights. These countries experienced significant economic transformations, characterized by rapid GDP growth, substantial increases in foreign direct investment, and improvements in infrastructure and institutional quality. However, the transition also came with social and economic costs, including increased competition, structural unemployment, and the need for significant public and private sector adjustments. By learning from these experiences, current and prospective EU members can better prepare for the challenges and opportunities that lie ahead.

In addition to economic and policy considerations, cultural and social dimensions play a crucial role in the integration process. The alignment of social norms, cultural values, and institutional practices between new and existing member states can facilitate smoother integration. This involves fostering mutual understanding and cooperation among diverse populations and addressing any potential social tensions that may arise from increased labour mobility and cultural exchanges. Efforts to promote cultural integration and social cohesion are vital for ensuring that the benefits of economic integration are broadly shared and contribute to a more inclusive and harmonious European Union.

Moreover, the strategic geopolitical implications of EU enlargement cannot be overlooked. Expanding the EU to include new member states, particularly from the Western Balkans and Eastern Partnership countries, enhances the EU's geopolitical influence and stability in these regions. This expansion serves as a counterbalance to the influence of other global powers, such as Russia and China, which have sought to assert their presence in these areas. By integrating these countries into the

EU framework, the Union can promote democratic governance, rule of law, and economic development, thereby contributing to regional peace and stability. The geopolitical benefits of enlargement, coupled with the economic and social advantages, underscore the importance of a comprehensive and well-coordinated approach to European integration.

4.1 Income Convergence

There are substantial income disparities among Western Balkans and the European Union. In 2022, incomes varied between 25.5% (Kosovo) and 45.5% (Montenegro) of the average GDP per capita (current prices, in purchasing power parity terms) of that of EU-27. This section addresses several important questions that have emerged almost two decades after the Eastern enlargement of the European Union (EU) in May 2004. It investigates whether the new EU member states and EU candidate countries have been able to achieve "catch up" with the "old" EU member states. Additionally, it explores whether European integration can still act as a driver of economic growth for current and future members and identifies the main driving forces behind such growth dynamics. The study considers significant events and challenges that have occurred during this period, including demographic changes, the Global Financial Crisis of 2008–09, the European sovereign debt crisis of 2008–12, and the recent poly-crisis involving the pandemic, energy crisis, and higher inflation during 2021–23.

The central research objective of this chapter is to examine the potential role of European integration as a catalyst for economic growth in new and prospective EU members. It does so by considering the prevailing European context and providing insights into the contemporary political, economic, and social dynamics within the EU. The primary motivation behind this study is to analyse the impact of European integration on accelerating economic growth and fostering income convergence in post-communist European economies. Situated within the broader framework of the EU, the paper aims to elucidate the complex interplay between European integration, economic growth, and income convergence.

To comprehensively capture the intricate relationship between European integration and economic growth, this study is guided by three interconnected yet distinctive objectives. Firstly, we endeavour to ascertain whether European integration contributes to the narrowing of income disparities among European nations, thereby shedding light on the potential equalizing effects that such integration may yield. Secondly, our focus shifts to the post-communist economies, commonly referred to as emerging Europe, with the aim of identifying and comprehending the principal driving forces that propel growth dynamics within this region. Lastly, we embark on a comparative evaluation, scrutinizing whether the experiences of rapidly reforming new EU member states can serve as a blueprint for EU candidate countries in the Western Balkans. Moreover, we investigate the feasibility of emulating or adapting these experiences for potential candidate countries within the Eastern Partnership, namely Ukraine, Georgia, and Moldova. These three objectives collectively underpin our study, furnishing it with both depth and direction as we navigate the intricate terrains of European integration and economic growth.

To establish a robust foundation for this study, we commence by conducting an extensive review of existing literature, encompassing diverse perspectives. This literature review serves to consolidate the theoretical framework that underpins our research. With a comprehensive understanding of the theoretical landscape, we proceed to undertake an empirical investigation, utilizing rigorous data sources and innovative analytical strategies. The primary objective is to elucidate the tangible implications of European integration on the economic trajectory of post-communist economies in Europe, with particular emphasis on the role of governance.

In the subsequent sections, we present the structure and organization of the paper. The subsequent section provides a detailed account of the materials and methods employed in exploring the European context and examining the intricate relationship between European integration and growth dynamics. Subsequently, the third section expounds upon the outcomes derived from the utilization of Machine Learning Algorithms (MLAs), which aid in deciphering the underlying mechanisms driving the observed growth dynamics. Finally, the concluding section synthesizes the key insights gleaned from our study, offering pertinent policy recommendations aimed at fostering informed discourse and actionable measures in the realm of European integration. The structure of the paper is as follows. In the next section, we present materials and methods to explore the European context and the nexus between European integration and growth dynamics. The third section elaborates the results from MLAs' inquiries into mechanisms behind the growth dynamics. The last section conveys concluding remarks and policy recommendations.

To expand on the concept of income convergence, it is essential to consider the heterogeneity among the post-communist economies and their diverse experiences with European integration. Countries that have successfully implemented structural reforms, embraced good governance practices, and adhered to EU standards have generally exhibited more robust economic growth and faster income convergence with Western Europe. This pattern suggests that while EU integration provides a framework and incentives for economic modernization, the outcomes heavily depend on domestic policy choices and institutional capacities. For instance, the Baltic States, which pursued aggressive reforms and integration strategies, have outperformed many of their peers in terms of income convergence and overall economic development.

Furthermore, the role of external shocks and macroeconomic stability cannot be overlooked when analysing income convergence. The Global Financial Crisis of 2008–09 and the subsequent European sovereign debt crisis had profound impacts on the economic trajectories of many new EU member states and candidate countries. Those with sound fiscal policies, diversified economies, and robust financial sectors were better equipped to weather these crises and maintain growth momentum. In contrast, countries with structural vulnerabilities, high levels of public debt, and reliance on volatile sectors faced prolonged economic disruptions and slower convergence. This highlights the importance of macroeconomic resilience and the capacity to implement counter-cyclical policies in sustaining long-term growth and convergence.

Finally, addressing demographic challenges is crucial for sustaining income convergence in the long run. Many countries in emerging Europe face declining populations and ageing demographics, which can constrain labour supply, productivity, and economic growth. Policies aimed at enhancing labour market participation, attracting skilled immigration, and investing in human capital are vital for mitigating these demographic pressures. Additionally, leveraging technological advancements and fostering innovation ecosystems can help offset the adverse effects of demographic trends by boosting productivity and creating new economic opportunities. Therefore, a comprehensive approach that combines structural reforms, macroeconomic stability, and demographic resilience is essential for achieving and sustaining income convergence in the context of European integration.

4.2 Macroeconomic Perspective on European Integration

The Eastern enlargement of the EU in May 2004 with ten new member states, and three more thereafter in 2007 and 2013, created a unique historical opportunity for deepening economic integration and accelerating economic growth on the European continent. On 1 May 2004, the EU was enlarged with eight countries from Central and Eastern Europe (Czechia, Estonia, Hungary, Latvia, Lithuania, Poland, the Slovak Republic, and Slovenia) and two Mediterranean countries (Malta and Cyprus). Bulgaria and Romania joined the EU on first January 2007, whereas Croatia on first July 2013. The EU accession process encouraged high degrees of trade and financial integration with the "old" Europe, harmonization of the legislation, institutional capacity building, labour mobility, etc. Sizeable net international capital inflows also supported higher productivity, accelerated growth, and income convergence. Europe was largely promoted as an engine of convergence that brought benefits for millions (e.g. Gill and Raiser 2012).

The transformational recession in the 1990s brought a dramatic deterioration in living standards of post-communist economies. The initial adverse transition shock in terms of declining output and employment was unprecedented. With strong assistance of the World Bank Group, the International Monetary Fund, and other International Financial Institutions, subsequent privatization, enterprise restructuring, and macroeconomic stabilization laid the foundations for a strong growth rebound. The EU integration prospects motivated important structural and institutional reforms, facilitated faster transition to a market economy, and strengthened the resilience of these economies to unfavourable shocks. Bold trade liberalization reforms also enabled trade creation and trade diversion from the Soviet-led political and economic bloc (Council for Mutual Economic Assistance, COMECON) to Western Europe. Foreign savings inflows—primarily originating from Western Europe—supplemented the low levels of domestic savings, thereby strongly accelerating investment activity. It is important to highlight that growth dynamics were also characterized by slowdowns and breaks, either due to civil wars and political

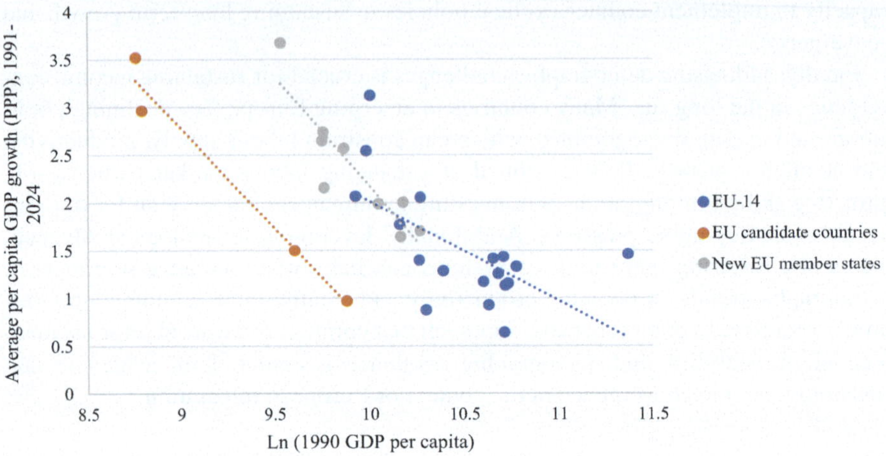

Fig. 5 Initial conditions vs. growth performance in Europe (1990–2023, 1990 = 100). Notes: [1] GDP per capita is expressed in Purchasing Power Parity terms and in 2017 constant international dollars. [2] Due to missing observations, the initial data only for Bosnia and Herzegovina refers to 1996, for Serbia 1997, and for Kosovo 2000. Source: World Economic Outlook database, The International Monetary Fund (October 2024)

unrests as was the case in South Eastern Europe (e.g. Kešeljević and Spruk 2021), stop-and-go macroeconomic policies or reform reversals (e.g. Szekely and Ward-Warmedinger 2018), etc. Depending on their pace of political, structural, and institutional reforms, the post-communist economies effectively split into front-runners and late reformers.

The front-runners were the eight transition countries from Central and Eastern Europe (CEE), including the Baltic States. The initial conditions were favourable at least in terms of political, geographical, and cultural proximity to Western Europe. Their successful institutional convergence and creation of functioning market economies led to the largest Eastern enlargement of the EU, which took place in May 2004. Pre-EU accession period and initial years of EU membership witnessed remarkably high economic growth rates in the new EU member states (Fig. 5).

The Baltic countries (Latvia, Lithuania, and Estonia) were leading the way in the two-speed catch-up process, while other CEE countries have lagged somewhat behind (e.g. Abiad et al. 2009). Inspired by their successful economic transformation and political integration, three other countries from Southeastern Europe (Bulgaria, Romania, and Croatia) later also managed to fulfil the formal EU entry requirements. While the EU membership is a politically legitimate goal per se, the higher economic growth rates and income convergence are not guaranteed. For this reason, we investigate whether these new EU member states continued the catching-up behaviour with respect to the "old" Europe.

The late reformers were the six countries from the Western Balkans (Albania, Bosnia and Herzegovina, Kosovo, Montenegro, North Macedonia, and Serbia). Their domestic support for joining the EU has always been rather high, while the transformative power of Europe widely praised for promoting democracy and supporting societal and economic change (Börzel and Lebanidze 2017). The European Council and the EU-Western Balkans Summit of Thessaloniki in June 2003 signalled the EU commitment to embrace other South-eastern European countries. One at a time, they upgraded their status into EU candidate countries, and few of them (Montenegro and Serbia) even opened the EU negotiating chapters.

Based on their EU membership status, we distinguish two groups of post-communist European economies: 13 new EU member states and six EU candidate countries with different growth performance. The three convergence clubs in Europe could be broadly categorized as follows:

Western Europe includes the more developed economies of the EU, such as Germany, France, the UK (until its departure from the EU), and the Nordic countries. These countries had already achieved high levels of development by 1990 and have continued to grow, albeit at a slower pace, since then. This is a rather heterogeneous group in terms of growth performance, but this is beyond the scope of the paper.

Central and Eastern Europe (CEE) includes the countries that joined the EU in 2004, 2007, and 2013, such as Poland, Hungary, and Bulgaria. These countries started from a lower base of income per capita in 1990 but have generally grown at a faster rate than the Western European countries, partly driven by the process of catching up and partly by their EU accession. The convergence process in these countries has been facilitated by substantial inflows of foreign direct investment, EU structural funds, and the adoption of EU regulatory frameworks. The economic performance of CEE countries underscores the transformative impact of EU membership, which has spurred modernization and integration into the global economy.

The Western Balkans and Eastern Partnership countries include those that are currently EU candidate countries or potential candidates, such as Albania, North Macedonia, Serbia, Armenia, and Georgia. These countries have also grown since 1990, but their growth and convergence process has generally been slower than the CEE countries. The Western Balkans, in particular, have faced significant challenges related to political instability, weak governance, and incomplete economic reforms. Despite these obstacles, the prospect of EU membership continues to serve as a powerful incentive for these countries to pursue necessary reforms and align with EU standards.

Figure 6 presents the GDP per capita of Western Balkan countries—Albania, Kosovo, North Macedonia, Bosnia and Herzegovina, Montenegro, and Serbia—relative to the GDP per capita of the EU-27, adjusted for purchasing power parity (PPP), over the period from 2010 to 2023. This measure helps to assess the economic convergence of these countries with the EU-27 average. Throughout this period, Montenegro and Bosnia and Herzegovina generally maintained a higher percentage, indicating relatively better economic performance compared to their peers. Serbia shows a steady upward trend, suggesting gradual convergence. North Macedonia remains relatively stable, with minor fluctuations. Albania and Kosovo, on the other hand, exhibit lower values, indicating slower progress in closing the income gap with the EU-27. The upward or downward trends in these lines reflect

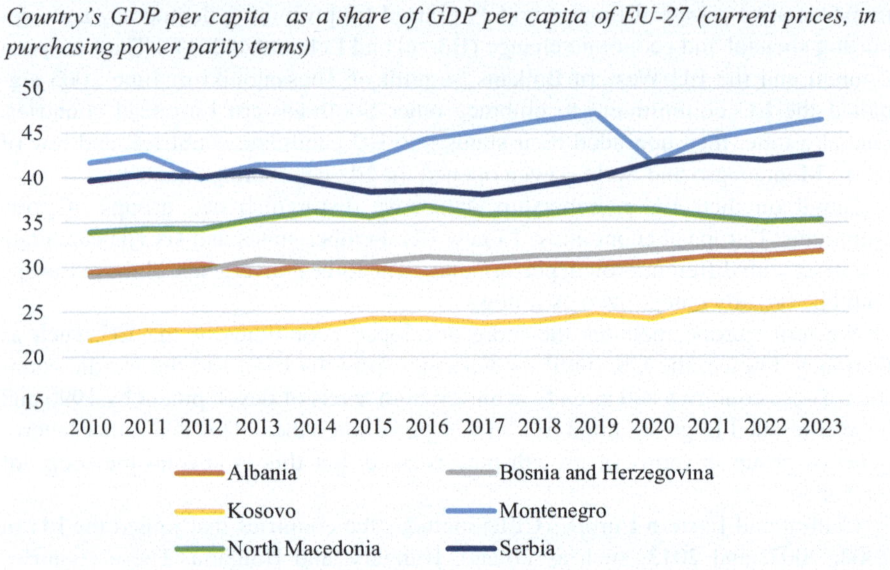

Fig. 6 Income convergence in Europe (2010–2023). *Country's GDP* per capita *as a share of GDP* per capita *of EU-27 (current prices, in purchasing power parity terms)*. Note: [1] Gross domestic product per capita, current prices, Purchasing power parity; international dollars. [2] The values for 2023 are estimates. Source: IMF World Economic Outlook database, October 2024

the economic developments and policy impacts in these countries over the years. The estimates for 2023 suggest ongoing but varied levels of economic convergence among these nations, highlighting both the challenges and progress in aligning with broader European economic standards. The source is the IMF World Economic Outlook database, April 2024.

The analysis of these convergence clubs highlights the differing pathways and outcomes of European integration across the region. For the CEE countries, the combination of EU accession, structural reforms, and significant financial support has facilitated a robust convergence process. However, the Western Balkans and Eastern Partnership countries face a more arduous journey, marked by persistent structural challenges and geopolitical complexities. These disparities underscore the need for tailored policies and sustained support to ensure that all countries in the region can benefit from the integration process and achieve sustainable economic growth.

Furthermore, the economic performance of these convergence clubs is not only influenced by their integration into the EU but also by their internal policies and external economic environments. For instance, the CEE countries have benefited from strong trade linkages with Western Europe, a stable macroeconomic environment, and effective utilization of EU funds. In contrast, the Western Balkans have faced disruptions due to regional conflicts, slower reform implementation, and less favourable investment climates. Understanding these nuanced factors is crucial for devising effective strategies that address the unique challenges and leverage the specific strengths of each group.

Finally, the role of governance and institutional quality cannot be overstated in the context of income convergence. Countries that have managed to implement strong governance frameworks and uphold the rule of law tend to attract more investment and experience faster economic growth. The experiences of the CEE countries demonstrate the positive impact of good governance on economic performance, while the ongoing struggles in the Western Balkans highlight the adverse effects of weak institutions. Strengthening governance structures and fostering institutional development are essential for ensuring that all countries can achieve their full economic potential within the European integration framework.

The transformative power of European Integration has been a multidimensional topic of extensive research and debate. We provide a brief summary of the key themes emerging from the literature:

Trade Integration: The EU, through its Single Market, has provided a platform for trade integration, reducing tariffs and non-tariff barriers. Studies have shown that this increases trade among member states, which can stimulate growth and convergence. By facilitating the free movement of goods, services, capital, and labour, the Single Market has enhanced competition and efficiency, leading to higher productivity and economic growth. However, the benefits of trade integration are not uniformly distributed, with some regions and sectors experiencing more significant gains than others.

Economies of Scale: By creating a single market, European integration allows firms to access a larger customer base and achieve economies of scale. Research highlights that larger markets enable firms to lower their per-unit costs and invest more in research and development, fostering innovation and competitiveness. However, potential risks include market diversion, where trade shifts from more efficient to less efficient producers due to preferential treatment. This can undermine overall efficiency and lead to suboptimal resource allocation if not managed carefully.

Single European Currency and Schengen Agreement: The adoption of a common currency (Euro) and the removal of internal borders (Schengen) further facilitate trade. Studies have suggested these developments can enhance economic growth by reducing transaction costs, eliminating exchange rate uncertainties, and improving price transparency. However, they also underscore the importance of economic and institutional readiness for these steps, as the benefits of the euro and Schengen area membership depend heavily on sound fiscal and monetary policies and robust governance frameworks.

Financial Integration: European integration has promoted financial openness, with a higher degree of capital account liberalization. The literature points to an increase in net international capital inflows, including Foreign Direct Investment (FDI) and portfolio investment inflows, promoting investment and growth in the region. Financial integration has enabled better allocation of capital, facilitated access to funding for businesses, and supported economic diversification. However, it also necessitates strong regulatory frameworks to manage financial stability risks and prevent crises.

Solidarity and Cohesion Funds: The EU provides structural and investment funds to new EU member states and Instrument for Pre-Accession (IPA) funds for candidate countries. Research suggests these funds play a key role in reducing regional disparities, supporting infrastructure development, and stimulating economic growth. By targeting less developed regions, these funds help to bridge the development gap and promote social and economic cohesion. The effective utilization of these funds is crucial for maximizing their impact, requiring transparent governance and efficient project management.

Institutional Integration: The process of transposing acquis communautaire (EU law) into national laws facilitates institutional convergence. Studies have found improvements in rule of law, political stability, regulatory quality, control of corruption, voice and accountability, and government effectiveness following EU accession. Institutional integration strengthens governance frameworks, enhances public sector efficiency, and builds investor confidence. However, the success of this process depends on the commitment of national governments to implement and enforce these reforms consistently.

However, the literature also cautions that the effectiveness of European integration as a transformative force can be influenced by a range of factors, including the initial conditions in individual countries, the pace and depth of their integration process, and their capacity to implement and enforce structural and institutional reforms. Countries with stronger institutional frameworks and political stability are better positioned to reap the benefits of integration. Conversely, those with weaker governance and higher levels of corruption may struggle to achieve sustained growth and convergence.

Moreover, it is essential to address potential negative side effects, such as economic and social disparities, to ensure that the benefits of integration are broadly shared. Economic integration can exacerbate regional inequalities if growth is concentrated in already developed areas. Policymakers must design inclusive policies that support lagging regions and vulnerable populations, promoting balanced development and social cohesion. By fostering a more inclusive approach, the EU can enhance the overall resilience and sustainability of the integration process, ensuring long-term prosperity for all member states.

4.3 Growth Dynamics

Despite the numerous methodological obstacles, the growth literature has been blossoming. Early inquiries into growth dynamics for European transition economies focused on the role of exchange rate stability as an instrument of macroeconomic stabilization (e.g. De Grauwe and Schnabl 2008; Schnabl 2009). Exchange rate stability was found to deliver lower levels of inflation, promote international trade, and create a growth-conducive environment.

Subsequent studies shifted the emphasis from macroeconomic stabilization to the traditional channels of trade and financial integration. They explored the interplay among exports, investment, and net FDI inflows in emerging Europe. For example, Weber (2011) used reduced-form vector autoregressions (VARs) for Eastern European economies during the 1993–2009 period and found that exports, investment, and FDI in particular, are robust determinants of growth. Trade openness was used as a merely standard explanatory variable in most growth regressions for emerging Europe (e.g. Fetahi-Vehapi et al. 2015; Campos et al. 2019).

Other studies explored the role of international financial integration, namely either FDI or foreign capital (e.g. Lipsey 2006; Prasad et al. 2007; Abiad et al. 2009). Deeper capital market integration was found to improve the allocation of capital and ultimately encourage a sustained real economy growth (e.g. Orlowski 2020). Schnabel and Seckinger (2019, p. 71) also document the stabilizing role of foreign bank presence, which had a "more than four times stronger growth effect during the crisis than in normal times". Still, the overall effect of the Global Financial Crisis 2008–09 appears to reduce income convergence in Europe at the regional level (Cabral and Castellanos-Sosa 2019).

Trade and financial integration could not entirely explain growth dynamics in emerging Europe. The applied work expanded its interest towards the role of financial development, political integration, and institutional quality. Friedrich, Schnabel, and Zettelmeyer (2013, p. 536) used industry-level data and found that "the effect of financial integration on sectoral growth differentials was found to be strongest in countries that are most highly politically integrated". This is one of the most influential studies documenting important complementarities between political and financial integration. These results were challenged by Kalaitzoglou and Durgheu (2016), documenting that "neither political nor financial integration" affects growth, but the introduction of the single European currency. The results are relevant only for those emerging European economies that fulfilled the Maastricht criteria and joined the euro area.

An important corollary of the study by Glawe and Wagner (2021) is that some CEE and most SEE countries appear to be caught in a low-level institutional equilibrium. They argue that the institutional clusters of countries can also explain the income clubs in Europe. Other studies investigated the impact of the design of intergovernmental relations (e.g. Rodríguez-Pose and Krøijer 2009) or economic freedom (e.g. Vukotić and Baćović 2006) on growth.

In emerging Europe, the quality of human capital was also regarded as a salient growth driver (Crespo Cuaresma et al. 2013). It has usually been proxied by the volume of capital (educational attainment or average years of education) or an assessment of the quality of labour force. At microeconomic level, Conti and Sulis (2016) found that the skill level of the workforce strongly impacts technology adoption, total factor productivity, and economic growth.

Demographic factors also tend to play a prominent role. The empirical literature explored the impact of age structure of European societies on their economic growth prospects (Crespo Cuaresma et al. 2014, 2016). Despite the large immigration wave in Europe—during the refugee crisis in 2015—the unfavourable long-term demographic trends are likely to cause a growth slowdown and to reduce the speed of income convergence.

Box 2 Growth Empirics Challenges

Growth empirics—the empirical investigations of economic growth—has faced a range of challenges that can complicate the task of developing robust, reliable, and widely applicable findings. These challenges, acknowledged by many scholars (e.g. Pack 1994; Bosworth and Collins 2003; Durlauf et al. 2005; Ciccone and Jarociński 2010), can be categorized into the following areas:

1. Open-endedness of theoretical frameworks: Economic growth is influenced by a wide range of factors, from macroeconomic policy and institutional quality to human capital and technological innovation. This creates an open-ended nature for theoretical frameworks, making it hard to formulate and test hypotheses precisely.
2. Specification problems: The specification of econometric models for growth can be a complex task. It requires making choices about which variables to include, how to measure these variables, and what functional form to use for the relationship between the variables. Errors in specification can lead to biased and inconsistent estimates.
3. Measurement errors: Many variables in growth models, such as human capital or institutional quality, are difficult to measure accurately. Measurement errors can introduce bias into the estimates and reduce the reliability of the findings.
4. Missing data observations: Data for many variables may be unavailable or incomplete for many countries, particularly during the early transition period. This can limit the scope of the analysis and the robustness of the findings.
5. Problematic replicability: Findings from one study may not always be replicable in different contexts, due to differences in data, methodology, or the underlying economic conditions.
6. Model uncertainty: There is often uncertainty about the "correct" model to explain growth, including which variables to include.
7. Specification uncertainty: Another source of uncertainty stems from the challenging specification of the relationships among variables in the model, given competing theories about the drivers of growth.
8. Heterogeneity uncertainty: There may be uncertainty about how to group countries for analysis, given the significant heterogeneity in economic structures, policies, and performance.

These challenges have led to a mixed empirical record for growth econometrics. Despite the intellectual appeal and theoretical elegance of many growth

(continued)

models, their empirical performance has often been less than satisfactory, with limited ability to explain the variations in growth rates across countries and over time. Some empirical growth papers carry limited policy inference, conditional on the data used and the chosen specification. Beyond that context, the estimates would not be robust even to slightly altered empirical specifications. Last but not least, there have been instances where the prior views of researchers have been changed by the "convincing" estimation results (see Brock and Durlauf 2001). As a result, there is an ongoing need for more robust, rigorous, and nuanced empirical research on economic growth.

A small strand of literature focused on the role of public finance. Maşca et al. (2015) highlight that a small dimensional public sector, productive public investments, and prudent public debt strategy generate growth-conducive effects. Rant et al. (2021) find that during 1995–2018, slower rates of convergence across the EU member states were correlated with higher public and private debt ratios.

From a "big picture" perspective, Campos et al. (2019) use the synthetic control method on data from the previous EU enlargements between 1973 and 2004. They conclude that without European integration, per capita incomes of CEE would have been, on average, approximately 10% lower in the first 10 years after joining the EU. Furthermore, they find little evidence that the effects of EU accession decrease over time after each enlargement. Czasonis and Quinn (2012) find mixed evidence in favour of the income convergence for the Eastern European economies, but their study was conducted more than one decade ago. In contrast, a later study produced by Nagy and Šiljak (2022) does find income convergence during the 2004–2018 period. The higher rates of economic growth in post-communist economies in Europe were supported by economic openness, inflation, and government integrity.

D'Andrea (2022) conducted a comprehensive survey of the growth literature in European context, by applying a Bayesian approach on 70 explanatory variables. The findings were consistent with neoclassical growth theories since savings and the initial level of GDP per capita had been found to be reliable predictors of growth. Additional robust factors were the percentage of manufacturing in the GDP, demographic factors, fiscal positions, wage and labour contract regulation, and fixed capital accumulation. This limitation suggests the need for further research that can incorporate institutional variables and explore their potential impact on growth within the European context. This could include factors such as the quality of governance, rule of law, and regulatory effectiveness, which are thought to play a key role in shaping economic outcomes.

We identify several important gaps in the empirical literature on the role of European integration as a growth engine. Firstly, the literature is inconclusive to what extent the European integration drives growth dynamics and income convergence (Campos et al. 2019). Are lower-income countries simply more likely to grow faster as suggested by the hypothesis of income convergence? If they do grow faster, is there an interplay with the political, institutional, and structural reforms

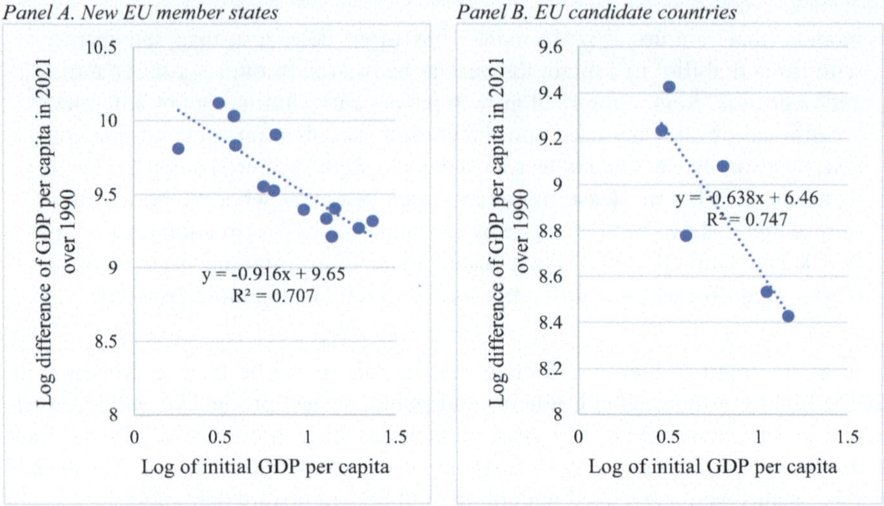

Fig. 7 Unconditional convergence within Europe. Note: The implied rate of convergence is calculated by using the formula ($\lambda_u = -\log(1 + \beta_u)/n$), using statistically significant coefficients (β_u) of cross-country regressions on annual data for the entire period (n). Source: Authors' calculations

motivated by prospective EU membership? Secondly, many studies are not so recent, and their findings may be of reduced practical relevance. The validity of this point stems from the fact that growth performance has been unstable.

These studies collectively illustrate the multifaceted nature of the growth process and the diverse ways in which European integration can potentially contribute to growth. They also highlight the need for further research to deepen our understanding of these complex relationships.

Cross-country-income inequalities are a pervasive issue that influences social, economic, and political landscapes of countries worldwide. For an analysis of income inequalities in the context of European integration, we use several metrics to compare and contrast income inequality among the various "convergence clubs". By investigating these measures, we can gain a clearer understanding of how European integration impacts income inequality both within and across these groups. The observations provided here yield insights into the dynamics of income inequalities in Europe.

During crises, cross-country income inequalities, measured by metrics such as the mean log deviation of per capita GDP or standard deviation of logarithms, seem to diminish (Fig. 7). The implied rate of convergence for the new EU member states and EU candidate countries is 8.26% and 3.39% per annum, respectively, during 1990–2022. This could be due to several reasons: for instance, countries with higher incomes may be more exposed to the global economic shocks that often trigger crises, causing their incomes to fall more than lower-income countries. At the same time, counter-cyclical fiscal and monetary policies can help buffer the impact of crises on lower-income countries.

Regarding the EU-14 (the 14 countries that were EU members before the 2004 enlargement), income variations seem to be widening. It is important to note that this trend is not uniform: countries such as Greece, Portugal, and Spain are lagging, while Ireland is performing well. This heterogeneity may be linked to the differing economic structures, fiscal positions, and reform trajectories of these countries. On a more positive note, GDP per capita disparities within new EU member states and EU candidate countries appear to be narrowing. This suggests that the convergence process within these two groups is ongoing, likely driven by factors such as EU integration, structural reforms, and investment in human capital and infrastructure. However, it is also important to bear in mind that this convergence process may be uneven and that the level of income in these countries still remains below that of the EU-14.

The analysis of income dynamics reveals that the benefits of European integration are not evenly distributed across the continent. For the new EU member states, integration into the EU has provided significant opportunities for growth and convergence, largely due to access to the single market, structural funds, and institutional reforms. These countries have been able to leverage EU membership to attract foreign investment, modernize their economies, and improve living standards. Nevertheless, the initial conditions and the pace of reforms have varied widely, resulting in different trajectories of income convergence among these nations.

In contrast, the EU candidate countries, primarily located in the Western Balkans, face more significant challenges. Despite aspirations for EU membership and ongoing reforms, these countries have struggled with persistent economic and political instability, weaker governance frameworks, and less effective implementation of structural policies. Consequently, their convergence process has been slower and more uneven. The disparities in income levels between these candidate countries and the more advanced EU economies underscore the need for targeted support and policies that address the unique challenges they face in their path to integration.

These trends underline the complexity of income dynamics in Europe and the multiple factors that can influence income inequalities both across and within countries. They also highlight the continued relevance of the convergence debate in the context of European integration. Addressing income inequalities requires a multifaceted approach that includes fostering economic growth, improving governance, investing in human capital, and ensuring that the benefits of integration are widely shared. Policymakers must focus on creating inclusive growth strategies that can help bridge the gap between different regions and socio-economic groups within Europe.

Furthermore, the role of structural funds and cohesion policies in mitigating income disparities cannot be overstated. These funds play a crucial role in supporting less developed regions, enhancing their infrastructure, and improving their competitiveness. However, the effectiveness of these funds depends on their efficient allocation and the capacity of recipient countries to absorb and utilize them effectively. Ensuring transparency, accountability, and good governance in the management of these resources is essential to achieving their intended outcomes and promoting equitable growth across Europe.

5 Governance and Institutional Challenges

5.1 Governance Gaps in Post-Communist Economies

The term "governance gaps" often refers to the deficiencies in the structure, capacity, or practices of institutions that shape the decision-making process in a country. These gaps can exist in various forms and can have significant implications for the effectiveness and legitimacy of governance. In the context of emerging Europe, governance gaps can pertain to various areas such as:

Rule of Law: The rule of law is a cornerstone of good governance. It involves aspects such as the independence and efficiency of the judiciary, the enforceability of contracts, and the protection of property rights. In some parts of emerging Europe, issues such as corruption, judicial inefficiency, or political interference in the legal system can pose challenges to the rule of law. These challenges undermine public trust in legal institutions and hinder economic development by creating an unpredictable business environment. Effective reforms in the judiciary, along with measures to combat corruption, are essential for strengthening the rule of law in these countries.

Public Administration: Effective public administration is critical for the implementation of policies and the provision of public services. However, some emerging European countries may face challenges in this area, such as bureaucratic inefficiency, lack of transparency, and difficulty in coordinating across different levels of government. These issues can result in slow policy implementation, misallocation of resources, and reduced public service delivery quality. Enhancing the capacity of public institutions through training, adopting best practices, and improving coordination mechanisms can significantly improve governance outcomes.

Democratic Governance: This involves aspects such as the conduct of free and fair elections, the protection of civil and political rights, and the effectiveness of political representation. In some emerging European countries, these democratic principles may be under pressure due to issues like political polarization, media censorship, or the concentration of power. Such conditions can erode democratic norms and weaken the accountability of political leaders. Strengthening democratic institutions, ensuring media freedom, and promoting inclusive political processes are crucial for safeguarding democratic governance.

Economic Governance: Good economic governance involves sound fiscal management, effective regulation, and a supportive environment for businesses. However, challenges can arise from issues such as fiscal imbalances, inefficient state-owned enterprises, or excessive red tape. Poor economic governance can lead to macroeconomic instability, stifled private sector growth, and reduced foreign investment. Implementing transparent fiscal policies, restructuring state-owned enterprises, and streamlining regulatory frameworks are essential steps towards improving economic governance.

Addressing these governance gaps is critical for the long-term social, economic, and political development of emerging Europe. It is also a key part of the process of European integration, as adherence to principles of good governance is a requirement for EU membership. The prospect of EU membership can itself be a powerful

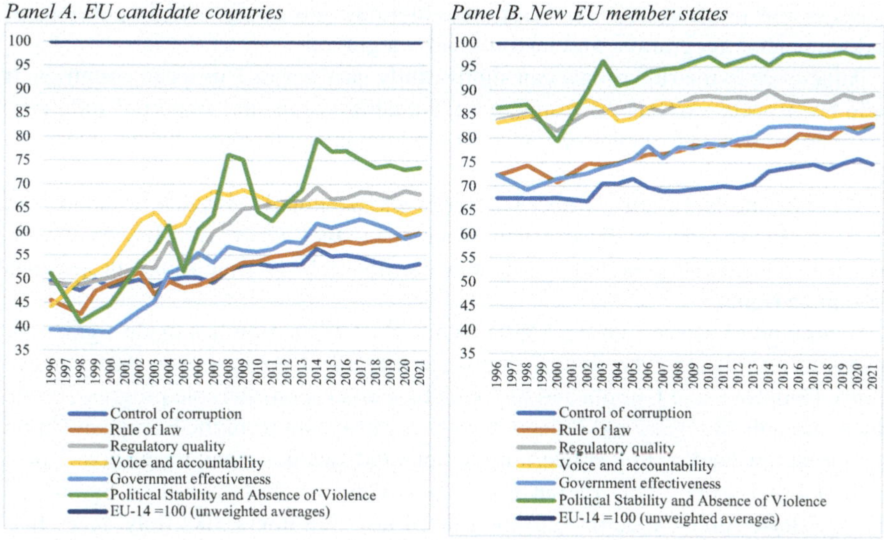

Fig. 8 Institutional gaps in emerging Europe (1996–2021, EU14 average = 100). Note: EU 14 refers to the unweighted average for EU-15 minus the United Kingdom. Source: Authors' calculations based on data from Worldwide Governance Indicators, World Bank (February 2024)

driver of governance reforms in these countries. By aligning their governance structures with EU standards, emerging European countries can improve their institutional capacity, enhance public trust, and create a more conducive environment for sustainable development. Moreover, the EU's emphasis on governance as a precondition for membership underscores the importance of robust institutions in achieving long-term stability and prosperity.

As presented in Fig. 8, a striking similarity is that the progress across all six dimensions follows the same pattern or order in the two groups of economies: the smallest gap is observed for political stability and absence of violence, followed by the gap in regulatory quality and voice and accountability. Wider institutional gaps are observed in government effectiveness and rule of law, while the most significant disparity compared to "old" Europe refers to the control of corruption. From 2014 onwards, we observe worrisome deterioration or stagnation along the governance indicators in most EU candidate countries, indicating some backsliding in terms of the institutional quality. The estimated progress in the control of corruption for the EU candidate countries in 2021 was 53.3% of that one for the EU-14 economies. Political stability and absence of violence also witnessed noticeable deterioration in SEE economies compared to the more advanced European economies.

5.2 Rule of Law and Democratic Backsliding

In the new EU member states, we highlight the stagnation in terms of voice and accountability and the more recent backsliding in the control of corruption. In the next section, we critically review the existing body of empirical literature in order to assess how much attention the empirical literature has given to the importance of trade, financial integration, and institutional integration.

Adherence to the rule of law can significantly vary across European countries. It includes aspects such as government accountability, fair and impartial judiciary, transparent laws and regulations, respect for human rights, and citizens' access to justice.

Western and Northern Europe: Countries like Denmark, Sweden, Finland, and the Netherlands generally have strong adherence to the rule of law. They have well-established legal and judicial systems, low corruption levels, and robust protections for human rights.

Central and Eastern Europe (CEE): While the CEE region has made significant strides in establishing the rule of law since the fall of communism, performance varies. Countries like Estonia and Slovenia have made considerable progress, while others, notably Hungary and Poland, have faced criticism from the European Union for rule of law backsliding concerning judicial independence and media freedom.

Southern Europe: This region has a mixed record. Countries like Spain and Portugal have robust adherence to the rule of law, but others, like Italy, face challenges with judicial efficiency and corruption.

Southeast Europe (Western Balkans): Countries in the Balkans are making efforts to improve the rule of law as part of their EU accession process. However, they still face challenges in areas such as judicial independence, corruption, organized crime, and protection of minority rights.

Eastern Partnership Countries: Ukraine, Moldova, and Georgia are working to reform their judicial and legal systems, often in cooperation with the EU. However, they continue to face significant challenges related to corruption, weak institutions, and in some cases, unresolved conflicts.

The World Bank's Worldwide Governance Indicators (WGI) provide insights into six dimensions of governance, including Rule of Law and Regulatory Quality. The rule of law reflects the extent to which agents have confidence in and abide by the rules of society. This encompasses the quality of contract enforcement, property rights, the police, and the courts, as well as the likelihood of crime and violence. Regulatory Quality, on the other hand, captures perceptions of the ability of the government to formulate and implement sound policies and regulations that permit and promote private sector development.

General trends until 2021 suggested that:

Western Europe: Countries such as Germany, France, the UK, and the Nordic countries typically score highly on both Rule of Law and Regulatory Quality, indicating effective governance, solid legal frameworks, and efficient regulatory policies.

Central and Eastern Europe: There is a varied picture in this region. Some countries, such as Estonia, have received high scores, indicating strong institutions. In contrast, others have faced challenges in these areas.

Southern Europe: Countries like Spain and Portugal generally have good scores, although issues such as corruption and judicial inefficiency can be areas of concern, notably in Italy and Greece.

Southeast Europe (Western Balkans): These countries tend to have lower scores, reflecting ongoing challenges with corruption, judicial independence, and institutional capacity. However, many of these countries are working to improve in these areas as part of their EU accession process.

Eastern Partnership Countries: These countries generally have lower scores, reflecting significant challenges related to corruption, weak institutions, and political instability.

6 An Innovative Methodological Approach to Convergence in Europe

Machine Learning (ML) methods have emerged as a promising alternative to traditional econometric techniques, presenting notable advantages such as enhanced flexibility, the ability to handle non-linear relationships, and the capacity to analyse vast and intricate datasets. In this study, we employ regression trees as our ML algorithm of choice. Regression trees employ decision rules derived from the data to predict outcomes, making them well-suited for capturing complex relationships and unveiling interactions between variables. Moreover, regression trees facilitate the examination of heterogeneous effects, wherein the impact of a variable may vary across different subsets of the sample.

By leveraging regression trees, we aim to overcome the limitations of conventional econometric approaches and gain deeper insights into the relationship between European integration and economic growth in the context of post-communist economies. This methodology enables us to uncover intricate patterns and non-linear dynamics that may exist within the dataset, providing a more nuanced understanding of the mechanisms driving growth in these economies. Additionally, regression trees offer a flexible and interpretable framework for analysing complex relationships and identifying key drivers of growth, facilitating policy formulation and decision-making processes.

The study employs a machine learning approach to analyse the role of European integration as a growth driver, using a combination of data from four databases: IMF's World Economic Outlook (October 2024), Penn World Table 10.01, World Bank's World Development Indicators, and Total Economy Database by Groningen University. These databases collectively provide a rich set of economic, social, and institutional indicators that can be used as predictors of growth. This comprehensive dataset allows for a detailed examination of various factors influencing economic growth, ensuring that the analysis is robust and well-grounded in empirical evidence.

The method employed for the analysis in this study is a regression tree, a powerful machine learning algorithm widely used in data analysis and prediction tasks. A regression tree aims to fit the available data by constructing a hierarchical structure of binary splits. The process begins at the root node of the tree, where the entire dataset is considered. At each subsequent node, the algorithm selects a predictor variable and a corresponding splitting rule that divides the data into two branches based on the value of that variable. This iterative process continues until the data is divided into homogeneous groups or the tree reaches a predefined depth.

The splitting rule is determined by evaluating various candidate rules and selecting the one that maximizes the difference in growth rates between the two resulting branches. This criterion ensures that the splits effectively partition the data into distinct regions within the predictor space, enhancing the algorithm's ability to capture nonlinear relationships and interactions among variables. The regression tree continues to recursively split the data at each node, resulting in a tree-like structure with multiple levels. This process halts when certain stopping criteria are met, such as a minimum number of observations per node or a maximum tree depth.

Once the regression tree is constructed, predictions can be made by traversing the tree from the root to a leaf node, where the predicted response value is determined. The predictions are obtained by aggregating the response values of observations falling into the same leaf node. This approach allows for localized analysis, capturing the heterogeneity of the data and providing insights into the specific characteristics and dynamics associated with different segments of the predictor space.

The utilization of a regression tree in this analysis capitalizes on its capability to effectively handle nonlinearity, capture intricate relationships, and identify significant predictors within the context of European integration and economic growth in post-communist economies. The hierarchical structure of the regression tree provides a lucid and interpretable framework, enabling a comprehensive understanding of the underlying patterns present in the data while segmenting it into distinct regions based on the predictor variables. This methodological approach not only enhances the interpretability of the results but also facilitates the identification of critical factors influencing growth dynamics.

The outcome is a tree structure in which each leaf node represents a unique segment within the predictor space. The predicted growth rate for observations falling within each segment is obtained by calculating the mean growth rate of the data points residing in that particular segment. This approach allows for a localized analysis, capturing the heterogeneity of the data and providing insights into the specific characteristics and dynamics associated with different segments of the predictor space. By leveraging the strengths of the regression tree methodology, this study can provide valuable insights into the multifaceted process of growth in post-communist economies within the context of European integration. The methodology's flexibility, ability to handle non-linear relationships, and capacity to reveal interactions and heterogeneous effects contribute to a comprehensive and nuanced analysis of the complex dynamics underlying economic growth in these economies.

Moreover, regression trees can accommodate a large number of predictor variables, allowing for a comprehensive analysis of various factors that influence economic growth. This flexibility is particularly advantageous in the context of European integration, where multiple dimensions and drivers of growth need to be considered. The ability to include a wide range of variables ensures that the analysis captures the multifaceted nature of economic growth and the diverse factors that contribute to it.

Additionally, regression trees have the ability to uncover interactions and heterogeneous effects, which are often present in complex economic systems. This capability enables a more nuanced understanding of the relationship between European integration and economic growth, as it allows for the examination of how the impact of different variables varies across different subsets of the sample. By revealing these interactions, the analysis can provide more targeted and effective policy recommendations.

By leveraging the strengths of the regression tree methodology, this study can provide valuable insights into the multifaceted process of growth in post-communist economies within the context of European integration. The methodology's flexibility, ability to handle non-linear relationships, and capacity to reveal interactions and heterogeneous effects contribute to a comprehensive and nuanced analysis of the complex dynamics underlying economic growth in these economies. This approach not only enhances our understanding of the factors driving growth but also provides a robust framework for informing policy decisions aimed at fostering sustainable economic development in the region.

The construction of a regression tree follows a specific process designed to segment or divide the predictor space (the set of possible values for predictor variables $X_1, X_2, \ldots, Xp$) into J non-overlapping regions ($R_1, R_2, \ldots, R_J$).

For each observation that falls into a specific region, R_J, the same prediction is made. This prediction is the mean of the response values for the training observations in that region. In the context of this study, the response value is the growth rate, so the prediction for an observation is the average growth rate for the other countries in the same region (in terms of the predictor space, not geographic region).

The regions are constructed to be high-dimensional rectangles, or boxes, in the predictor space (Fig. 8). This choice is made for simplicity and to facilitate interpretation of the resulting predictive model. The objective is to find boxes $R_1, R_2, \ldots, R_J$ that minimize the Residual Sum of Squares (RSS), a common measure of prediction error, so that:

$$RSS = \sum_{j \in J} \sum_{i \in R_j} \left(yi - \hat{y}R_J \right)^2 \tag{1}$$

To achieve this, a top-down, greedy approach is used, known as recursive binary splitting. This approach starts at the top of the tree (with all observations) and successively splits the predictor space into two new branches at each step. The specific split (i.e. the variable and value to split on) is chosen to minimize the RSS for the resulting two branches. The process continues recursively, considering all the observations within each branch for the next split, until a stopping criterion is reached.

In essence, each node in the tree represents a decision point where the data is split based on the value of one of the predictor variables. The splitting process is guided by the goal of minimizing the prediction error, leading to a tree structure that partitions the data into regions that are as homogeneous as possible in terms of the response variable.

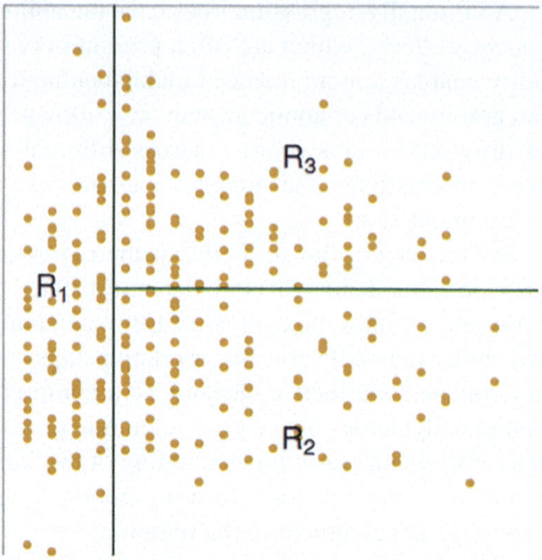

Fig. 9 An illustration of a three-region partition. Source: James et al. (2017), p. 329

This recursive binary splitting method allows the regression tree to handle complex, non-linear relationships between the predictor variables and the response variable. By dividing the data into smaller and more homogeneous groups, the tree can make more accurate predictions for new observations, as each prediction is based on the average response value within the relevant region of the predictor space.

The result is a hierarchical tree structure where each leaf node represents a specific segment of the predictor space, and the prediction for each observation is determined by the mean response value of the training observations that fall into the same segment (Fig. 9). This method not only improves predictive accuracy but also provides a clear and interpretable model that can be easily visualized and understood, making it a powerful tool for analysing the relationship between European integration and economic growth in post-communist economies.

The outlined process is a comprehensive method for constructing a regression tree and selecting an optimal model size that balances the trade-off between fit and complexity. It involves the following steps:

Tree Growing via Recursive Binary Splitting: The first step is to grow a large regression tree on the training data using recursive binary splitting. This process continues until each terminal node (leaf) of the tree contains fewer than a specified minimum number of observations. This produces a large, complex tree that fits the training data closely.

Tree Pruning with Cost Complexity Pruning: The second step is to prune the large tree obtained in Step 1 to avoid overfitting. This is done using cost complexity pruning (also known as weakest link pruning), which controls the trade-off between the tree's complexity and its fit to the training data. This method introduces a complexity parameter (α) that penalizes the tree's number of terminal nodes. It produces a sequence of best subtrees for each value of α.

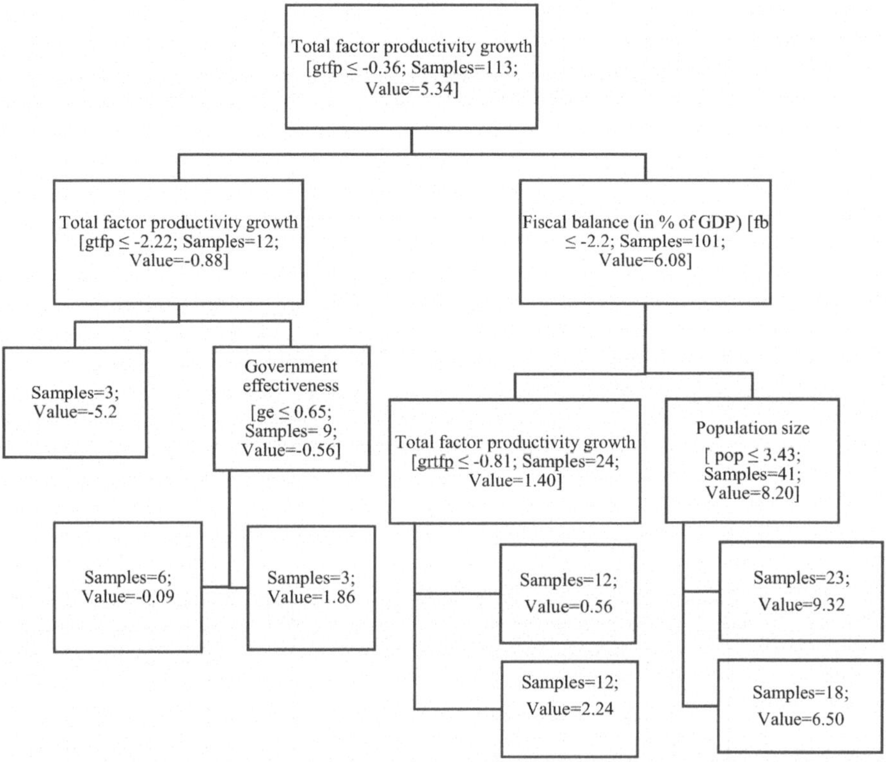

Fig. 10 Pruned regression trees of growth drivers in new EU member states (1990–2007). Source: Authors' calculations based on data for 1990–2007

Cross-validation to Choose α: The third step is to use K-fold cross-validation to select the optimal value of α. The training data is divided into K folds (subsets) and the process from Steps 1 and 2 is repeated K times, each time leaving out one of the folds from the training data. For each fold, the mean squared prediction error on the left-out data is calculated as a function of α. The average error across all K folds is then computed for each α, and the α that minimizes this average error is chosen.

Selection of the Optimal Subtree: Finally, the optimal subtree is selected from the sequence of best subtrees obtained in Step 2. This is the subtree that corresponds to the chosen value of α from Step 3. This subtree represents the best trade-off between fit and complexity and is the final model selected from the regression tree analysis.

The first set of results from the pruned regression trees refer to the new EU member states for 35 variables as potential growth drivers (Figs. 10 and 11). We split the period under consideration into two sub-periods: 1990–2007 (before the Global Financial Crisis of 2008–09) and 2008–2021 (during and after the crisis). The growth of total factor productivity (TFP) is a reliable predictor of high growth performance in both sub-periods. As illustrated in Fig. 4, high-growth performers

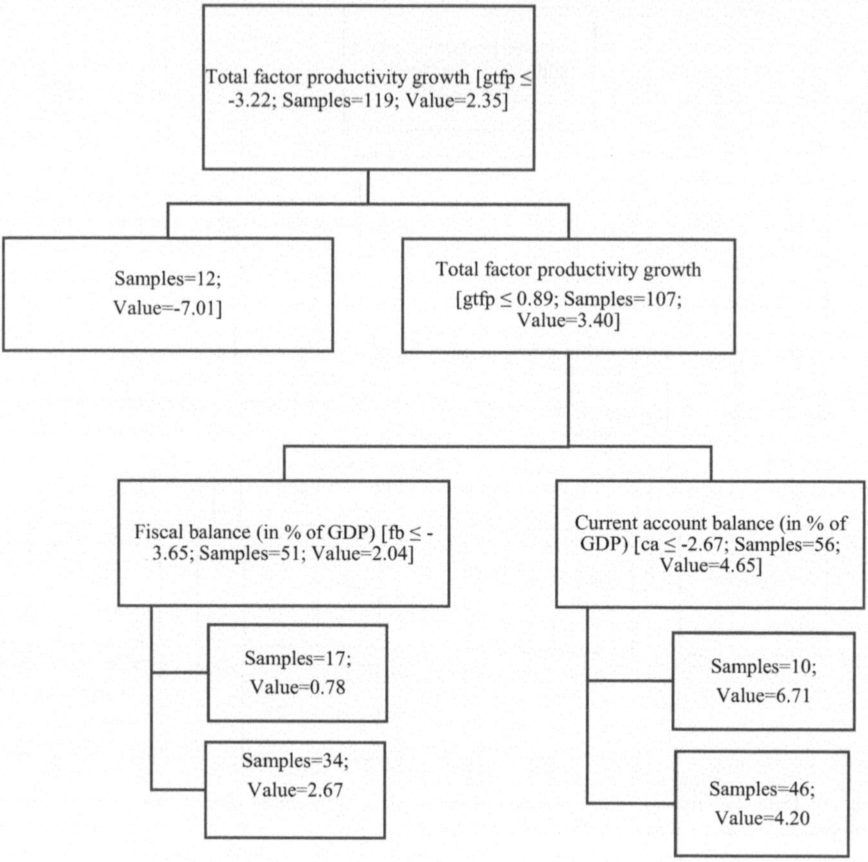

Fig. 11 Pruned regression trees of growth drivers in new EU member states (2008–2022). Source: Authors' calculations based on data for 2008–2022

before the Global Financial Crisis (GFC) 2008–09 were those witnessing TFP growth higher than −0.36, smaller budget deficits or budget surpluses (fiscal balance higher than −2.2% of GDP), and large populations (higher than 3.43 million inhabitants). During 2008–2021, high-growth performers were characterized by growth of TFP higher than 0.89% and a current account balance higher than −2.67% of GDP (Fig. 10).

This approach allows for a detailed understanding of the factors driving economic growth in different periods and under varying economic conditions. By identifying key predictors of growth, such as TFP, fiscal balance, and current account balance, the study provides valuable insights into the mechanisms through which European integration can influence economic performance. The use of regression trees, with their ability to handle non-linear relationships and interactions between variables, offers a robust and flexible methodology for analysing complex economic phenomena.

Fig. 12 Pruned regression trees of growth drivers in EU candidate countries (1990–2007). Source: Authors' calculations based on data for 1990–2007

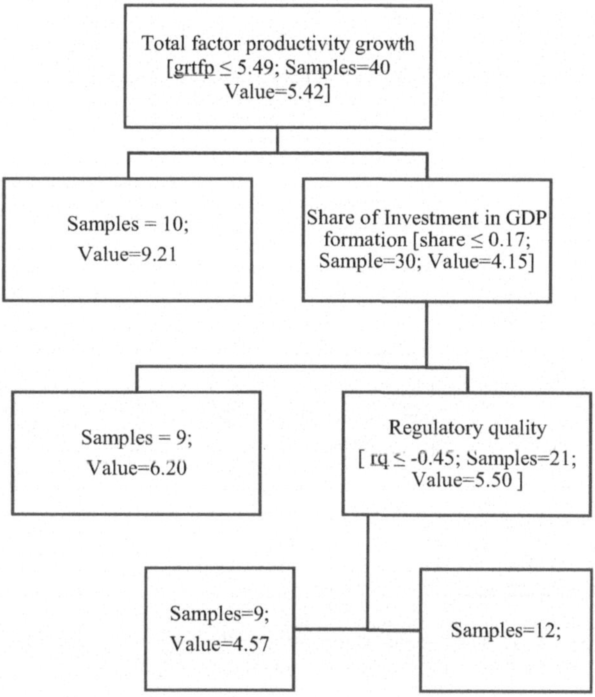

It is not uncommon to use the opposite of the current account balance as a proxy for the net international capital inflows (e.g. Blanchard and Giavazzi 2002). In this context, the high-growth performers would be post-communist economies attracting net international capital inflows in excess of 2.67% of GDP per annum. This appears to be an important growth driver in a post-crisis world in which investors are more risk averse.

The pruned regression trees for the EU candidate countries from Western Balkans are presented in Figs. 12 and 13. As illustrated in Fig. 12, high-growth performers among present EU candidate countries (before GFC 2008–09) were those witnessing high growth of TFP (on average, above 5.5% per annum), gross domestic investment share higher than 17% of GDP, and progress in regulatory quality index above −0.45 [range: −2.5; 2.5], as defined by the World Bank governance indicators framework.

During 2008–2021, the pruned regression tree suggests that the most reliable predictors of real GDP per capita growth were net international capital inflows in excess of 2.5% of GDP, and rule of law index above −0.17 [range: −2.5; 2.5], as defined by the World Bank governance indicators. From a policy perspective, creating a business-friendly environment—characterized by adherence to rule of law as well as satisfactory regulatory quality—was conducive to sizeable net international capital inflows that were driving higher rates of economic growth.

To address the criticisms and limitations associated with traditional approaches to growth regression, this study incorporates novel methodological advancements.

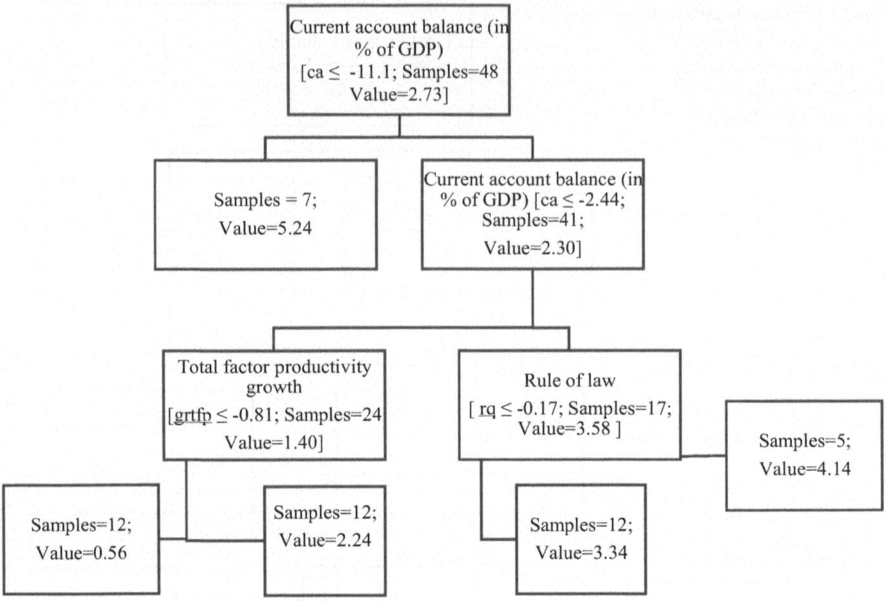

Fig. 13 Pruned regression trees of growth drivers in EU candidate countries (2008–2022). Source: Authors' calculations based on data for 2008–2022

While growth regression analyses have been widely employed in economic research, a phenomenon of "growth regression fatigue" has emerged among researchers, journal editors, referees, and readers. This fatigue arises from recurring challenges inherent in traditional econometric approaches, including concerns related to model uncertainty, specification uncertainty, and heterogeneity uncertainty.

Our results align well with Paul Krugman's famous assertion that "Productivity isn't everything, but in the long run, it's almost everything", as it finds strong evidence supporting the role of Total Factor Productivity (TFP) in driving economic growth. The analysis underscores the significance of efficiency gains and technological advancements in determining long-term economic performance.

However, the study recognizes that TFP alone does not provide a comprehensive explanation for growth variations across European countries. It reveals that other factors, both economic and institutional, contribute to the understanding of growth dynamics. Within the European sample, positive associations are observed between growth and indicators of good governance, trade openness, and bank profitability. Conversely, inflation exhibits a negative impact on growth, while gross national saving demonstrates a positive association with growth.

Further examination of the sample, disaggregated into EU member states and EU candidate countries, unveils some divergent findings. In the case of EU member states, factors such as fiscal consolidation, government effectiveness, and net international capital inflows emerge as conducive to growth. On the other hand, for EU candidate countries, the study highlights the crucial role of the rule of law, regulatory quality, and net international capital flows in fostering growth.

These results underscore the multifaceted nature of economic growth and emphasize that various factors collectively shape a country's growth trajectory. Productivity improvements, economic policies, institutional quality, and international economic linkages all contribute significantly to the growth dynamics observed across European countries. The findings of this study shed light on the complex interplay between these factors and provide valuable insights for policymakers seeking to promote sustainable economic growth in the context of European integration. The findings of this study validate the European Commission's approach to emphasize the importance of institutional quality in the EU integration process. The Commission's strategy to structure the EU accession negotiations around the "Fundamentals" cluster of chapters, which deal with areas such as judiciary and fundamental rights, justice, freedom and security, and public administration reform, is well-aligned with evidence that good governance and strong institutions are critical for economic growth. This cluster of chapters is typically the first to open and the last to conclude, signifying their paramount importance in the negotiation process.

However, the study also reveals that systematic differences in institutional quality persist between groups of countries within Europe. Despite significant progress observed in some countries in Southeast Europe, such as Romania and Croatia, gaps in institutional quality with respect to the EU-27 average remain substantial.

In addition, the study finds that democratic backsliding, a regression in democratic quality and governance standards, is detrimental to growth. This underscores the importance of continued focus on institutional and democratic reforms, not only for the sake of democratic values but also for the tangible economic benefits that they can deliver.

The implications of these findings are clear: promoting strong institutions and democratic governance should remain at the forefront of the EU's enlargement policy, both for potential future member states and within the existing EU member states. These elements are crucial for fostering economic convergence and ensuring the long-term success of the European integration project.

The study's findings highlight a crucial period of institutional development in countries on the path to EU membership (see Fig. 8). Specifically, it is during the EU accession period, when countries are negotiating their membership and aligning their institutions with EU standards, that the most significant progress in rule of law is observed. This can likely be attributed to the strong incentives and rigorous benchmarks set by the EU during this process, which drive comprehensive institutional and legal reforms in candidate countries.

However, the momentum appears to slow once countries become EU members. While there is still progress in the rule of law observed during the early years of EU membership, the pace of improvement is not as marked as during the accession period. This could be due to a variety of factors, such as the relaxation of external pressures following accession, difficulties in implementing reforms, or shifts in political priorities.

These findings underscore the importance of the EU accession process as a transformative period for candidate countries. They also signal a potential need for continued efforts to support and incentivize institutional development even after countries join the EU. This could help ensure that the progress made in the rule of law during the accession period is sustained and further built upon during the early years of EU membership.

This study acknowledges the instances of democratic backsliding in some new EU member states, such as Hungary, where there has been noticeable deterioration in areas like the rule of law, corruption, and economic governance. This points to a significant challenge: while several countries may have met the criteria for EU accession when they joined, changes often leaned towards cosmetics, with a greater emphasis on the volume rather than the quality of legislation passed.

For instance, Croatia, despite passing an average of three laws per day during the period between 2008 and 2010, has since faced criticism for its failure to uphold the rule of law and for pervasive systemic corruption. Such situations highlight that the mere transposition of EU legislation into national law is not sufficient—it must be accompanied by effective implementation and enforcement, along with a genuine commitment to uphold EU values and standards.

In light of these challenges, this study recommends that the EU enhances its monitoring of rule of law adherence among its member states and candidate countries. This could involve producing regular, thorough assessments of rule of law compliance, corruption levels, and the quality of economic governance. Such efforts would not only help to identify and address instances of democratic backsliding, but would also encourage continuous improvement in institutional quality, promoting a more effective and sustainable European integration process.

The study presented a comprehensive analysis of the role of European integration as a growth driver in emerging Europe. It explored various factors, including trade integration, financial integration, institutional integration, human capital, and demographic factors, to understand their impact on economic growth. The empirical strategies employed, ranging from conventional econometrics to machine learning algorithms like regression trees, provided valuable insights into the complex relationships underlying growth dynamics.

The findings of the study aligned with the notion that productivity growth, particularly Total Factor Productivity, is a robust predictor of economic growth. This highlights the crucial role of efficiency gains and technological progress in driving long-term economic performance. However, the analysis revealed that productivity growth alone is not sufficient to explain growth variations across European countries.

The study identified additional factors that contribute to growth in emerging Europe. For the entire European sample, good governance indicators, trade openness, bank profitability, gross national saving, and low inflation were found to be associated with higher growth rates. The results indicated that countries with better governance, open trade policies, strong financial sectors, higher saving rates, and lower inflation tend to experience faster economic growth.

However, differences across groups of countries within Europe were evident. Among EU member states, fiscal consolidation, government effectiveness, and net international capital inflows were identified as growth-conducive factors. This suggests that countries that maintain sound fiscal policies, exhibit effective governance, and attract foreign capital experience higher growth rates. In contrast, for EU candidate countries, the rule of law, regulatory quality, and net international capital flows were significant drivers of growth. This implies that countries aspiring for EU membership should prioritize reforms to enhance the rule of law and regulatory frameworks while attracting international investment.

The study also shed light on the importance of institutions and their role in shaping economic growth. It confirmed that good governance and strong institutions are fundamental for sustainable development. The European Commission's approach of bringing institutions to the forefront, with a particular focus on the "Fundamentals" cluster during EU accession negotiations, is in line with the findings. It is during the EU accession period that the largest progress in the rule of law was observed, highlighting the transformative power of the integration process. However, the study also revealed that progress in institutional quality slows down once countries become EU members. This indicates the need for continued efforts to strengthen and maintain good governance throughout the EU integration process.

Furthermore, the study highlighted challenges such as democratic backsliding, where countries exhibit regression in democratic quality and governance standards. It emphasized that democratic backsliding is detrimental to growth, underscoring the crucial link between strong institutions and economic performance. To address this, the study stressed the importance of regular and thorough assessments of adherence to the rule of law in all EU member states and candidate countries. Such assessments can help identify shortcomings and guide policy interventions to strengthen institutions and ensure the proper functioning of democratic systems.

In conclusion, this study offers significant contributions to the understanding of the intricate interplay between European integration and economic growth in emerging Europe. It highlights that while productivity growth remains a vital driver of economic performance, a range of additional factors including good governance, trade openness, financial stability, regulatory quality, and the rule of law also exert significant influence. These findings underscore the multifaceted nature of growth dynamics and emphasize the importance of comprehensive approaches to promote inclusive and sustainable economic development.

The study emphasizes the need for continuous efforts to strengthen institutions, uphold democratic standards, and pursue economic reforms. These measures are crucial for creating a conducive environment that supports robust economic growth and fosters convergence among member states and candidate countries in emerging Europe. By addressing these challenges, European integration can continue to act as a catalyst for economic development and facilitate the convergence of economies within the region.

The insights provided by this study hold significant implications for policymakers and stakeholders involved in shaping the economic trajectory of emerging Europe. It underscores the importance of promoting institutional quality, ensuring transparency, enhancing trade relations, and maintaining financial stability to unlock the full potential of European integration. By pursuing these objectives, emerging

Europe can harness the benefits of integration and foster sustained and inclusive economic growth in the years to come.

7 Future Directions

The analysis presented in this chapter underscores the significant role of European integration as a catalyst for economic growth and convergence among post-communist European economies. The regression tree methodology applied in this study provided valuable insights into the multifaceted drivers of growth, revealing the importance of total factor productivity (TFP), good governance, and financial stability as key determinants.

The findings highlight that new EU member states and EU candidate countries have made notable progress in income convergence, although the pace and extent of this convergence vary across different groups. While the new EU member states have generally experienced higher growth rates and better alignment with EU standards, the Western Balkans and Eastern Partnership countries still face substantial challenges in catching up with their Western counterparts. The convergence process has been driven by several factors, including access to the single market, adoption of EU standards, financial integration, and the benefits of cohesion policies.

However, the study also identifies persistent governance gaps, particularly in the areas of rule of law, regulatory quality, and control of corruption, which continue to hinder the growth potential of several emerging European economies. Addressing these governance challenges is crucial for sustaining the momentum of economic integration and ensuring that the benefits of EU membership are equitably distributed.

Moreover, the impact of global economic shocks, such as the Global Financial Crisis and the recent poly-crisis involving the pandemic, energy crisis, and inflation, underscores the need for resilient economic policies and robust institutional frameworks to mitigate vulnerabilities and support long-term growth.

While European integration has proven to be a powerful engine of economic growth and convergence, its success hinges on the continuous efforts of both current and prospective EU members to uphold democratic principles, strengthen institutional quality, and implement structural reforms. By fostering an environment conducive to sustainable development, the European Union can continue to advance the economic prosperity and cohesion of its diverse member states, paving the way for a more integrated and resilient Europe.

7.1 Trade Integration with the European Union

The Western Balkans has established strong trade links with the EU-27, particularly with major economies such as Germany and Italy. This high degree of European trade integration of the WB6 countries can be attributed to a combination of geographical proximity, political frameworks, and economic interactions.

Geography plays a significant role in facilitating trade between the Western Balkans and the EU. As gravity models of international trade suggest, countries that are geographically closer tend to trade more with each other. For instance, Belgrade, the capital of Serbia, is only 371 kilometres from Budapest, the capital of Hungary. Similarly, Sarajevo, the capital of Bosnia and Herzegovina, is 400 kilometres from Zagreb, the capital of Croatia. This proximity reduces transportation costs and enhances the efficiency of trade logistics, thereby fostering stronger trade relationships.

Trade liberalization has also been a crucial factor in enhancing trade integration. The gradual reduction and eventual abolition of tariffs under the Stabilization and Association Agreements (SAAs) have significantly facilitated trade. The SAAs, which constitute the framework of relations between the EU and the WB6 countries, have paved the way for the implementation of the Stabilization and Association Process, promoting trade liberalization and economic cooperation. This has allowed WB6 countries to access the large EU market more easily, boosting their exports and imports.

Foreign capital inflows, particularly in the form of Foreign Direct Investment (FDI), have played a pivotal role in strengthening trade ties. Large net inflows of FDI in the region have supported much stronger trade relationships between the WB6 and the EU-27. For example, significant German greenfield investments in the automotive component industry in Macedonia have promoted Macedonian exports to Germany. The outsourcing of certain segments of the value chain, especially those requiring low-skill labour, has become a common practice in various industries, such as the textile industry. Empirical research indicates that the small economies of the Western Balkans, abundant with inexpensive labour, have been particularly attractive for cost-driven FDI, which complements trade by integrating these countries into the broader European production network.

Foreign exchange arrangements have also facilitated international trade. The nature of these arrangements, which are mutually reinforcing, has supported trade integration. Due to the high degree of trade integration with the EU, some countries have opted for the unilateral adoption of the euro as their domestic currency and de facto legal tender, such as Montenegro and Kosovo in 2002. Bosnia and Herzegovina has a currency board arrangement where the Convertible Mark (CM) is fully backed by euros. Macedonia has maintained a de facto fixed exchange rate of the Macedonian denar with respect to the euro since 2002. Serbia has chosen a managed float exchange rate regime, while Albania operates under a free-floating exchange rate regime. These stable currency arrangements and unilateral euroizations promote international trade with European businesses, reinforcing the trade ties between the WB6 and the EU.

As a result of these factors, the share of WB6 trade with the EU-27 in their total international trade of goods over the past decade has been substantial, varying from 39.6% in Montenegro (2015) to 67.6% in Albania (2013). Figure 14 presents the share of international trade of the Western Balkan countries—Bosnia and Herzegovina, Montenegro, North Macedonia, Albania, Serbia, and Kosovo—with the EU-27 as a percentage of their total international trade over the period from

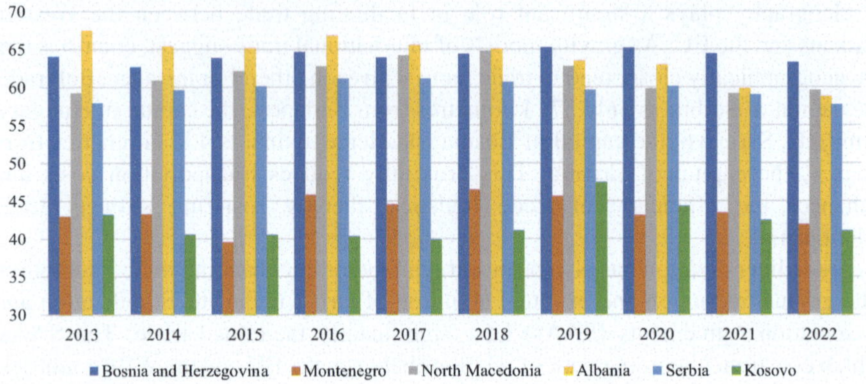

Fig. 14 Trade integration of Western Balkans with EU-27 (2013–2022). Share of international trade of WB6 with EU-27 in their total international trade (2013–2022, in percent). Source: Authors' calculations based on data from Eurostat (2024)

2013 to 2022. This percentage highlights the degree to which these economies are integrated with the European Union, indicating the importance of the EU as a trading partner.

Bosnia and Herzegovina and Serbia consistently maintain high levels of trade integration with the EU, with shares typically around or above 60%. This indicates a strong and stable economic relationship, facilitated by geographical proximity, historical ties, and significant economic reforms aimed at aligning with EU standards. Albania and Montenegro also exhibit substantial integration with the EU, although their trade shares show more fluctuations over the years. These fluctuations could be attributed to varying economic conditions, changes in domestic policies, and shifts in global market dynamics.

North Macedonia demonstrates a particularly strong and relatively stable trade relationship with the EU, especially from 2016 onwards. This stability suggests successful implementation of trade agreements and sustained efforts to enhance economic integration with the European market. The country's strategic location and efforts to improve its business environment likely contribute to this steady trade relationship.

Kosovo, while showing the lowest levels of trade integration with the EU among the Western Balkan countries, still has a substantial portion of its total international trade with the EU. This underscores the EU's role as a key trading partner for Kosovo, despite the challenges it faces in terms of economic development and political recognition.

In sum, the data indicates that the EU remains a crucial trading partner for the Western Balkans, with varying degrees of reliance among the countries. The trend over the years also reflects changes in trade policies, economic developments, and possibly the impact of EU accession processes on trade relationships. The efforts of these countries to align their economic policies with EU standards, attract foreign investment, and enhance trade liberalization have played significant roles in shaping

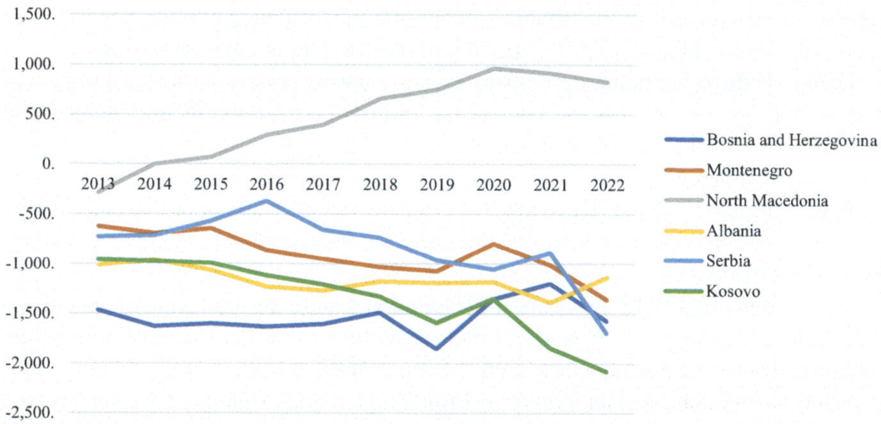

Fig. 15 Trade balances of WB6 countries with respect to EU-27, in million EUR (2013–2022). Source: Authors' calculations based on data from Eurostat (2024)

their trade dynamics with the EU. This integration is not only a testament to the economic interdependence between the Western Balkans and the EU but also highlights the potential benefits of further economic reforms and closer political ties in promoting regional stability and growth.

It is interesting to highlight that except for Macedonia (Fig. 15), all WB6 countries recorded trade deficit with the EU-27. It displays the net exports of goods and services for six Western Balkan countries—Bosnia and Herzegovina, Montenegro, North Macedonia, Albania, Serbia, and Kosovo—over the period from 2013 to 2022. Net exports are calculated as the difference between a country's exports and imports, and positive values indicate a trade surplus, while negative values indicate a trade deficit. North Macedonia stands out with a significant increase in net exports, moving from a deficit position in 2013 to a trade surplus by 2022, peaking around 2020. This improvement suggests substantial growth in export activities or a decrease in imports. Conversely, Kosovo exhibits the largest trade deficit, with its net exports declining steadily, reflecting either rising imports, falling exports, or both.

The other countries in the Western Balkans display varied trends in their net export levels. Bosnia and Herzegovina and Montenegro exhibit relatively stable net export levels with minor fluctuations, generally remaining in a deficit position. This indicates consistent challenges in balancing their trade, with imports exceeding exports over the years. These deficits suggest ongoing structural issues in their economies, such as limited export diversification and competitiveness in the global market (see Fig. 14).

Albania's net exports show a pattern of fluctuations, reflecting periods of both improvement and decline, but generally trending downward. This trend indicates Albania's struggle to maintain a positive trade balance, facing challenges in boosting its export capacity while managing import levels. The fluctuating trade balance underscores the volatility in Albania's economic performance and the need for targeted policies to enhance export growth and reduce dependency on imports.

Serbia, on the other hand, demonstrates a fluctuating pattern with slight improvement in net exports towards the later years, though it still remains in a deficit. The observed improvements in Serbia's trade balance suggest progress in enhancing its export performance, possibly due to increased foreign direct investment and improved industrial output. However, the persistence of a trade deficit highlights the ongoing need for economic reforms and strategic investments to achieve a sustainable trade surplus.

These trends highlight the economic challenges and varying levels of success in trade balance among the Western Balkan countries. The data reveals that while some countries, like Serbia, show signs of improvement in their trade balance, others, such as Bosnia and Herzegovina, Montenegro, and Albania, continue to face significant trade deficits. These deficits impact their overall economic stability and growth prospects, indicating the necessity for comprehensive trade and economic policies. Enhancing export capacity, diversifying the economic base, and improving competitiveness are crucial steps for these countries to achieve a more favourable trade balance and foster long-term economic growth. The analysis underscores the importance of tailored economic strategies that address the specific needs and challenges of each country within the Western Balkan region.

7.2 Financial Integration with the European Union

Albania The investments from European Union countries into Albania over the years 2013–2022 demonstrate considerable variations across different countries and a general trend in investment behaviour. Total investment from EU countries initially increased sharply from EUR 2.5 billion in 2013 to a peak of EUR 5.9 billion in 2015. In the subsequent years, investment levels experienced slight fluctuations but generally remained above EUR 5 billion, reflecting sustained interest and economic commitment by the EU in Albania. Italy, as one of the major investors, had significantly high investments, peaking at EUR 3809.0 million in 2015. Although there was a slight decrease thereafter, Italy remained a substantial contributor throughout the period. This consistent investment indicates strong economic ties between Italy and Albania, driven by historical connections and geographical proximity. Greece started with EUR 589.0 million in 2013, peaked at EUR 931.7 million in 2015, and then saw a reduction over the following years. This decline may reflect changing economic dynamics or bilateral issues between Greece and Albania. Despite these fluctuations, Greece's investments signify its ongoing economic engagement with Albania. Germany exhibited fluctuations in its investment levels but remained a notable investor. German investments increased significantly from EUR 29.0 million in 2016 to EUR 96.0 million in 2020, highlighting Germany's growing interest in the Albanian market. This increase could be attributed to Germany's strategic economic policies and Albania's improving business environment. Estonia, although starting from lower investment levels, showed an impressive increase over the decade, culminating at EUR 47.0 million in 2022. This growth indicates Estonia's rising interest and confidence in Albania's economic potential. Similarly, the Netherlands and Hungary showed significant increases later in the decade, with the Netherlands leaping to EUR 1204.0 million and Hungary to EUR 188.4 million by 2022. These substantial increases suggest a growing interest in the Albanian market from these countries, driven by favourable investment opportunities and economic conditions. Several other countries, such as Denmark, France, and Poland, displayed considerable variability in their investment levels. This variability could be due to changing economic conditions, strategic shifts in investment priorities, or specific bilateral relations. Investments from countries like Bulgaria, Czechia, and Croatia, although smaller in scale, show continuous albeit modest engagement in Albania. These investments reflect a steady interest in maintaining economic ties and exploring business opportunities in Albania. The share of EU investments in Albania's total inward FDI stock displayed a decreasing trend from 68.4% in 2013 to 50.2% in 2022 (see Fig. 15). This decline suggests that while the EU remains a significant investor, its relative dominance may be diminishing in the face of increasing investments from non-EU countries or other global economic shifts. This trend highlights the growing diversification of Albania's investment sources and the country's integration into the global economy. It also underscores the importance for Albania to continue fostering a conducive investment climate to attract and retain diverse international investments.

Bosnia and Herzegovina Direct investment from EU countries into Bosnia and Herzegovina has shown varied trends from 2013 to 2022, reflecting diverse levels of commitment across member states. The total EU-27 investment generally exhibited a positive trajectory, growing from EUR 3069.9 million in 2013 to EUR 4381.4 million by 2022, signalling a strengthening economic engagement by the EU in Bosnia and Herzegovina. Country-specific trends highlight Germany as consistently one of the top investors, with investments increasing substantially from EUR 242.0 million in 2013 to EUR 674.0 million in 2022. This steady increase indicates a robust economic relationship between Germany and Bosnia and Herzegovina, driven by Germany's strategic interest in the region's market potential and economic stability. Croatia exhibited a remarkable spike, particularly notable in 2015 with EUR 1119.8 million, reflecting its geographic and economic proximity to Bosnia and Herzegovina. This peak can be attributed to Croatia's significant cultural and historical ties, which facilitate cross-border investments and economic collaborations. Italy saw a significant rise in investments from EUR 175.7 million in 2013 to EUR 430.4 million in 2022, indicating growing Italian business interest in the region. The increase in Italian investments suggests a strategic move to capitalize on emerging opportunities in Bosnia and Herzegovina, driven by Italy's broader regional economic policies. Slovenia demonstrated consistent growth in investment, culminating at EUR 586.3 million in 2022. This trend highlights the strong economic ties between Slovenia and Bosnia and Herzegovina, likely facilitated by geographical proximity and similar market conditions. Slovenia's continuous investment growth reflects a stable and growing economic partnership.

Bulgaria and Czechia showed relatively small but fluctuating investment levels, suggesting niche or limited engagements. These countries' investments are likely driven by specific business opportunities rather than a broad strategic interest, leading to varied investment patterns over the years. The Netherlands and Sweden exhibited substantial variations, with Sweden particularly ramping up its investments in 2018 but seeing fluctuations afterward. This indicates episodic large-scale investments influenced by specific projects or market conditions, rather than consistent long-term strategies. Hungary and Poland have shown increasing investment trends, likely driven by regional strategies and expanding market presence. These trends suggest a focused effort by Hungary and Poland to enhance their economic footprint in Bosnia and Herzegovina, leveraging regional proximity and market expansion strategies. Denmark displayed a significant jump in 2016, possibly due to specific large-scale investments. This spike points to targeted investments in particular sectors or projects that prompted a substantial one-time increase, rather than sustained annual growth. Overall, the investment landscape from EU countries into Bosnia and Herzegovina over the past decade indicates a complex interplay of strategic interests, regional proximity, and specific economic opportunities. This diverse investment pattern underscores the multifaceted nature of EU economic engagement with Bosnia and Herzegovina, reflecting both broad and targeted investment approaches across different member states.

North Macedonia The total direct investment inflows from EU countries underscore a strong interest in the business environment of North Macedonia, growing substantially from EUR 2.0 billion in 2013 to EUR 3.3 billion in 2022. This represents around half of the total inward FDI stock into the economy of North Macedonia, indicating a robust commitment by EU investors to the region. Investment inflows from various EU member states reveal upward trends and significant contributions over the years. Notable among these contributors are Slovenia, Greece, Germany, Italy, Bulgaria, and the Netherlands. Slovenia stands out as a consistent investor, with its investments increasing steadily from EUR 401.0 million in 2013 to EUR 491.1 million in 2022. The strong political and economic relations between these two former Yugoslav republics facilitate this steady inflow of Slovenian capital into North Macedonia. In addition to investments, bilateral trade relations between the two countries are exceptionally strong, further bolstering their economic partnership. Greece is another major regional investor, with its investments growing significantly from EUR 269.9 million in 2013 to EUR 465.7 million in 2022. This growth reflects the strategic economic ties and mutual interests shared between Greece and North Macedonia, underpinned by geographical proximity and historical connections. Germany registered a significant increase in investments, rising to EUR 391.0 million in 2020, followed by a minor reduction to EUR 345.0 million by 2022. This highlights Germany's substantial investment footprint in North Macedonia, establishing it not only as a principal trading partner but also as a key

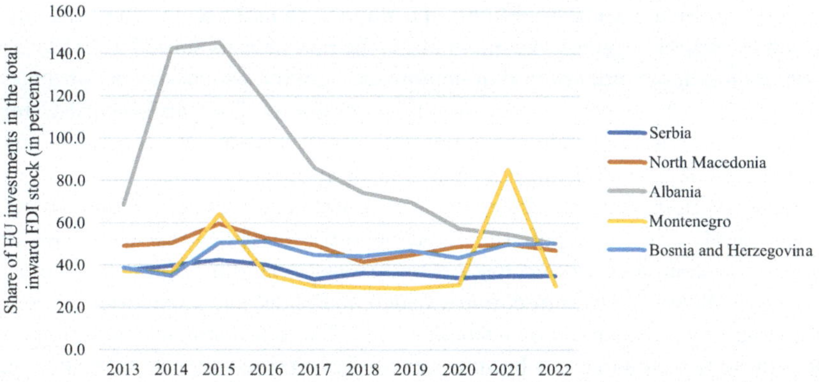

Fig. 16 Share of EU direct investment positions in total inward FDI stocks of Western Balkan countries (2013–2022, in percent). Notes: [1] Aggregate data for EU investments in Kosovo has a lot of missing observations. [2] EU direct investment positions, flows, and income, by countries (BPM6) [bop_fdi6_geo__custom_11943169]. Source: Authors' calculations based on data from Eurostat (July 2024)

investor in various sectors of the Macedonian economy. Italian direct investments have shown a steady increase from EUR 152.1 million in 2013 to EUR 177.9 million in 2022, maintaining a consistent investment interest. This steady growth reflects Italy's strategic engagement and economic interests in North Macedonia, leveraging opportunities in a growing market. Bulgaria, too, has displayed a steady upward trajectory, with investments growing from EUR 57.6 million in 2013 to EUR 159.2 million in 2022. This steady increase in Bulgarian investments underscores the strengthening economic ties and the strategic importance of North Macedonia as a regional partner. The investment stocks of EU member states reflect not only their financial stakes but also suggest a deeper economic integration and partnership with North Macedonia. The sustained and growing investment trends indicate a solid confidence in the Macedonian market and its potential for future growth. These investments from the EU are not just financial commitments; they are also indicative of stronger economic ties, greater collaboration, and a shared vision for regional development and prosperity (Fig. 16).

Montenegro EU investments in Montenegro have demonstrated dynamic patterns over the period from 2013 to 2022, reflecting shifts in both the scale and the source of funding from various EU member states. The total EU investments exhibited significant fluctuations, with notable peaks in 2015 and 2021, indicating sporadic large-scale investments. The share of EU investments in Montenegro's total inward FDI stock varied considerably, peaking at 85.3% in 2021 but generally maintaining around 30%. This indicates that while EU investments are substantial, they are not always dominant in Montenegro's overall FDI landscape. For instance, the total EU investment stocks increased dramatically to EUR 2926.9 million in 2015, driven largely by a major investment from the Netherlands amounting to EUR 1646.0 million. This significant spike highlights the impact of large-scale, one-time investments on overall FDI figures. Again, in 2021, the investments surged to EUR 4254.6 million, indicating another period of heightened activity, which may be attributed to specific large-scale projects or favourable economic policies attracting EU investors. Key consistent contributors include Italy, with investments generally ranging around the EUR 250–500 million mark but dipping in the later years, reflecting possible shifts in investment strategies or economic conditions. Slovenia showed a relatively stable investment pattern, increasing towards EUR 207.8 million by 2022, suggesting sustained economic interest and robust bilateral relations. Smaller but steady investments came from countries such as Poland and Luxembourg, demonstrating ongoing engagement on a smaller scale. These investments, although not as large as those from major contributors, indicate a diversified interest in Montenegro's economic potential across various EU member states. Croatia and Greece also maintained significant investment levels, with neighbouring Croatia's investment stock peaking at EUR 261.4 million in 2017. This regional proximity likely facilitates economic ties and investment flows, enhancing economic integration between Montenegro and its EU neighbours. This fluctuating investment pattern from the EU contrasts with the more stable contributions from non-EU countries. The data suggests that varying interest by EU countries towards Montenegro is influenced by geopolitical shifts and economic policies. This variability in EU investment patterns highlights the importance of targeted economic policies and stable political environments in attracting consistent FDI flows from the EU, contributing to Montenegro's economic growth and development. The investment landscape in Montenegro reflects a complex interplay of regional dynamics, economic opportunities, and strategic interests of EU member states. The peaks and troughs in investment figures underline the need for Montenegro to maintain an attractive investment climate to capitalize on the sporadic yet substantial influxes of EU capital. These investments are crucial for fostering economic growth, enhancing infrastructure, and integrating Montenegro more closely with the European economic framework.

Kosovo Germany leads as the primary EU country in terms of direct investment stocks in Kosovo, holding 17.5% of the total foreign direct investment (FDI). This substantial share underscores the strong economic ties and confidence that Germany has in Kosovo's market potential. Close behind is non-EU member Switzerland, with 16.2% of the total FDI, indicating robust bilateral economic relations and a significant Swiss economic footprint in Kosovo. These investments are strategically channelled into critical sectors such as real estate, leasing activities, financial services, and energy. The focus on these sectors highlights a strategic approach to supporting infrastructure development and enhancing economic stability in Kosovo. The real estate and leasing sectors, for instance, are vital for urban development and business expansion, providing necessary facilities for both local and foreign businesses. Investments in financial services are crucial for strengthening the financial infrastructure, improving access to capital, and fostering a more dynamic business environment. In the energy sector, investments are essential for ensuring sustainable and reliable energy supplies, which are critical for industrial growth and overall economic development. Given Kosovo's strategic position and its growing energy needs, investments in this sector also align with broader efforts to integrate the region's energy markets with those of the EU, promoting energy security and sustainability. The strategic investment patterns of Germany and Switzerland reflect both the economic opportunities present in Kosovo and the broader geopolitical interest in stabilizing and integrating the region economically with EU standards. These investments not only contribute to immediate economic growth but also support long-term structural improvements, aligning Kosovo's economic infrastructure more closely with European norms and practices. The prominent roles of Germany and Switzerland in Kosovo's FDI landscape illustrate the interconnectedness of economic and geopolitical strategies. By channelling investments into key sectors, these countries are not only fostering economic growth but also contributing to the stability and integration of Kosovo within the broader European economic framework. This strategic alignment is vital for Kosovo's continued development and its aspirations for closer ties with the European Union.

Serbia The EU investment stocks in Serbia have shown a notable progression over the years 2013–2022. The total EU investment stocks have consistently grown from EUR 12.5 billion in 2013 to EUR 19.3 billion by 2022, indicating a strengthening and deepening of economic relations. Germany has been a significant contributor, with investments peaking at EUR 2118 million in 2022, highlighting its pivotal role in the Serbian market. The robust investment from Germany reflects the country's confidence in Serbia's economic potential and the strategic importance of its market. Similarly, the Netherlands has shown substantial investment increases, culminating at EUR 4626 million in 2022, making it one of the largest EU investors in Serbia. The significant Dutch investments underscore the Netherlands' strategic economic interests and its focus on fostering long-term business relationships within the region. Other significant contributors include Italy and Luxembourg, with consistent investments over the years, indicating stable economic interests in the region. Italy's investments were particularly robust, reaching EUR 1712.3 million in 2022, reflecting the strong historical and economic ties between the two countries. Luxembourg's investments remained significant as well, indicating a strategic positioning in Serbia's market, particularly in financial services and high-value sectors. Additionally, Slovenia and Hungary have shown notable investment activity. Slovenia's investments increased significantly to EUR 1732 million by 2022, showcasing the strong economic linkages and bilateral cooperation. Hungary's investments reached EUR 1320 million, indicating a focused engagement in Serbia's economic landscape and reflecting regional strategic interests. Conversely, investments from Greece, initially high, have seen a decline, reflecting potential shifts in economic strategies or market dynamics. This decline might be attributable to broader economic adjustments within Greece or changing investment priorities. Smaller EU countries like Estonia and Lithuania, while contributing less in absolute terms, demonstrate a continued interest in maintaining economic ties with Serbia. Their investments, though modest, signify ongoing engagement and potential for future growth.

The increasing trend in EU investment stocks in Serbia, coupled with the diversification of contributing countries, underscores the growing economic integration between Serbia and the European Union. This reflects not only the economic strategies of individual EU countries but also Serbia's growing importance as a key market and investment destination in the Balkans. This trend is supported by the share of EU investments in Serbia's total inward FDI stock, which has shown slight fluctuations but generally indicates a significant EU stake in the Serbian economy. The steady increase in EU investments in Serbia highlights the mutual benefits and strategic interests that underpin the economic relationship. The diverse range of investing countries and the substantial capital inflows underscore the confidence of EU investors in Serbia's market potential and its strategic importance in the broader European economic landscape. This growing economic integration is likely to continue, driven by Serbia's ongoing efforts to align with EU standards and the mutual benefits of closer economic ties.

A recent study by Ardakani et al. (2024) investigates the impact of membership in the European Monetary Union (EMU) on economic and financial outcomes, using propensity score matching to address self-selection bias. The primary aim is to understand if the adoption of the euro and integration into the EMU leads to significant changes in key economic indicators, including inflation volatility, GDP growth, bond yields, and fiscal health.

The EMU was established to foster market integration by eliminating exchange rate volatility, reducing transaction costs, and harmonizing financial regulations. The European Central Bank (ECB) plays a crucial role in managing the euro and implementing monetary policies aimed at maintaining price stability. The effectiveness of the EMU has been a subject of extensive research, with mixed findings on its impact on price stability, interest rate convergence, and yield spreads.

The study utilizes data from 1990 to 2019, covering 19 EMU member countries and 20 non-member European countries. To address the self-selection bias, the authors employ propensity score matching, a method commonly used in applied microeconomics. This approach allows for the estimation of the average treatment effect on the treated (ATT) by comparing EMU and non-EMU countries with similar covariate distributions. The study also conducts robustness checks, including different sample periods and sensitivity analyses.

Key findings indicate that EMU membership significantly reduces the volatility of inflation, GDP growth, and bond yields. This indicates a stabilizing effect of the EMU on these key macroeconomic indicators. The study also reveals that EMU membership is associated with higher debt-to-GDP ratios, particularly in the post-crisis period. This suggests that fiscal challenges were more pervasive than previously thought. The effectiveness of the EMU varies across different countries and periods. For instance, while some countries experienced reduced volatility in economic indicators, others saw an increase in fiscal imbalances.

The findings carry significant implications for policymakers. The EMU's role in reducing volatility should be leveraged by offering guidance and tools to help member states stabilize key economic metrics. Enhanced fiscal oversight is needed to monitor and address fiscal imbalances across all member states, not just the traditionally problematic ones. Given the varying impacts of EMU membership, a one-size-fits-all approach may not be suitable. Collaborative efforts among member states to share experiences and solutions are crucial.

Ardakani et al. (2024) provide a comprehensive analysis of the impact of EMU membership on economic and financial outcomes. The study highlights the stabilizing effects of the EMU on inflation and growth volatility while also pointing out the fiscal challenges associated with membership. The findings underscore the importance of tailored policy approaches and enhanced fiscal oversight to ensure the long-term success and stability of the EMU.

The findings of this study hold particular relevance for Western Balkan countries aspiring to join the EMU. These countries, including Albania, Montenegro, North Macedonia, and Serbia, face unique economic challenges and opportunities as they seek closer integration with the European Union (EU). The potential benefits of EMU membership, such as reduced inflation and growth volatility, could provide a stabilizing influence on their economies, which are often characterized by higher economic fluctuations and vulnerabilities.

However, the study also underscores the importance of addressing fiscal imbalances, a critical consideration for Western Balkan countries. As these nations prepare for potential EMU membership, they must focus on strengthening their fiscal frameworks and ensuring sustainable debt levels. The experience of current EMU members suggests that robust fiscal oversight and adherence to fiscal rules are essential to maximize the benefits of monetary integration.

Furthermore, the heterogeneous impact of EMU membership observed in this study implies that Western Balkan countries must be prepared for varied outcomes. Policymakers in these countries should tailor their economic strategies to their specific contexts, leveraging the lessons learned from existing EMU members to navigate the complexities of monetary union.

The ability to conduct an independent monetary policy of WB-6 countries is strongly dependent on the choice of the exchange rate arrangements. In that context, WB-6 can be divided into two groups of countries with: (1) fixed exchange rate regimes (unilateral use of euro in Kosovo and Montenegro, a currency board arrangement in Bosnia and Herzegovina, and de facto fixed exchange rate regime in North Macedonia) and (2) flexible exchange rate regimes (inflation targeting and floating exchange rate regime in Albania and Serbia).

Unilateral Use of the Euro Kosovo and Montenegro have already adopted the euro as a legal tender and a de facto currency. These two Western Balkans countries have no independent monetary policy. They are unilaterally euroized and fully rely on the credibility of the ECB and the euro as a global reserve currency. In a sense, these WB countries are passive members of the euro area. Their central banks are focused on strengthening the soundness, solvency, and efficient functioning of their financial systems as well smooth functioning of the payment systems.

Currency Board Arrangement Bosnia and Herzegovina has tied its currency (the convertible mark, KM) to the euro through a currency board arrangement. The central bank maintains monetary stability by issuing domestic currency with full coverage in freely convertible foreign exchange funds under fixed exchange rate (1 KM: 0.51129 euro). The intention is to reduce exchange rate volatility and promote monetary stability by fixing the domestic currency against the euro as chosen anchor currency. The adoption of the currency board arrangement has given Bosnia and Herzegovina a stable and trusted currency as well as a low inflation rate. Such a macroeconomic environment promotes significant bilateral trade and investment relations with the EU member states.

De Facto Fixed Exchange Rate Regime The monetary policy of North Macedonia is based on exchange rate targeting. Even though officially classified as a managed exchange rate arrangement, the country has a de facto fixed exchange rate regime linked to the euro, thereby preserving the ability to change the exchange rate in case of large shocks. With a fixed exchange rate regime, the ability to set monetary policy is very limited and dependent on the country's degree of financial openness. Since the country uses the euro as an anchor currency, the exchange rate against the other major currencies reflects the performance of the euro in international markets. To illustrate this, imagine hugging a dolphin, placing your full trust in its good intentions, and letting the dolphin decide how to swim or float.

Managed Floating Regime The National Bank of Serbia chose inflation targeting and a managed floating exchange rate regime to ensure price stability. After the pandemic outbreak in 2020, the central bank of Serbia signalled a public commitment to a stable exchange rate relative to the euro. Although Albania has a flexible exchange rate regime, it has remained broadly stable. In sum, Albania and Serbia have a significant space for pursuing an accommodative (independent) monetary policy, because of their flexible exchange rate regimes.

If we exclude Montenegro and Kosovo, the other four Western Balkans countries have historically had a high degree of currency substitution (euroization). Put differently, a large portion of the deposits and loans in the financial systems are either in euros or are linked to the value of the euro (euro-indexed deposits or loans). The currency and assets substitution (in the case of Western Balkans known as "euroization") are features of the countries in transition, which in the past faced with financial and monetary crisis in the system, and hence diminished credibility of the domestic currency (e.g. Besimi, Pugh, and Adnett 2006). The substantial presence of foreign-owned banks in the financial system can also be an important euroization factor.

The central banks of WB-6 countries closely follow the monetary policy decisions made by ECB and the daily movements of the key interest rates. The ECB and the national banks of the EMU member states also provide substantial technical cooperation for the national central banks of the EU candidate and potential candidate countries from Western Balkans. The areas vary from central bank statistics, payment systems, money laundering, bank supervision, financial stability, internal audit, information technology, to implementation of other central banking standards. After all, the ECB and the national supervisory authorities of the euro area countries are also home supervisors of many multinational banks that have a presence in the Western Balkans. Therefore, the monetary policy coordination and technical cooperation are mutually beneficial. The ultimate goal of these programmes is to prepare the central banks of the WB-6 region for membership of the European System of Central Banks (ESCB), once the respective countries join the EU.

7.3 The Potential Benefits of Further European Integration

7.3.1 The European Union's Perspective

The future enlargement of the European Union (EU) can be generally seen as a win-win situation because of the political, economic, and cultural benefits it will bring. This complex approach to Europe's growth will help in establishing the EU as a paramount global actor, boost its economic power, and increase its cultural multiplicity.

Important Geopolitical Benefits One major strategy the EU uses to assert itself in regions critical to its interests is expansion. By accepting nations from the Western Balkans, the European Union will be able to establish itself firmly within a historically unstable region, thereby reducing external influences exerted by rival powers such as Russia and China. This strategic enlargement not only strengthens the EU's external borders but also enhances stability and peace in a region that has experienced much conflict before.

Through enlargement, the EU effectively exports its values and norms—democracy, rule of law, human rights, and market economy—helping to stabilize its neighbourhood. It is through this expansion that the region acts as both a buffer zone and bridge, thereby promoting security among all member states. As scholar Frank Schimmelfennig argues, the EU's enlargement policy serves as a key instrument in its foreign policy toolkit, promoting peace and stability through the projection of its normative power (Schimmelfennig 2001). By integrating the Western Balkans in the Union, the EU not only mitigates the risk of regional instability but also curtails the influence of non-EU actors who might otherwise fill the geopolitical void.

Significant Economic Advantages Enlargement offers significant economic advantages. New member states often undergo substantial reforms to meet EU standards, leading to improved governance and economic policies. This alignment boosts their economic performance, which in turn contributes to the EU's overall economic health. Moreover, enlargement expands the single market, facilitating trade and investment flows. This increased market size allows for greater economies of scale, benefiting businesses throughout the Union.

Additionally, newer members often possess competitive advantages in certain sectors, such as agriculture or manufacturing, which can complement the economic profiles of existing members. The integration of these markets thus leads to more dynamic intra-EU trade relations and fosters a more competitive economy on a global scale. The economic rationale for enlargement is supported by the work of Baldwin et al. (1997), who highlight that the integration of new markets enhances economic efficiency and increases the EU's global competitiveness.

Cultural and Social Benefits Cultural enrichment is another significant benefit of EU enlargement. The Union's motto, "United in diversity", highlights the value placed on cultural plurality. Each new member adds to the cultural tapestry of the EU, bringing unique traditions, languages, and perspectives. This diversity not only enriches the cultural experience within the EU but also promotes mutual understanding and tolerance among its peoples.

Socially, enlargement can lead to improved rights and opportunities for citizens across the Union. As countries reform to meet EU criteria, improvements in areas like education, healthcare, and employment rights can occur, benefiting both new and existing member states. Furthermore, the free movement of people enhances cultural exchange and educational opportunities, helping to forge a pan-European identity. As Inglehart and Norris (2003) discuss, the cultural integration facilitated by EU enlargement contributes to the development of a collective European identity, fostering solidarity and cohesion among diverse populations.

Institutional and Structural Benefits Enlargement also necessitates institutional and structural reforms within the EU, which can lead to more efficient and effective governance. The integration of new members often provides momentum for the EU to reassess and refine its policies and procedures. This adaptation process can lead to innovative approaches in governance, from policymaking to administration.

Moreover, the challenges of integrating diverse economies and systems can foster greater flexibility and resilience in the EU's institutions, preparing them for future challenges. As argued by Börzel and Risse (2000), the process of enlargement drives institutional learning and adaptation within the EU, ultimately strengthening its capacity to address complex, multidimensional issues.

The structural benefits of enlargement also involve enhancing the EU's strategic capabilities. The inclusion of new member states can expand the EU's geopolitical reach, providing strategic advantages in terms of security, energy, and environmental policies. For instance, the integration of energy infrastructures and environmental regulations across a larger EU can enhance energy security and promote sustainable development, addressing critical challenges faced by the Union. Additionally, the expansion of the EU's judicial and regulatory frameworks ensures a more comprehensive and coherent application of European laws and standards, enhancing the rule of law and governance throughout the region.

Furthermore, the institutional reforms driven by enlargement can lead to a more democratic and transparent EU. The integration process often requires new member states to adopt rigorous standards of accountability and transparency, which can influence broader EU governance practices. This reciprocal influence can enhance the democratic legitimacy of EU institutions, fostering greater trust and engagement among citizens. The continuous evolution and improvement of EU institutions through the enlargement process underscore the Union's commitment to democratic values and effective governance, positioning it as a robust and adaptive global actor.

7.3.2 The Western Balkans' Perspective

Political and business leaders from Western Balkans, almost without exception, have repeatedly highlighted their aspirations for joining the Union. Public polls have consistently indicated large shares of populations supporting the prospective EU membership. In the eyes of ordinary people, the EU is still a symbol of economic prosperity and democracy, synonymous with the rule of law and respect for human rights and freedoms. The EU is perceived as a political union with a functioning market economy, a high living standard, and competent institutions (Kandikjan and Stojkov 2010; Taylor 2013).

The previous rounds of EU enlargements have reaffirmed the transformative power of the EU integration in fostering socio-economic development, political stability, and democratic consolidation (e.g. Börzel and Lebanidze 2017; Brsakoska Bazerkoska and Dokmanović 2017). The Western Balkans, drawing from these experiences, view EU membership as a gateway to stability, economic growth, and enhanced governance. The promise of joining the EU has galvanized reform efforts across the region, aligning policies and institutions with EU standards and best practices.

Political Stability Political stability is one of the most anticipated benefits of EU membership for the Western Balkans. Historically, the region has been plagued by political turbulence and conflict. EU membership is seen as a stabilizing force, offering a framework for resolving disputes and fostering cooperation. The EU's emphasis on democratic governance, rule of law, and human rights provides a foundation for political stability. As the region moves closer to EU membership, these principles are expected to be further entrenched in the political systems of Western Balkan countries, reducing the risk of political instability and conflict.

Economic Prosperity The economic benefits of EU membership are also highly valued in the Western Balkans. The integration into the EU's single market promises increased trade, investment, and economic growth. The region anticipates significant inflows of foreign direct investment (FDI) as a result of the stability and market access that come with EU membership. The alignment with EU economic policies and regulations is expected to improve the business environment, making the region more attractive to investors. Additionally, access to EU structural and cohesion funds can help address regional disparities and promote economic development, further enhancing the economic prospects of the Western Balkans.

Further Democratic Consolidation Democratic consolidation is another critical area where the Western Balkans expect to benefit from EU membership. The process of EU integration requires countries to implement extensive political and institutional reforms, strengthening democratic governance. This includes enhancing the independence and efficiency of the judiciary, ensuring free and fair elections, and protecting fundamental rights and freedoms. These reforms not only align the countries with EU standards but also promote the development of robust democratic institutions. The oversight and support from EU institutions during the accession process help ensure that these reforms are effectively implemented and sustained.

Societal Resistance However, there are societal players that could lose their political and economic power when a level-playing field is secured and when the scrutiny by EU institutions is enhanced. These groups, often entrenched in the existing power structures, might resist the changes required for EU accession. They might be the biggest winners from the prolonged EU accession process of the Western Balkans, benefiting from the status quo that allows them to maintain their influence and control. This resistance can slow down the reform process and create obstacles to the region's EU integration efforts.

The perspective of the Western Balkans on EU integration is overwhelmingly positive, viewing it as a pathway to political stability, economic prosperity, and democratic consolidation. The transformative power of EU membership is expected to address many of the region's historical and contemporary challenges. However, the journey towards EU membership is complex and fraught with challenges, particularly from those who stand to lose from the changes it necessitates. Despite these challenges, the aspiration for EU membership remains a unifying and motivating force in the Western Balkans, driving forward the necessary reforms and fostering hope for a better future.

8 What Lies Ahead?

The European Union (EU) integration of the Western Balkans is a complex and multifaceted process, marked by aspirations for membership and the challenges of meeting stringent accession criteria. As we delve into this intricate journey, it becomes clear that the process is not merely political but also encompasses significant economic and social dimensions. In this book, we explore the key themes surrounding the European integration and democratization of the Western Balkans, the region's security regionalization, and the specific challenges and opportunities faced by Albania and Kosovo in their EU integration journey.

Political and business leaders from the Western Balkans have consistently highlighted their aspirations for EU membership, a sentiment echoed by large segments of their populations. The EU is seen as a beacon of economic prosperity, democracy, and the rule of law. Public polls frequently show strong support for EU membership, reflecting a widespread belief in the transformative power of EU integration to foster socio-economic development and political stability. The previous rounds of EU enlargements have demonstrated the potential of EU integration to drive socio-economic and political reforms. Countries that joined the EU in the past have experienced significant improvements in governance, economic performance, and democratic consolidation. This sets a hopeful outlook for the Western Balkan countries aspiring to join the Union.

Despite numerous initiatives, the Western Balkans have experienced a stagnation in security regionalization. This stagnation can be attributed to several factors, including divergent political interests, historical animosities, and varying levels of commitment to regional cooperation among the countries. The region still grapples with issues such as organized crime, political instability, and economic disparities, which hinder the development of a cohesive regional security framework. External actors, particularly the EU and the United States, play a crucial role in the regional security dynamics of the Western Balkans. The EU, through various initiatives and frameworks such as the Stability Pact and the Regional Cooperation Council (RCC), has been instrumental in promoting regional cooperation. However, the influence of other global powers, like Russia and China, complicates the regional security landscape and poses challenges to the EU's efforts to foster stability and cooperation.

Albania's journey towards EU membership has been marked by significant milestones and persistent challenges. The country has made notable progress in areas such as judicial reform and the fight against corruption. However, it still faces substantial hurdles, including the need for further reforms in public administration and the judiciary. The opening of accession negotiations in July 2022 was a historic step, reflecting Albania's commitment to meeting EU standards and the EU's recognition of these efforts. Economic integration and trade agreements with the EU have been crucial in supporting Albania's reform agenda and economic development. The Stabilization and Association Agreement (SAA) has facilitated increased trade and investment flows, contributing to economic growth. However, challenges remain in fully aligning Albania's regulatory framework with EU standards and addressing structural economic issues such as unemployment and regional disparities. To sustain progress, Albania must continue to address critical challenges in areas like justice reform, public administration, and energy policy. Strengthening the rule of law, enhancing administrative capacity, and improving energy infrastructure are essential for Albania's successful integration into the EU. These reforms will not only facilitate compliance with EU accession criteria but also promote sustainable economic growth and social development.

Kosovo's path towards EU integration is influenced by its unique political and economic context. The EU has played a pivotal role in supporting Kosovo's regional integration through initiatives like the Common Regional Market (CRM) and the Stabilization and Association Agreement (SAA). These frameworks aim to enhance economic cooperation, attract foreign investment, and promote political stability in Kosovo and the broader Western Balkan region. Kosovo faces numerous challenges, including political instability, governance issues, and limited international recognition. However, the country also has significant opportunities to leverage EU support for economic and social development. Reforms in areas such as governance, the rule of law, and economic policy are crucial for Kosovo's progress towards EU membership. The EU's ongoing support and the potential for deeper regional integration provide a pathway for overcoming these challenges. The geopolitical landscape of the Western Balkans has been further complicated by the Russian invasion of Ukraine. This event has underscored the strategic importance of the region for the EU and highlighted the need for enhanced security and political stability. The EU's response to the invasion, including increased support for Western Balkan countries, reflects a renewed commitment to integrating the region and countering external influences that threaten stability and democratic governance.

The next chapters highlight the multifaceted nature of the Western Balkans' journey towards EU integration. While the region faces significant challenges, including political instability, economic disparities, and security concerns, the potential benefits of EU membership provide a strong incentive for continued reforms and cooperation. The EU's support and strategic engagement are crucial in facilitating the integration process and promoting stability, prosperity, and democratic governance in the Western Balkans. The path to EU membership is complex and requires sustained efforts from both the Western Balkan countries and the EU. However, the transformative potential of EU integration offers a promising future for the region, aligning it more closely with European values and standards.

As we explore these themes in greater depth with the help of our contributors, we invite you to join us in examining the dynamic interplay of politics, economics, and society that shapes the Western Balkans' quest for EU membership. This journey is not just about meeting criteria and ticking boxes; it is about embracing a shared vision for a united, prosperous, and stable Europe.

References

Abiad A, Leigh D, Mody A (2009) Financial integration, capital mobility, and income convergence. Econ Policy 24(58):241–305

Alesina A, La Ferrara E (2005) Ethnic diversity and economic performance. J Econ Lit 43(3):762–800

Ardakani OM, Kishor NK, Song S (2024) Does membership of the EMU matter for economic and financial outcomes? Contemp Econ Policy 42(3):416–447. https://doi.org/10.1111/coep.12638

Baldwin R, Wyplosz C (2015) The economics of European integration. McGraw-Hill Education

Baldwin RE, Francois JF, Portes R (1997) The costs and benefits of eastern enlargement: the impact on the EU and Central Europe. Econ Policy 24:125–170. https://doi.org/10.1111/1468-0327.00018

Bechev D (2011) Constructing South East Europe: the politics of Balkan regional cooperation. Palgrave Macmillan, Hampshire

Belloni R, Brunazzo M (2017) After "Brexit": the Western Balkans in the European waiting room. Eur Rev Int Stud 4(1):21–38

Besimi F, Pugh G, Adnett NJ (2006) The monetary transmission mechanism in Macedonia: implications for monetary policy (2006). Centre for Research on Emerging Economies Working Paper No. 02-2006, Available at SSRN: https://ssrn.com/abstract=989209

Blanchard O, Giavazzi F (2002) Current account deficits in the Euro Area: the end of the Feldstein-Horioka puzzle? Brook Pap Econ Act 2(2002):147–186. https://www.jstor.org/stable/1209205

Börzel TA, Lebanidze B (2017) The transformative power of Europe beyond enlargement: the EU's performance in promoting democracy in its neighbourhood. East Eur Polit 33(1):17–35
Börzel TA, Risse T (2000) When Europe hits home: Europeanization and domestic change. Eur Integr Online Pap 4(15)
Börzel TA, Risse T (2009) The transformative power of Europe: the European Union and the diffusion of ideas, KFG working paper series, no. 1. Freie Universität Berlin
Bosworth B, Collins SM (2003) The empirics of growth: an update. Brook Pap Econ Act 34(2):113–206
Bourguignon F, Demertzis M, Sprenger R (2022) Managing diversity in the European Union. Bruegel Blueprint Series
Brock WA, Durlauf SN (2001) What have we learned from a decade of empirical research on growth? Growth empirics and reality. World Bank Econ Rev 15(2):229–272. https://doi.org/10.1093/wber/15.2.229
Brsakoska Bazerkoska J, Dokmanović M (2017) The transformative power of the EU in the Western Balkans: enlargement as a tool for democratization. SEER J Lab Soc Aff East Eur 20(3–4):137–148
Cabral R, Castellanos-Sosa FA (2019) Europe's income convergence and the latest global financial crisis. Res Econ 73(1):23–34. https://doi.org/10.1016/j.rie.2019.01.003
Campos NF, Coricelli F, Moretti L (2019) Institutional integration and economic growth in Europe. J Monet Econ 103(May):88–104. https://doi.org/10.1016/j.jmoneco.2018.08.001
Ciccone A, Jarociński M (2010) Determinants of economic growth: will data tell? Am Econ J Macroecon 2(4):222–246. https://doi.org/10.1257/mac.2.4.222
Conti M, Sulis G (2016) Human capital, employment protection and growth in Europe. J Comp Econ 44(2):213–230. https://doi.org/10.1016/j.jce.2015.01.007
Crespo Cuaresma J, Havettová M, Lábaj M (2013) Income convergence prospects in Europe: assessing the role of human capital dynamics. Econ Syst 37(4):493–507. https://doi.org/10.1016/j.ecosys.2013.02.004
Crespo Cuaresma J, Lábaj M, Pružinský P (2014) Prospective ageing and economic growth in Europe. J Econ Ageing 3(April):50–57. https://doi.org/10.1016/j.jeoa.2014.05.003
Crespo Cuaresma J, Loichinger E, Vincelette GA (2016) Aging and income convergence in Europe: a survey of the literature and insights from a demographic projection exercise. Econ Syst 40(1):4–17. https://doi.org/10.1016/j.ecosys.2015.07.003
Czasonis M, Quinn MA (2012) Income convergence in Europe: catching up or falling behind? Acta Oecon 62(2):183–204
D'Andrea S (2022) Are there any robust determinants of growth in Europe? A Bayesian model averaging approach. Int Econ 171(October):143–173. https://doi.org/10.1016/j.inteco.2022.06.001
Ellis T (2023) Without Greece, There Can Be No EU. Ekathimerini. February 27. https://www.ekathimerini.com/opinion/interviews/1210891/without-greece-there-can-be-no-eu/
Encyclopædia Britannica (2023) European Union. Britannica. https://www.britannica.com/topic/European-Union
Dabrowski M, Myachenkova Y (2018) The Western Balkans on the road to the European Union. Bruegel Policy Contribution, Issue 2018/04
De Grauwe P, Schnabl G (2008) Exchange rate stability, inflation, and growth in (South) Eastern and Central Europe. Rev Dev Econ 12(3):530–549. https://doi.org/10.1111/j.1467-9361.2008.00470.x
Der Spiegel (2009) Erdogan has gambled away political capital. Der Spiegel, 7 April
Durlauf SN, Johnson PA, Temple JRW (2005) Growth econometrics. Handb Econ Growth 1:555–677. https://doi.org/10.1016/S1574-0684(05)01008-7
Dustmann C, Frattini T (2014) The fiscal effects of immigration to the UK. Econ J 124(580):F593–F643
Economides S (2020) From fatigue to resistance: EU enlargement and the Western Balkans. Dahrendorf Forum. https://www.dahrendorf-forum.eu/publications/from-fatigue-to-resistance-eu-enlargement-and-the-western-balkans/

Economides S, Featherstone K, Hunter M (2024) The European Union and the Western Balkans: enlargement, integration and challenges. Routledge

Elbasani A (ed) (2013) European integration and transformation in the Western Balkans: Europeanization or business as usual? Routledge, London

Eurobarometer (2009) Views on European Union enlargement - analytical report. European Commission, Directorate-General Communication

Eurobarometer (2023) Public opinion in the European Union. European Commission, Directorate-General Communication

Featherstone K (2005) Introduction: modernization and the structural constraints of Greek politics. West Eur Polit 28(2):223–241

Fetahi-Vehapi M, Sadiku L, Petkovski M (2015) Empirical analysis of the effects of trade openness on economic growth: an evidence for South East European countries. Procedia Economics and Finance 19(January):17–26. https://doi.org/10.1016/S2212-5671(15)00004-0

Franks J et al (2018) Economic convergence in the Euro Area: coming together or drifting apart? IMF Working Paper

Friedrich C, Schnabel I, Zettelmeyer J (2013) Financial integration and growth: why is emerging Europe different? J Int Econ 89(2):522–538. https://doi.org/10.1016/j.jinteco.2012.07.003

Gill IS, Raiser M (2012) Golden growth: restoring the lustre of the European economic model. World Bank Group, Washington, D.C.. Available at: http://documents.worldbank.org/curated/en/539371468036253854/Main-report

Glawe L, Wagner H (2021) Convergence, divergence, or multiple steady states? New evidence on the institutional development within the European Union. J Comp Econ 49(3):860–884

Grabbe H (2006) The EU's transformative power: Europeanization through conditionality in Central and Eastern Europe. Palgrave Macmillan

Inglehart R, Norris P (2003) The true clash of civilizations. Foreign Policy 135:63–70

James G, Witten D, Hastie T, Tibshirani R (2017) An introduction to statistical learning with applications in R, 2nd edn. Springer, New York

Kalaitzoglou I, Durgheu B (2016) Financial and economic growth in Europe: is the Euro beneficial for all countries? J Econ Integr 31(2):414–471

Kandikjan V, Stojkov A (2010) 'Economic integration of the Republic of Macedonia into the European Union - from stabilisation to association to accession. In: Annual Proceedings of the Law Faculty in Honor of Professor Todor Rushkov, pp 221–268. [in Macedonian]

Karjalainen T (2023) EU's enlargement policy and security concerns. Eur Foreign Aff Rev

Kešeljević A, Spruk R (2021) Long-term effects of Yugoslav war. Defence Peace Econ 34(4):410–436. https://doi.org/10.1080/10242694.2021.2007334

Lavenex S, Schimmelfennig F (2009) EU rules beyond EU borders: theorizing external governance in European politics. J Eur Publ Policy 16(6):791–812

Lipsey RE (2006) Measuring the impacts of FDI in Central and Eastern Europe, Working paper series. National Bureau of Economic Research. https://doi.org/10.3386/w12808

Maşca SG, Cuceu IC, Văidean VL (2015) The fiscal policy as growth engine in EU countries. Proc Econ Finance 32(January):1628–1637. https://doi.org/10.1016/S2212-5671(15)01489-6

Moravcsik A (1998) The choice for Europe: social purpose and state power from Messina to Maastricht. Cornell University Press

Moravcsik A, Vachudova MA (2003) National interests, state power, and EU enlargement. East Eur Polit Soc 17(1):42–57. https://doi.org/10.1177/0888325402239682

Nagy SG, Šiljak D (2022) Is the European Union still a convergence machine? Acta Oecon 72(1):47–63. https://doi.org/10.1556/032.2022.00003

O'Brennan J (2014) The EU's engagement with the Western Balkans: uneven and unsatisfactory. J Contemp Eur Stud 22(2):219–234

Orlowski LT (2020) Capital markets integration and economic growth in the European Union. J Policy Model 42(4):893–902. https://doi.org/10.1016/j.jpolmod.2020.03.012

Pack H (1994) Endogenous growth theory: intellectual appeal and empirical shortcomings. J Econ Perspect 8(1):55–72. https://doi.org/10.1257/jep.8.1.55

Papadimitriou D, Phinnemore D (2004) Europeanization, conditionality and domestic change: the Twinning exercise and administrative reform in Romania. J Common Mark Stud 42(3):619–639. https://doi.org/10.1111/j.0021-9886.2004.00521.x
Papadimitriou D, Phinnemore D (2008) Romania and the European Union: from marginalisation to membership? Routledge
Politico (2021) European Commission rebuffs Charles Michel's bid for 2030 enlargement target. Politico, 15 October. Available at: https://www.politico.eu/article/european-commission-snub-charles-michel-2030-enlargement-target/. Accessed 15 Oct 2021
Prasad ES, Rajan RG, Subramanian A (2007) Foreign capital and economic growth. Brook Pap Econ Act 2007(1):153–209
Rant V, Marinč M, Porenta J (2021) Debt and convergence: evidence from the EU member states. Financ Res Lett 39(March):101617. https://doi.org/10.1016/j.frl.2020.101617
Risse T (2010) A community of Europeans? Transnational identities and public spheres. Cornell University Press
Rodríguez-PoseA, KrøijerA (2009) Fiscal decentralization and economic growth in Central and Eastern Europe. Growth Chang 40(3):387–417. https://doi.org/10.1111/j.1468-2257.2009.00488.x
Schimmelfennig F (2001) The community trap: Liberal norms, rhetorical action, and the Eastern enlargement of the European Union. Int Organ 55(1):47–80
Schnabel I, Seckinger C (2019) Foreign banks, financial crises and economic growth in Europe. J Int Money Financ 95(July):70–94. https://doi.org/10.1016/j.jimonfin.2019.02.004
Schnabl G (2009) Exchange rate volatility and growth in emerging Europe and East Asia. Open Econ Rev 20(4):565–587. https://doi.org/10.1007/s11079-008-9084-6
Schimmelfennig F (2014) EU enlargement and differentiated integration: discrimination or equal treatment? J Eur Publ Policy 21(5):681–698. https://doi.org/10.1080/13501763.2014.897744
Sedelmeier U (2014) Anchoring democracy from above? The European Union and democratic backsliding in Hungary and Romania after accession. J Common Mark Stud 52(1):105–121
Shore C (2000) Building Europe: the cultural politics of European integration. Routledge
Smith ME (2003) Europe's foreign and security policy: the institutionalization of cooperation. Cambridge University Press
Smith J (2019) Europe as a political project: a political and historical analysis. Eur Politics Soc 20(2):210–228
Szekely IP, Ward-Warmedinger M (2018) Reform reversals: areas, circumstances and motivations. Comp Econ Stud 60(4):559–582
Taggart P, Szczerbiak A (2013) Coming in from the cold? Euroscepticism, government participation and party positions on Europe. J Common Mark Stud 51(1):17–37
Taydas Z, Kentmen-Cin C (2017) Determinants of public opinion towards EU enlargement: evidence from Turkey. J Eur Integr 39(3):283–300
Taylor P (2013) The EU's future and the Western Balkans: enlargement or retrenchment? J Contemp Eur Res 9(4):538–547
Vinci A (2000) EU and Balkan leaders hold key summit. CNN. November 24th, 2000. https://edition.cnn.com/2000/WORLD/europe/11/23/balkan.summit/index.html
Vukotić V, Baćović M (2006) Economic freedom and economic growth in South East Europe. Transit Stud Rev 13(1):81–91. https://doi.org/10.1007/s11300-006-0098-8
Warsaw Institute (2020) Can western Balkans serve as a role model of integration for eastern partnership? Warsaw Institute. https://warsawinstitute.org/can-western-balkans-serve-as-role-model-of-integration-for-easternpartnership/
Weber E (2011) Foreign and domestic growth drivers in Eastern Europe. Econ Syst 35(4):512–522. https://doi.org/10.1016/j.ecosys.2011.02.001
Wunsch N, Olszewska Z (2022) Navigating EU enlargement in a complex world. European Policy Centre
Young J (2017) Brexit: all you need to know about the UK leaving the EU. BBC News. Available at: https://www.bbc.com/news/uk-politics-32810887. Accessed 15 Oct 2021

The European Integration and Western Balkans: What Now?

Ivica Bocevski

Abstract

Is there a real perspective for the full integration of the Western Balkans Six in the European Union, or is the accession process already dead? "Something is rotten in the state of the European integration of the Western Balkans" is not just a poetic way to describe the state of affairs regarding full accession, but a reality. The European Union, and previously the European Economic Community, was quite efficient in previous cycles of European enlargement. Virtually all the accession processes were completed within the mandate of a single European Commission once the negotiation processes had been started with the respective countries. Furthermore, in the pre-accession period, the European Union invested heavily in the removal of the "non-acquis political criteria", which were usually linked to the democratic insufficiencies of the candidate countries. The only notable exceptions to the "rule of a single European Commission" are the Turkish enlargement and the Western Balkans Six (WB6) accession process. Given the fact that most of the WB6 countries already have the necessary legal framework in place for cooperation with the EU and that the single market is by far the largest trading partner of the region, the only logical conclusion is that there is no political will for further enlargement of the European Union, and so the accession process has ground to a halt.

Keywords

Democratization · European Union · Western Balkans · Democratic stabilization · Democratic backsliding · Democratic breakdown

I. Bocevski (✉)
Center for Research and Policy Making, Skopje, North Macedonia

A. Stojkov, T. Warin (eds.), *Western Balkans and the Future of Europe*, The Future of Europe, https://doi.org/10.1007/978-3-031-86465-0_2

1 The European Union and the Democratization

Is there a real perspective for the full integration of the Western Balkans Six (WB6) in the European Union, or is the accession process already dead? “Something is rotten in the state of the European integration of the Western Balkans” is not just a poetic way to describe the state of affairs regarding full accession, but a reality. The EU—previously the European Economic Community, was quite efficient in previous cycles of European enlargement. Virtually all the accession processes were completed within the mandate of a single European Commission once the negotiation processes had been started with the respective countries. Furthermore, in the pre-accession period, the European Union invested heavily in the removal of the “non-acquis political criteria”, which were usually linked to the democratic insufficiencies of the candidate countries. The only notable exceptions to the “rule of a single European Commission” are the Turkish enlargement and the WB6 accession process. Given the fact that most of the WB6 countries already have the necessary legal framework in place for cooperation with the EU and that the single market is by far the largest trading partner of the region, the only logical conclusion is that there is no political will for further enlargement of the European Union, and so the accession process has ground to a halt.

The democratic nature of the European Union and its member states is enshrined in the Treaty of the European Union. Article 2 of the Treaty stipulates that “The Union is founded on the values of respect for human dignity, freedom, democracy, equality, the rule of law and respect for human rights, including the rights of persons belonging to minorities. These values are common to the Member States in a society in which pluralism, non-discrimination, tolerance, justice, solidarity and equality between women and men prevail” (Treaty of the European Union 2012). That being said, is there a link between European integration and the democratization processes in its member states, candidates, and potential candidates? Can the EU project its democracy in its neighbourhood and around the globe? The answer seems obvious because “no regional organization or influence has had a more powerful impact on democratization in its own neighbourhood than the EU” (Diamond 2008). The EU was created from six Western European countries, which underwent thorough and substantial re-democratization in the aftermath of World War II, and all successful emerging Mediterranean democracies after the collapse of the southern dictatorships were admitted to the EU as full member states. Leo Tolstoy wrote in Anna Karenina that “happy families are all alike; every unhappy family is unhappy in its own way”, and at first sight it may seem that all the success stories of the post-communist democratic transitions are also alike, as they are now members of the European Union, while the undecided cases are at various stages in their journey towards European integration, and the failed post-communist democratizations are all unsuccessful in their own way, without any prospect of becoming members of the European Union.

Actual evidence is, however, less than obvious, and as Sedelmeier concludes, “the link between democratization and European integration is not straightforward” because “it is not clear to which extent the EU actually had a causal influence and how its influence varied across countries and issues” and “even if the EU did have a causal impact, it is not obvious that its influence was always entirely positive for democracy in East Central Europe" (Sedelmeier 2010).

In their essence, the democratization processes in the Mediterranean and the post-communist countries confirm that "one of the firmest conclusions" was that "transitions from authoritarian rule and immediate prospects for political democracy [are] largely to be explained in terms of national forces and calculations" and that "external factors [tend] to play an indirect and usually marginal role, with the obvious exception of those instances when foreign occupying power was present", as Philippe C. Schmitter writes in the most authoritative study on the democratization process, *Transitions from Authoritarian Rule* in 1986. However, after the fifth enlargement of the European Union, there has been a steady inflation of scholarly articles in which the role of the "external factors of democratization" has been reassessed due to the successful European integration story of the post-communist ten that joined the European Union (Tolstoy's happy families or Donald Rumsfeld's "New Europe") in 2004 (*see also* Bunce et al. 2010). Despite all the triumphalism of this tectonic historic event in contemporary European history, Philippe C. Schmitter's argument is still rock solid when he claims that democratic transition and consolidation are primarily issues of domestic politics and can best be explained by following the micro and macro political vectors in every polity.

However, the role of the European Union has to be re-evaluated, since throughout its history, this entity has played a decisive role in the democratic stabilization of the emerging European democracies, following their democratic transitions from authoritarian and totalitarian regimes (e.g. Grabbe 2006). The primary democratic role of the European Union in the domestic affairs of its constituent countries is "preventive", implying that there has never been a case of complete democratic breakdown in any of the European member states. This specific role of the European Union was a by-product of its institutional development and the events of the wider geostrategic environment of the European continent. It confirms the postulates of the intergovernmentalist approach to the European Union since the institutional development of the EU has led towards the broadest possible acceptance by the domestic national elites of the necessity to preserve the democratic regimes as a minimal condition for access to the common market and the other benefits provided by full membership.

The attractiveness of the EU continues to motivate countries to apply for membership. However, none of these countries are seduced by the special Cytherean "soft power" of a European Venus, as Robert Kagan defines the European way of foreign policy (Kagan 2003). The applicants' positions result from a cold-blooded cost–benefit analysis, and even though their elites and societies are aware of the massive reform process necessary for full accession to take place, the final prize (full membership) far "outweighs the costs, particularly those of exclusion, that applicants make concessions even when no coercion is threatened" (Moravcsik and Vachudova 2003). Furthermore, "a seat at the Council table gives small and medium-sized countries more say in world affairs through the EU's collective weight. And it is also beneficial in disputes with their neighbours; while those members left outside have much less influence" (Grabbe and Sedelmeier 2009).

Thus, full membership in the European Union brings enormous economic, societal, and other benefits to the societies, states, and markets involved. The emulation of the Western European economic order and welfare state cuts across the political and societal spectrum, assuring guarantees for different segments of the society with divergent and conflicting political interests, while access to the potential of the common market provides for substantial gains and a slow convergence towards the living standards of the Western societies. Full membership also exponentially multiplies the "costs" of undemocratic regime change carried by a potential authoritarian elite, thus leading to the preservation of democratic political regimes in the member states. This does not mean that the member states will inevitably reach the highest levels of democratization and liberalization, nor does it mean that European integration creates some kind of "deus ex machina" leading towards "ever more democratic and liberal countries". As Charles Tilly argues, "sunny optimism about the durability and inevitable advance of democratization seems utterly displaced" (Tilly 2007), and in the case of the full member states of European Union, there has not been a clear "path dependency" leading towards full democratic consolidation. Recent evidence from the Central and Eastern European countries shows that some form of deconsolidation can take place over time, and media freedom and the independence of the regulatory bodies can be a challenge even for some of the founding member states. However, the conclusion that there has not been any case of full democratic breakdown in the European Union holds even after 70 years after the inception of the European Union and five major waves of enlargement (1973, 1981–1987, 1995, 2004, and 2013–?), two of which comprised the incorporation of countries emerging from decades of authoritarian and totalitarian systems. The fifth wave began with the Croatian accession in 2013, but so far none of the other stabilization and association agreement countries (i.e. the WB6) have joined the European Union, so the wave is more of a ripple at the moment than a full enlargement wave.

2 When Conditionality Meets Sovereignty and Great Power Politics

The former Yugoslav countries are a perfect example for the idea that nothing is predetermined in history and politics. Former Yugoslavia had a form of association with the European Economic Community since the early 1970s, and unlike other communist countries, the citizens of Yugoslavia had the freedom to travel both in Western and in Eastern Europe without any visa restrictions. In economic terms, former Yugoslavia had a thorough and deep cooperation with the Western European countries. The irony of history for the Western Balkan nations is that their Eastern border was the "Iron Curtain" until 1989, so for the citizens of the Warsaw Pact countries the "free world" began at the Yugoslav border. In a few months, this very same border may become a Schengen frontier for the citizens of the former Yugoslav countries (except for Slovenia and Croatia) and the entry point to the European Union. In a way, the fate of the post-Yugoslav countries (except for Slovenia) contradicts the findings of Lucan Way and Steven Levitsky, who argue that "Western leverage (governments' vulnerability to external pressure) and linkage to the West (the density of a country's ties to the United States, the European Union, and Western-led multilateral institutions)" explain the divergent paths of the post-communist countries (Levitsky and Way 2005). The level of Western leverage and linkage to the former Yugoslavia was by far the greatest compared with any other post-communist country, using any statistic possible. Still, the country collapsed.

In the early 1990s, it was popular to explain the collapse of former Yugoslavia, which was followed by bloody wars, as a resurgence of "ancient hatreds", "primordial conflicts", "tribal instincts", "balkanization", and other deprecating and pejorative expressions. However, the essence of the Yugoslav crisis was the inability of the federation to manage the "segmental institutions" of its constituent parts (Roeder 2007).

In the aftermath of the Kosovo crisis in 1999, the European Union began the Stabilization and Association Process (a modified version of the Association process, with an emphasis on stabilization in order to accentuate the post-conflict situation in the Western Balkans), with the objective of preparing the participant countries for full membership in the European Union. At the Thessaloniki European Council in June 2003, all of the EU's member states declared their "unequivocal support to the European perspective of the Western Balkan countries" and that "the future of the Balkans is within the European Union". The Thessaloniki Declaration gave a concrete prospect of membership to Albania, Bosnia and Herzegovina, Croatia, Macedonia, and Yugoslavia (now succeeded by Serbia, Montenegro, and Kosovo).

Two decades after the end of the violent conflicts, Croatia has been a member of the EU since 2013 and entered the eurozone and the Schengen area in 2023, Montenegro and Serbia have been negotiating for almost a decade, Albania will probably start the negotiation process in the coming period, the Macedonian European integration was stuck in the antiquity (through the Greek veto) and is now lost somewhere in the Middle Ages (through the Bulgarian veto), Bosnia and Herzegovina has finally become a candidate country (after Ukraine and Moldova), and Kosovo is expected to complete its visa-liberalization process.

Nonetheless, these recent developments in the region signal the limits of the democratic conditionality. Namely, one role of the European Union in the Western Balkans, as a foreign power seeking to exert its influence in order to pacify the region, meets another of its role, as a "Staatenverbund" (association of sovereign states) that the Western Balkan countries aspire to join as full members. Gergana Noutcheva observes that "in the Western Balkans, the question of whether the EU is genuinely concerned about spreading its norms, or is acting out of a rational interest to secure stability on the Continent, has been more prominent in the political thinking on the receiving end of EU conditionality, as a result of which compliance with conditions tied to sovereignty has been either fake or partial or imposed by external actors. When the EU's policy lacks strong normative foundations, political leaders in non-EU countries tend to reject EU-sponsored ideas about what is right and appropriate for the governance and external relations of their states and tend to revert to domestic sources of legitimacy, no matter whether these are based on rationality or identity" (Noutcheva 2009).

On the other hand, the countries of the region have recently shown that they can cope with very demanding, comprehensive, and wide-ranging reform, even in the most sensitive areas. The visa-liberalization process has ended with success in all six countries, even though it incurred considerable institutional and financial costs. The opening of the accession negotiations, with a clear timeframe for concluding the process, can lead to the same effects already witnessed in the ten post-communist countries that have already joined the EU (Hughes et al. 2004; Haughton 2007; Epstein 2008).

In reality, the processes observed by Ganev (2002, 2007), Noutcheva (2009), and Sasse (2008) are part of the same phenomenon, with the major difference in their status vis-à-vis the European Union. The incorporation of the Balkan countries in the EU will prevent any backsliding into a full democratic breakdown, as witnessed in Central, Eastern, and Southeastern Europe.

3 Implications for Western Balkans

We analysed the role of the European Union in the democratization processes of former European authoritarian and totalitarian states, as well as the institutionalization of the EU's role as a "democratizing agent". The other external influences (the US security umbrella, NATO integration, and the role of political actors in shaping the diverse outcomes of transitions) were not taken into consideration, although they must be an integral part of any thorough analysis of the influence of external factors on emerging democracies. This article only focused on the European Union and has argued that the most important role of the EU in democratization is the role of democratic stabilization, which is only possible after a country's full accession to the Union. This finding can be reinforced by the fact that the only emerging third-wave democracy left out of the third enlargement (Turkey) has experienced a military coup and a full democratic breakdown. The same political dynamic can also be observed in post-communist countries. It seems that democratic conditionality can exert the influence of the European Union and lead towards a change of the political elite in candidates and potential candidates (Slovakia 1998, Croatia 1999, Serbia 2000), but the structural deficiencies of the domestic political systems still remain. Furthermore, the countries left without any clear EU perspective easily descend into some kind of "hybrid regimes", "democracies with adjectives", or full authoritarianism, as has been the case with the Russian Federation and Belarus. Of course, the logic of democratic stabilization does not come from beliefs in European supranationalism, it comes from a cold-blooded analysis of the costs and benefits of European integration. The key ingredient of democratic stabilization is the threat of exclusion from the common market and the joint European institutions, which keep the elites and societies "locked in" the preservation of a democratic regime. This notion also sets the limits of the democratization potential of the European Union, as demonstrated by evidence from the recent enlargement and the early exercising of democratic conditionality in the Western Balkans. Whenever the process goes beyond the intergovernmentalist approach and into redefining the basic tenets of the democratic constitutional order, the results are ambiguous at best. This is where the limits of the democratic stabilization potential of the European Union are clearly drawn. Explicitly, enlargement cannot be a nation-building exercise.

The key dilemma for the future of the democratizing role of the European Union is whether the Union will continue its enlargement or has come close to defining the final and definite frontiers of European integration. Without the possibility of full accession to the common market and participation in EU-wide decisions, it is highly unlikely that the democratic stabilization role of the EU will function in its neighbourhood and throughout the globe. The other challenge is the possibility of exporting the model. The world is experiencing a growing number of "alphabet soup" emulations of the EU, although none of them has come even close to the depth and width of European integration. Wallace (1994) has argued that "the experience of deep integration within Western Europe does not ... provide a model for others to follow. Its historical development was rooted in stages of economic development and security framework that have now both disappeared. The institutional structure that West European governments agreed to under those past circumstances has managed to respond to the very difficult challenges posed by the economic and industrial transformation in the 1970s and 1980s. Political, economic and security motivations have been entangled in the evolution of West European regional integration from the 1940s to the 1990s" (Wallace 1994). The last possibility of "expanding the model" still has not been tested, like expanding the OECD into a common-market, globalized EU-like model, with the possibility of open global membership in the future. Given the real structure of the contemporary world, this can be an interesting idea for contemplation but appears too idealistic for any serious analysis.

The best conclusion for any text examining the democratization of the post-communist countries would be the warning given by Sir Ralf Dahrendorf in his essay *Reflections on the revolution in Europe*, with the appropriate subtitle "Letter intended to have been sent to a Gentleman in Warsaw" (echoing Edmund Burk's "letter to a gentleman in Paris" from another tumultuous and revolutionary period of modern European history). Dahrendorf cautions that it may take a mere 6 months for a constitutional reform, and 6 years for an economic reform, but "sixty years are barely enough to lay" the social foundations required for an open society to emerge, or as he puts it, "transform the constitution and the economy from fair-weather to all weather institutions capable of withstanding the storms generated within and without" (Dahrendorf 1990).

Unfortunately, in the case of the Western Balkans, the European Union will forego its most successful policy (the democratic stabilization of the member states) if the process of enlargement does not continue.

References

Bunce V, McFaul M, Stoner-Weiss K (2010) Democracy and authoritarianism in the postcommunist world. Cambridge University Press, New York

Dahrendorf R (1990) Reflections on the revolution in Europe: in a letter intended to have been sent to a gentleman in Warsaw. Times Books, New York

Diamond L (2008) The spirit of democracy: the struggle to build free societies throughout the world. Times Books/Henry Holt and Company, New York

Epstein R (2008) In pursuit of liberalism: international institutions in Postcommunist Europe. The Johns Hopkins University Press, Baltimore

Ganev V (2002) The Balkans: different, but why and how? Rom J Polit Sci 2

Ganev V (2007) Preying on the state: the transformation of Bulgaria after 1989. Cornell University Press, Ithaca

Grabbe H (2006) The EU's transformative power: Europeanization through conditionality in Central and Eastern Europe. Palgrave Macmillan

Grabbe H, Sedelmeier U (2009) The future shape of the European Union. In: Egan M, Nugent N, Paterson WE (eds) Research agendas in EU studies: stalking the elephant. Palgrave Macmillan

Haughton T (2007) When does the EU make a difference? Conditionality and the accession process in Central and Eastern Europe. Polit Stud Rev 5(2)

Hughes J, Sasse G, Gordon C (2004) Europeanization and regionalization in the EU's enlargement to Central and Eastern Europe: the myth of conditionality. Palgrave Macmillan, New York

Kagan R (2003) Of paradise and power: America and Europe in the new world order. Alfred A. Knopf: Distributed by Random House, New York

Levitsky S, Way L (2005) International linkage and democratization. J Democr 16(3)

Moravcsik A, Vachudova MA (2003) National interests, state power and EU enlargement. East Eur Polit Soc 17(1)

Noutcheva G (2009) Fake, Partial and imposed compliance: the limits of the EU's normative power in the Western Balkans. J Eur Publ Policy 16(7)

Roeder P (2007) Where nation-states come from: institutional change in the age of nationalism. Princeton, Princeton University Press

Sasse G (2008) The politics of EU conditionality: the norm of minority protection during and beyond EU accession. J Eur Publ Policy 15(6)

Sedelmeier U (2010) The EU and democratization in Central and Southeastern Europe since 1989. In: Ramet S (ed) Central and southeast European politics since 1989. Cambridge University Press, Cambridge

Tilly C (2007) Democracy. Cambridge University Press, New York

Treaty of the European Union, (Official Journal C326, page 0001–0390, October 26, 2012)

Wallace W (1994) Regional integration: the West European experience. Brookings Institution, Washington

The European Integration of the Western Balkans and Its Impact on the EU as a Geopolitical Entity

Aleksandar Spasov

Abstract

In an age of intensified geopolitical competition in the world, the European Union strives to constitute itself as a geopolitical entity having a role in international relations that is beyond a common market and customs union. EU's strategy to achieve "strategic autonomy" and political declarations on "European sovereignty" as a strategic ambition are steps in that direction. Still, the EU's development unlike the development of nation-states is connected to a process called "EU enlargement". The EU enlargement had undergone several phases in the last decades and now is directed towards the eastern part of the continent and towards the remaining part of the southeastern part of the continent, known as the Western Balkans. The article analyses the European integration of the Western Balkan countries through geopolitical perspective and identifies the geopolitical consequences both for the EU and the region if the current stalemate in the process continues.

Keywords

European Union · Western Balkans · Enlargement · Geopolitics

1 EU and the Western Balkans Between Promises and Geopolitics

Twenty-one years ago, in June 2003, the European Union on the EU-Western Balkans Summit in Thessaloniki, Greece (hereinafter: Thessaloniki Summit) "reiterated its unequivocal support to the European perspective of the Western Balkan

A. Spasov (✉)
Legal Theory and Legal Philosophy at Ss. Cyril and Methodius University, Iustinianus Primus Faculty of Law, Skopje, North Macedonia
e-mail: a.spasov@pf.ukim.edu.mk

A. Stojkov, T. Warin (eds.), *Western Balkans and the Future of Europe*, The Future of Europe, https://doi.org/10.1007/978-3-031-86465-0_3

countries" and declared that "the future of the Balkans is within the European Union".[1] The Western Balkans (hereinafter: WB) was a term created to replace "South Eastern Europe", a term that referred to a larger geographical area that included countries such as Bulgaria, Romania, and Slovenia which at the time of the Thessaloniki Summit were already in the advanced stage on their path to the EU membership that will happen in 2004 for Slovenia and in 2007 for Bulgaria and Romania. Therefore, the term Western Balkan countries referred to a group of countries not only geographically located in the western part of the Balkan Peninsula, but also in the early stages of the EU integration. The countries mentioned in the Declaration "Albania, Bosnia and Herzegovina, Croatia, the former Yugoslav Republic of Macedonia, Serbia and Montenegro",[2] with exception of Croatia that became EU member in 2013, will change their status and even names, but, essentially, will continue to be in the process without end in the foreseeable future for the past two decades. In meantime, the State Union of Serbia in Montenegro dissolved in 2006 in two independent countries, Republic of Serbia and Montenegro[3] and Kosovo declared independence and constituted itself in an independent country named as Republic of Kosovo in 2008[4] (a status that is not recognized by 5 current members of the EU and Kosovo, also, is not a member of the United Nations. Republic of Macedonia or as mentioned in the Declaration with the "provisional UN reference" following the 1995 Interim Accord "the former Yugoslav Republic of Macedonia" changed its official name to Republic of North Macedonia, as a consequence of the "Prespa Agreement" between the country and Greece that brought to a resolution of the decades long name dispute.[5] Following the mentioned events, the WB group of countries now consists of six countries: North Macedonia, Albania, Serbia, Montenegro, Bosnia and Herzegovina, and Kosovo.

The mentioned countries are in different stages of their EU integration path. Serbia and Montenegro are in the accession negotiations for more than a decade with moderate to slow progress in opening and especially closing the Negotiation Framework's chapters, Albania and North Macedonia started their accession negotiations in 2023 according to the new Methodology adopted by the European Commission in 2020,[6] but are currently facing obstacles in continuing the accession

---

[1] EU-Western Balkans Summit Thessaloniki, 21 June 2003, Declaration, available at: https://ec.europa.eu/commission/presscorner/detail/en/PRES_03_163

[2] EU-Western Balkans Summit Thessaloniki, 21 June 2003, Declaration, available at: https://ec.europa.eu/commission/presscorner/detail/en/PRES_03_163

[3] Serbia and Montenegro Union: Background and Pending Dissolution, Congressional Research Service, available at: https://crsreports.congress.gov/product/pdf/RS/RS21568/7

[4] *Rohan, Albert,* Kosovo's Path to Independence, European Council on Foreign Relations, available at: https://ecfr.eu/article/commentary_kosovos_path_to_independence/

[5] Final Agreement for the Settlement of the Differences as described in the United Nations Security Council Resolutions 817 (1993) and 845 (1993), the Termination of the Interim Accord of 1995, and the Establishment of the Strategic Partnership Between the Parties, available at: https://vlada.mk/sites/default/files/dokumenti/spogodba-en.pdf

[6] Revised Enlargement Methodology: Questions and Answers, European Commission, available at: https://ec.europa.eu/commission/presscorner/detail/sl/qanda_20_182

talks, Bosnia and Herzegovina is supposed to start the accession negotiations in 2024,[7] and Kosovo just recently was awarded a visa liberalization,[8] striving to be a awarded also a candidate status in the future.

In the past two decades since the Thessaloniki Summit, the geopolitical context in Europe significantly changed. Unlike in 2003 when the shared optimism on the future of the continent based on peaceful cooperation of the countries, functional democracy, protection of human rights, rule-of-law based order, and vibrant market economy prevailed both among the political actors and in the population, the last decade is marked by growing instability, war in the east started by the Russian aggression on Ukraine in 2014 and 2022, growing right wing populism, authoritarian tendencies, and euroscepticism both in the member states and in the candidate countries.

The EU expressed its ambition to constitute itself in a "geopolitical entity" rather than only common market in order to be able to respond to the newly created circumstances. These EU ambitions were expressed as early as 2013 when the concept of "EU Strategic Autonomy" started circulating[9] and were accelerated since the famous speech of the French President Macron at the University of Sorbonne in 2017 that declared the ambitions to constitute EU as a political community with its sovereignty.[10]

The essence of these ideas is that in a growing instable, hostile, and competitive global geopolitical context, the EU must find a balance between being self-sustainable and fully dependent in different areas starting from defence and security and continuing with internal production of essential goods, supply chains, critical raw materials, digital technologies and AI and last, but not least, protection of its democratic political system and human rights. The content of the concept of "EU Strategic Autonomy" is changing, shifting, and expanding depending on the changing circumstances, as can be seen in the latest document on the topic issued by the Spanish Presidency of the EU in the second half of 2023.[11]

The concept of the EU Strategic Autonomy can also be understood as implicit acceptance that the optimistic expectations from the ongoing globalization resulting in interdependent world that peacefully cooperates or that the globalization means

[7] Bosnia and Herzegovina, European Neighbourhood Policy and Enlargement Negotiations, European Commission, available at: https://neighbourhood-enlargement.ec.europa.eu/enlargement-policy/bosnia-and-herzegovina_en

[8] Kosovo, European Neighbourhood Policy and Enlargement Negotiations, European Commission, available at: https://neighbourhood-enlargement.ec.europa.eu/enlargement-policy/kosovo_en

[9] EU Strategic Autonomy (2013–2023), from Concept to Capacity, European Parliament, available at: https://www.europarl.europa.eu/RegData/etudes/BRIE/2022/733589/EPRS_BRI(2022)733589_EN.pdf.

[10] Sorbonne Speech of Emmanuel Macron, Ouest France, available at: https://international.blogs.ouest-france.fr/archive/2017/09/29/macron-sorbonne-verbatim-europe-18583.html

[11] Open Strategic Autonomy for a Competitive and Resilient EU, Spanish Presidency, Council of the European Union, available at: https://spanish-presidency.consilium.europa.eu/en/programme/open-strategic-autonomy-spanish-presidency-eu-council-resilient-eu2030/

the "end of history" are over. In such circumstances, EU must be prepared to act in a dominantly hostile environment in order to secure its survival and welfare.

Having in mind the described context of both processes, the chapter analyses the impact that the stalemate in the European integration of the WB countries has on the ambitions of the EU to constitute itself as a geopolitical entity. The stalemate of the European integration of the WB countries creates and/or strengthens internal processes in the WB countries such as democratic backsliding, rising populism, weaker socioeconomic development, increased depopulation of the region, increased malign influence by extra-regional actors, and higher probability of instability that are not only harming these countries, but can also have a very negative spillover effect for the EU that can potentially harm the position of the EU as a geopolitical power. Therefore, the relatively small countries of the WB, both in area and in population, if left in a limbo, can have disproportionate negative effect on the EU based on their important position as a crossroad of continents and geopolitical rivalries.

2 The Stalemate in the EU Integration of the WB Countries

The stalemate in the European integration of the WB countries is evident both in the length of time of the accession process and in the negative developments in the countries connected to the process or the backsliding in significant reform areas. Although, ahead of the December meeting of the European Council in 2023, in the "2023 Communication on EU Enlargement Policy" from the Commission to the European Parliament, the Council, the European Economic and Social Committee and the Committee of the Regions, once again, was reiterated that "… The Western Balkans have a historic window of opportunity to strongly bind their future to the European Union" and that "accession is and will remain a merit-based process fully dependent on the objective progress achieved by each enlargement partner", concluding that "the enlargement countries will have to act with determination to implement the necessary reforms and make tangible and irreversible progress, starting with the fundamentals of the EU accession process… the rule of law, in particular the independence and functioning of the judiciary and the fight against corruption, fundamental rights, the economy, the functioning of democratic institutions and public administration reform continue to be the cornerstones of the enlargement policy",[12] now, deep in 2024, in the majority of the WB countries there is not satisfying progress in the reforms.

Earlier in 2023, during the Bled Strategic Forum in Slovenia, the President of the European Council, Charles Michel, even set the year 2030 as a year when both sides, the EU and the candidate countries, must be ready to enlarge.[13]

[12] 2023 Communication on EU Enlargement Policy, Council of the European Union, available at: https://data.consilium.europa.eu/doc/document/ST-15094-2023-INIT/en/pdf

[13] Michel: We Must Be ready, on Both Side, to Enlarge by 2030, European Western Balkans, available at: https://europeanwesternbalkans.com/2023/08/28/michel-we-must-be-ready-on-both-sides-to-enlarge-by-2030/

Despite these optimistic statements by EU institutions and officials, the reality check clearly shows that the state of affairs is far less promising both in the track record of the past decades and in the present. For the purposes of this analysis, we will look at the time length in the EU integration of the WB countries, the progress in the rule of law and the functioning of the democratic institutions and the optimism for the process in the population.

Given the stage of the EU integration they are in, the WB countries can be divided into three functional groups (there are no formal groups of countries in the process since the process is based on individual merits, however informal groups in the reality of the process exist). In the first group are Serbia and Montenegro, in the second group are North Macedonia and Albania, and in the third group are Bosnia and Herzegovina and Kosovo.

Serbia applied for membership in 2009, got the candidate status in 2012, started the accession negotiations in 2013. More than a decade after the accession negotiations started, Serbia opened 22 out of 35 chapters, but only 2 of them are provisionally closed.[14]

Montenegro applied for membership in 2008, got the candidate status in 2010, started the accession talks in 2012. Again, more than a decade after the accession negotiations started, all 33 screened chapters have been opened, of which only 3 are provisionally closed.[15]

North Macedonia is a unique example in negative terms for the length of time of the process.[16] The country was the first among today's group of WB6 to become a candidate country for membership already in 2005. However, the country could not start the accession talks until 2022, mostly because of the dispute with Greece over the constitutional name (Greek veto) which was resolved in 2018 with the "Prespa Agreement",[17] then because of the French request for the new methodology for the accession talks in late 2019 (French veto), just when North Macedonia and Albania were supposed to start the accession negotiations and finally because of the Bulgarian objections (Bulgarian veto) on the implementation of the bilateral Treaty of Friendship, Good-Neighbourliness and Cooperation[18] over "different reading" of various historical issues back to the early middle ages.

---

[14] Serbia, European Neighbourhood Policy and Enlargement Negotiations, European Commission, available at: https://neighbourhood-enlargement.ec.europa.eu/enlargement-policy/serbia_en

[15] Montenegro, European Neighbourhood Policy and Enlargement Negotiations, European Commission, available at:https://neighbourhood-enlargement.ec.europa.eu/enlargement-policy/montenegro_en

[16] North Macedonia, European Neighbourhood Policy and Enlargement Negotiations, European Commission, available at: https://neighbourhood-enlargement.ec.europa.eu/enlargement-policy/north-macedonia_en

[17] Final Agreement for the Settlement of the Differences as described in the United Nations Security Council Resolutions 817 (1993) and 845 (1993), the Termination of the Interim Accord of 1995, and the Establishment of the Strategic Partnership Between the Parties, available at: https://vlada.mk/sites/default/files/dokumenti/spogodba-en.pdf

[18] Dogovor za prijatelstvo, dobrososedstvo I sorabotka megju Republika Makedonija I Republika Bugarija, available at: https://mfa.gov.mk/en/document/1712/treaty-friendship

Albania applied for membership in 2009, got the candidate status in 2014, started the accession talks in 2022 when the Commission started the screening process. In July 2023, the European Commission submitted to the Council the screening report on Cluster 1—Fundamentals, including benchmarks for opening accession negotiations on this cluster.[19]

Albania, alongside North Macedonia, also went through a prolongation of the start of the accession negotiations because of the previously mentioned French request for a new methodology but was informally coupled with North Macedonia and had to wait until the Negotiation framework for North Macedonia was adopted following the Bulgarian objections.

Bosnia and Herzegovina applied for membership in 2016. The EU Commission in 2019 identified 14 key priorities that the country had to fulfil ahead of the opening of the accession negotiations. In 2022, the country was awarded candidate status. In 2023, the European Council postponed the decision to open the accession negotiations for March 2024 until "necessary degree of compliance with the membership criteria is achieved" and, finally, the European Council reached a decision to open the accession negotiations in March 2024 and invited the European Commission to prepare the Negotiation Framework. Although there is significant development in the EU integration process in relatively short period for Bosnia and Herzegovina, one has to have in mind that the country is only in the early stages of the process.[20]

Kosovo applied for membership in 2022, and it is considered a "potential candidate". EU member countries agreed to grant Kosovo a visa liberalization since the beginning of 2024 and the Stabilization and Association Agreement (SAA) is in force since 2016.[21]

The presented overview of the state of affairs in the EU integration process of the WB countries cannot be fully understood without the specifics of the integration process which, at least for some of them, differs from the standard pattern for the other candidate countries in the past. For example, North Macedonia faced unprecedented vetoes by Greece and Bulgaria. The last veto by Bulgaria was related to purely bilateral matters of historical nature that included Bulgarian objections on the right of the country and Macedonians to their own historical narratives and reading of history going as far as disputing the existence of Macedonians as a separate nation and the Macedonian language as a separate language. Objections of such nature, basically, have nothing to do with the Copenhagen criteria for EU membership from 1993[22] although the "cover story" presented by Bulgaria was that these

---

[19] Albania, European Neighbourhood Policy and Enlargement Negotiations, European Commission, available at: https://neighbourhood-enlargement.ec.europa.eu/enlargement-policy/albania_en

[20] Bosnia and Herzegovina, European Neighbourhood Policy and Enlargement Negotiations, European Commission, available at: https://neighbourhood-enlargement.ec.europa.eu/enlargement-policy/bosnia-and-herzegovina_en

[21] Kosovo, European Neighbourhood Policy and Enlargement Negotiations, European Commission, available at: https://neighbourhood-enlargement.ec.europa.eu/enlargement-policy/kosovo_en

[22] Enlargement, Accession criteria, European Commission, available at: https://neighbourhood-enlargement.ec.europa.eu/enlargement-policy/glossary/accession-criteria_en

bilateral issues are part of the criteria for "human rights and respect for and protection of minorities" and "good neighborly relations". The outcome of the dispute was that the Council of the EU when adopting the Negotiation Framework for North Macedonia in July 2022 conditioned the closure of the first Intergovernmental Conference and the opening of the first cluster "Fundamentals" with amending to the Constitution in order to include the Bulgarian community in North Macedonia in the Constitution.[23]

The described situation and especially the numerous provocative statements by Bulgarian officials in that period contributed towards a negative atmosphere in the country and fueled the nationalism and as a consequence the Parliament of North Macedonia failed to adopt the necessary amendment to the Constitution in order to continue with the accession talks.[24] The then opposition in the Parliament (in present constituting the ruling majority) opposed the proposal claiming that beside being "unfair", it does not provide a guarantee that it will be the last Bulgarian request in the process. Also, in the changed political circumstances after the parliamentary elections in North Macedonia in 2024, the now ruling majority has not changed its positions on the issue and is promising to re-negotiate the conditions in a "more favorable" direction for the country.[25] As a consequence, North Macedonia is in a situation of quasi "self-imposed" blockade.

Albania, after the imposed break in the process following the described developments, failed to open the clusters and continue with the accession negotiations because an elected mayor coming from the Greek minority in Albania of a small municipality of Himara in Albania and after the European elections earlier in 2024 elected as MEP on the list of the Greek ruling party "Nea Demokratia" was convicted and sentenced with prison because of corruption. Although Albania claims that the alleged corruption has been beyond reasonable doubt proven in the court proceedings, Greece claims that the only reason for the sentence was mayor's ethnicity which "shows that Albania is not protecting the Greek minority" in the country.[26] This case was sufficient reason for Greece to block the accession negotiations for Albania.

[23] Enlargement, Council Conclusions on North Macedonia and Albania, Council of the European Union, available at: https://data.consilium.europa.eu/doc/document/ST-11440-2022-INIT/en/pdf

[24] The author of this article was member of the Expert Group, representing the then President of the Republic of North Macedonia, formed by the Government of the Republic of North Macedonia that was tasked to prepare the draft amendments following the Conclusions of the Council of the EU. The draft amendments were prepared by the Expert Group, adopted by the then Government and sent to the Parliament that failed to adopt them due to the lack of the necessary two-third majority to amend the Constitution, as prescribed in the Constitution.

[25] EU and Bulgaria Unlikely to Accept VMRO's Proposal for Re-Negotiating Constitutional Change, European Western Balkans, available at: https://europeanwesternbalkans.com/2024/07/12/eu-and-bulgaria-unlikely-to-accept-vmros-proposal-for-re-negotiating-constitutional-change/

[26] Greek EU Law Maker to Remain in Albanian Prison, Politico Europe, available at: https://www.politico.eu/article/greece-mep-fredi-beleri-albania-politics-prison-crime-charges-judicial-outcome/

In Serbia's Negotiation Network, a new chapter under number 35 and under the title "Other issues" was added that is mostly dealing with the "normalizations of the relations between Belgrade and Prishtina" or the so-called Kosovo issue.[27] The normalization includes the implementation of the Brussels Agreement from 2013 as amended by the Ohrid Agreement from 2023.[28] Although the "normalization" does not formally include mutual official recognition, Serbia is expected to de facto recognize Kosovo with all attributes of a sovereign and independent state and not to block Kosovo's membership in international organizations and Kosovo is expected to form the "Association of Serbian municipalities" as an advanced level of self-government and autonomy in ten municipalities where the Serb community constitutes majority and to take additional measures to promote the rights of the Serbian community and preserve the Serbian cultural heritage in Kosovo. Unfortunately, both sides are failing to implement their obligations and the relations between both sides are deteriorating compared to the optimism back in 2013. Recent events near the town of Banjska[29] just confirm that the stalemate is not only producing *status quo,* but also creates instability that potentially erupt in an open conflict.

The bilateral relations between Belgrade and Prishtina are crucial for the EU integration of both countries. Serbia's accession to the EU is directly conditioned to that issue which means that even by meeting all other standards Serbia cannot join the EU unless the issue is resolved. Kosovo's fate is also at stake. For Kosovo the resolution of the issue means not only prospect for EU integration, but furthermore completion of the process of establishing the statehood by being recognized by remaining five EU member countries and becoming member of the United Nations and other international organizations.

Additionally, Serbia is failing to comply with the EU foreign and security policy by refusing to impose sanctions on Russia following the Russian invasion on Ukraine in February 2022. In a report issued by the European Parliament in 2022, it is stated that "Serbia has not aligned with the EU's restrictive measures against Russia since 2014 and its record on alignment with the CFSP is mixed and inconsistent".[30] These Serbian positions, although not in the current stage of the integration, can create a problem for the country's membership in the EU.

Montenegro is facing an ongoing political instability after 2020 elections when the citizens for the first time in their democratic history witnessed a change of government. The decades long rule of the Democratic Party of Socialists (DPS) of the

[27] General EU Position, Ministerial Meeting opening the Intergovernmental Conference on the Accession of Serbia in the European Union, 2014, available at: https://data.consilium.europa.eu/doc/document/AD%201%202014%20INIT/EN/pdf

[28] Chapter 35 in Serbia's EU Accession Process is Being Amended Based on the Ohrid Agreement, European Western Balkans, available at: https://europeanwesternbalkans.com/2024/02/29/chapter-35-in-serbias-eu-accession-process-is-being-amended-based-on-the-ohrid-agreement/

[29] *Moloney, Marita,* Kosovo Monastery Siege Ends After Heavy Gun Battles, BBC News, available at: https://www.bbc.com/news/world-europe-66905091

[30] EU Sanctions Against Russia: Alignment of the EU Enlargement Countries, European Parliament, available at: https://www.europarl.europa.eu/RegData/etudes/IDAN/2022/639327/EXPO_IDA(2022)639327_EN.pdf

former President and Prime Minister Milo Djukanovikj, marked by credible allegations of widespread high corruption and some undemocratic practices, was ended by a coalition of opposition parties of different orientation and, additionally, in informal coalition with the Montenegrin Bishop of the Serbian Orthodox Church.[31] Although often referred to as "political crisis", the crisis in Montenegro in its roots has the complex relations in the country between Montenegrins and Serbs and relations to Serbia. However, these relations are not just important for the inter-ethnic relations in the country but have much bigger geopolitical significance knowing the specific relations of Serbia to Russia.

An important sign of optimism is the recent conclusion of the 16th Intergovernmental Conference on which "EU confirmed that Montenegro has, overall, met the interim benchmarks set for Chapters 23 and 24".[32] This is a very important step forward, knowing that the mentioned chapters include criteria from the rule-of-law area (organized crime and high corruption, judiciary, public administration, etc.) that is part of the fundamentals in the new Methodology.

Bosnia and Herzegovina, beyond the shortcomings that are characteristic to all other countries in the region, is in constant internal political crisis due to the very complex institutional setting, set by the Dayton Agreement from 1995[33] that ended the war in the country. Divided in two entities, the Federation of Bosnia and Herzegovina (FBiH) and Republika Srpska (RS), predominantly inhabited by Bosniaks and Croats in FBiH and Serbs in RS, with very limited competences of the central authorities and in constant need of consensus in order to reach a decision on central level, the country is very often blocked in performing its functions. Unlike in the mid-2000s when the reforms were implemented due to, among other incentives, the prospect of EU integration, in the present the country is politically divided as never before after the end of the war. Both Serbs and Croats have special relations to Serbia and Croatia and follow the specific national interests of these countries including their foreign policy priorities which complicate the relations with the Bosniaks that often pressure for transfer of more competences from entities to the central level. One of the main factors for the opposition by both Serbs and Croats is also the demography whereby the Bosniaks constitute just over 50% of the total population of the country, according to the latest census conducted in 2023.[34]

Although, at least formally, there is not significant political actor that is confronting Bosnia's EU aspirations, still the internal political dynamics is creating different picture. Namely, RS and its leadership have very close relations with present day

---

[31] *D'Urso, Dario, Vetrini, Lada,* Montenegro's Political Transition: from Djukanovikj to Where?, FEPS, Renner Institut, CeSPI, available at: https://feps-europe.eu/wp-content/uploads/2023/08/Montenegro-political-transition.pdf

[32] Montenegro, European Neighbourhood Policy and Enlargement Negotiations, European Commission, available at: https://neighbourhood-enlargement.ec.europa.eu/enlargement-policy/montenegro_en

[33] Dayton Peace Agreement, OSCE, available at: https://www.osce.org/bih/126173

[34] *Petke, Sven, Petzke, Jan, Kalbe, Sebastian, Garcia Čaušević, Sharin,* Demographic Development in Bosnia and Herzegovina, Konrad Adenauer Stiftung, available at: https://www.kas.de/en/country-reports/detail/-/content/demographische-entwicklung-in-bosnien-und-herzegowina

Russia and President Putin which is an obstacle for the country to align with EU FSP because of lack of consensus in the institutions.[35] Croats have objections that are marginalized by Bosniaks in the FBiH and on central level and are pushing Croatia to condition the country with fulfilling their demands as a pre-condition for EU member Croatia to agree to the advance of the country in the EU integration process.[36]

WB6 countries show moderate progress or in the case of North Macedonia and Serbia even regression in the reforms in the area of the rule-of-law, that is fundamental for their EU integration. In the recent Rule-of-Law Report issued by the European Commission for the member countries and some of the candidate countries the mentioned shortcomings are registered in detail. As stated in the report "North Macedonia has undergone several waves of judicial reform and adopted a new justice strategy aiming to improve the independence, efficiency, and professionalism of the judiciary. However, the independence of the judiciary and the institutional capacity to protect it against undue influence remain a serious concern. The level of perceived judicial independence is very low… A comprehensive national anti-corruption strategy is in place, however its implementation lags behind. High risk of corruption remains prevalent in many areas".[37]

Serbia suffers from increased political pressure on the judiciary and as stated in the Report "political pressure on the judiciary and the prosecution service remains high. A number of steps have been taken to reduce the space for political influence on the judiciary and the prosecution services, although their effects in practice still need to be observed and there is little or no follow-up on cases of undue influence… Parliament's ability to ensure the exercise of necessary checks and balances is constrained by issues of effectiveness, autonomy, and transparency, including in terms of the oversight of the executive and the law-making process".[38]

Montenegro shows good progress in the area, also confirmed on the recent Intergovernmental Conference, still "the track record of investigations and prosecutions in cases of high-level corruption is stable, but the lack of trials and final decisions contributes to a perception of impunity".[39]

---

[35] *Vulović, Marina,* Crisis in Bosnia and Herzegovina: Years of Power Struggles Come to the Boil, Stiftung Wissenschaft und Politik, available at: https://www.swp-berlin.org/publikation/crisis-in-bosnia-and-herzegovina-years-of-power-struggles-come-to-the-boil

[36] Freedom in the World 2023, Bosnia and Herzegovina, Freedom House, available at: https://freedomhouse.org/country/bosnia-and-herzegovina/freedom-world/2023

[37] 2024 Rule of Law Report, Country Chapter on the Rule of Law Situation in North Macedonia, European Commission, available at: https://commission.europa.eu/document/download/e7197a43-7f00-4eac-b02d-818ac71345f0_en?filename=61_1_58090_coun_chap_northmacedonia_nm.pdf

[38] 2024 Rule of Law Report, Country Chapter on the Rule of Law Situation in Serbia, European Commission, available at: https://commission.europa.eu/document/download/862952fa-6e79-44c4-b629-174a441e3d2e_en?filename=62_1_58091_coun_chap_serbia_sb.pdf

[39] 2024 Rule of Law Report, Country Chapter on the Rule of Law Situation in Montenegro, European Commission, available at: https://commission.europa.eu/document/download/6e3ff77c-4a53-4e92-a030-9ea4cca3045c_en?filename=60_1_58089_coun_chap_montenegro_mn.pdf

Albania although went through a significant judicial reform since 2016 and performed satisfactory on level of legislation still the concerns remain on "attempted interference and pressure on the judicial system by public officials or politicians".[40]

Last, but not least the public perception and support for the EU integration is a key pillar to the process. It is not only because in every democratic society public policy must have a democratic legitimacy and, in this case, also a direct consent in a form of a referendum or other form of directly involving the citizens in making the decision, but also for the sake of successful implementation of the necessary reforms. The true meaning of the often-mentioned transformative power of the EU integration is not only the full membership of the country in the EU as a final goal, but also a sustainable transformation of the society into a functional democracy that works for the benefit of the citizens.

In the recent years, the support for the integration is decreasing in most of the WB countries although the EU membership as strategic goal remains by far one of the few issues of national consensus in almost all WB countries. However, the expectations of the citizens in WB countries that the EU is "serious" in offering the WB countries full membership are significantly decreasing.

In a recent poll in the WB countries conducted by the Washington-based International Republican Institute (IRI) the described tendencies are reflected in numbers. On the question "If a referendum were held today on our country joining the European Union, how would you vote?" 92% and 85% answered in favour of EU membership in Albania and Kosovo, correspondingly, 71% in Montenegro, 68% in Bosnia and Herzegovina and North Macedonia, and only 40% in Serbia. Although the numbers in Albania and Kosovo remain stable and high and there is an increase in the support in Montenegro, there is a decrease in Bosnia and Herzegovina and Serbia, whereby Serbia as the largest country in the region is far from the necessary 50% support for a majority support. Also, North Macedonia although has still satisfying support for the EU is far from the support of 90% plus that used to have a decade ago.

On the question "Is the European Union serious in its intention to offer membership to Western Balkan countries?" The answers show growing disillusion of the citizens with the realistic prospects of becoming EU members in the foreseeable future. Respectable 62% of the citizens of Kosovo are confident in the EU intentions (in a country that is in the least advanced stage of the process) and 59% of the citizens of Montenegro share the same believe (country that is in the most advanced stage of the process). Only Albania of the rest of the WB countries is slightly above 50% with 54% of the citizens that believe that EU is serious in its intentions. The remaining three countries have numbers far from the necessary 50%. Bosnia and Herzegovina stands at 44%, North Macedonia at 34%, and Serbia at only 30%. The example of North Macedonia is striking. Once a "poster country" of EU, with support for the integration of over 90% and still supporting the integration with 68%

[40] 2024 Rule of Law Report, Country Chapter on the Rule of Law Situation in Albania, European Commission, available at: https://commission.europa.eu/document/download/0154dce1-5026-45de-8b37-e3d56eff7925_en?filename=59_1_58088_coun_chap_albania_al.pdf

seems to have citizens that don't believe in what they support. Such disillusion will inevitably lead towards decreasing support for integration in future and will make the country vulnerable to the influence by malign extra-regional actors.

Finally, on the very indicative question in the survey "What should our country's foreign policy course be?" the answers are without doubt showing the shifting tendencies in North Macedonia and Montenegro (both countries NATO members) with significant number of respondents answering "both West and Russia" while in Serbia the absolute majority of the respondents answered either "both West and Russia" or "pro-Russian, but keep up relations with the European Union and the West". The number of respondents that opted for the mentioned two alternatives or only for Russia in Bosnia and Herzegovina correlates with the percentage of the Serb population in the country. Only Albania and Kosovo, having in mind their antagonism for Russia because of Russia's support for Serbia, show clear pro-western orientation.[41]

3 The Geopolitical Consequences from the Stalemate in the EU Integration of the WB

Almost a decade ago, the then US Secretary of State John Kerry told the US Senate Foreign Affairs Committee that "Serbia, Kosovo, Montenegro and Macedonia are the new front line between Russia and the West".[42]

Although Montenegro and North Macedonia in meantime became members of NATO, none of the WB countries in the past decade managed to advance in the integration process to a level of joining the EU or being very close to full membership. The EU being above all a peace project, with ambition to constitute itself as a geopolitical entity, lacks a functional geopolitical strategy towards the Western Balkans. The past decade is a missed opportunity both for the EU and the WB countries. The WB countries bear huge responsibility for the created situation. However, the fact that EU unlike in the case of central and eastern European countries did not manage to push the process of the WB countries also remains.

As already stated, the relatively small countries of the WB both in area and in population, if left in a limbo, can have disproportionate negative effect on the EU based on their important position as a crossroad of continents and geopolitical rivalries. WB countries are part of a larger geographical area of southeastern Europe on the border between Europe and Asia Minor, the shortest road to the Middle East. The whole region is a multicultural area where South Slavs live together with Albanians and where Eastern Orthodox Christianity meets Islam and Catholicism. The region has mixed heritage of both Ottoman and Austrian and central European civilization. Historically, the region was often a centre of major historical events. In

---

[41] Western Balkans Regional Poll, February–March 2024, International Republican Institute, available at: https://www.iri.org/resources/western-balkans-regional-poll-february-march-2024-mini/

[42] *Deren, Jean-Arnault, Geslin Laurent,* Balkans Are the New Front Line, Le Monde Diplomatique, available at: https://mondediplo.com/2015/07/04balkans

the Roman times, the most important road that connected the western with the eastern part of the Empire Via *Egnatia* was partially running through a territory that in the present is part of some of the WB countries. After the fall of the Byzantine Empire, the region was the main road in the advancement of the Ottoman armies that were aiming to conquer large part of Europe and managed to get to Vienna. The region was a place where former major European forces Austria-Hungary and Russian Empire with significant involvement of France and UK during the decline of the Ottoman Empire fought proxy wars by supporting different liberation movements. First World War started after the assassination of the Habsburg heir to the throne Archduke Franz Ferdinand in Sarajevo in June 1914. Finally, the Yugoslav wars of the nineties of the twentieth century were the antipode to the optimism after the fall of the Berlin Wall when Europe was uniting while the Balkans was stuck in civil wars.[43]

If it continues, the stalemate in the European integration of the WB countries may result in following negative geopolitical consequences, both for the WB countries and the Balkans. First, WB countries due to their complex history are vulnerable to malign foreign influence that aims to create instability that can also hurt the EU. In order to disturb the Western efforts to help Ukraine that is invaded by Russia, Russian strategy is to abuse the vulnerability of the region by fuelling the nationalism and reviving the old historical disputes. The strategy is applied mainly by spreading dis- and misinformation,[44] but in the case of Bosnia and Herzegovina also with active involvement by using local politicians, like RS president Milorad Dodik.[45]

Second, China shows great interest in the region. Some of the WB countries are members of the Chinese economic initiative with geopolitical ambitions "Belt and Road". China is intensively involved in investments in the infrastructure of the region, by offering loans, but also pushing for Chinese companies to build the infrastructure. The example of the Montenegrin highway in which project Montenegro almost ended up in debt slavery is just one of the many examples. Chinese initiative's "Belt and Road" true goal is to easily penetrate Europe by using the WB countries as the "weakest part of the chain".[46]

Third, due to their weak institutional capacities, WB countries have weak system of checking the true nature of the Foreign Direct Investments from third countries outside EU and the West, especially to prevent money laundering and financing of terrorism and other cross border illegal activities.

---

[43] Balkans, Britannica Encyclopedia, available at: https://www.britannica.com/place/Balkans

[44] *Bashevski, Vangel,* Russian Pseudohistorical Manipulation Reaches North Macedonia, META, available at: https://meta.mk/en/russian-pseudohistorical-manipulation-reaches-north-macedonia/

[45] *Bechev, Dimitar,* Between the EU and Moscow: How Russia Exploits Divisions in Bosnia, Carnegie Endowment for International Peace, available at: https://carnegieendowment.org/research/2024/06/bosnia-between-russia-eu?lang=en

[46] *McBride, James, Berman, Noah, Chatzky, Andrew,* China's Massive Belt and Road Initiative, Council on Foreign Relations, available at: https://www.cfr.org/backgrounder/chinas-massive-belt-and-road-initiative

Fourth, although North Macedonia and Albania are already members in NATO and NATO is present in Kosovo and Bosnia and Herzegovina, still EU should be also involved in supporting the WB countries to continue contributing in the European "hard security". The role of WB during the migrant crisis was essential since these countries are on the so-called Balkan route, but their integration in the EU will strengthen their capacities.[47]

The WB countries doubtless belong in the EU. However, this important statement that is repeated for decades must become a reality in order to secure the future of the region, but also to avoid a situation where EU can lose part of its body in favour of other geopolitical actors. In a situation of an intensive geopolitical competition that we are living in it is not a viable option both for the region and the EU.

References

2023 Communication on EU Enlargement Policy, Council of the European Union, available at: https://data.consilium.europa.eu/doc/document/ST-15094-2023-INIT/en/pdf

2024 Rule of Law Report, Country Chapter on the Rule of Law Situation in Albania, European Commission, available at: https://commission.europa.eu/document/download/0154dce1-5026-45de-8b37-e3d56eff7925_en?filename=59_1_58088_coun_chap_albania_al.pdf

2024 Rule of Law Report, Country Chapter on the Rule of Law Situation in Montenegro, European Commission, available at: https://commission.europa.eu/document/download/6e3ff77c-4a53-4e92-a030-9ea4cca3045c_en?filename=60_1_58089_coun_chap_montenegro_mn.pdf

2024 Rule of Law Report, Country Chapter on the Rule of Law Situation in North Macedonia, European Commission, available at: https://commission.europa.eu/document/download/e7197a43-7f00-4eac-b02d-818ac71345f0_en?filename=61_1_58090_coun_chap_northmacedonia_nm.pdf

2024 Rule of Law Report, Country Chapter on the Rule of Law Situation in Serbia, European Commission, available at: https://commission.europa.eu/document/download/862952fa-6e79-44c4-b629-174a441e3d2e_en?filename=62_1_58091_coun_chap_serbia_sb.pdf

Albania, European Neighbourhood Policy and Enlargement Negotiations, European Commission, available at: https://neighbourhood-enlargement.ec.europa.eu/enlargement-policy/albania_en

Balkans, Britannica Encyclopedia, available at: https://www.britannica.com/place/Balkans

Bashevski, Vangel, Russian Pseudohistorical Manipulation Reaches North Macedonia, META, available at: https://meta.mk/en/russian-pseudohistorical-manipulation-reaches-north-macedonia/

Bechev, Dimitar, Between the EU and Moscow: How Russia Exploits Divisions in Bosnia, Carnegie Endowment for International Peace, available at: https://carnegieendowment.org/research/2024/06/bosnia-between-russia-eu?lang=en

Bosnia and Herzegovina, European Neighbourhood Policy and Enlargement Negotiations, European Commission, available at: https://neighbourhood-enlargement.ec.europa.eu/enlargement-policy/bosnia-and-herzegovina_en

Chapter 35 in Serbia's EU Accession Process is Being Amended Based on the Ohrid Agreement, European Western Balkans, available at: https://europeanwesternbalkans.com/2024/02/29/chapter-35-in-serbias-eu-accession-process-is-being-amended-based-on-the-ohrid-agreement/

[47] Western Balkans Route, European Council, Council of the European Union, available at: https://www.consilium.europa.eu/en/policies/eu-migration-policy/western-balkans-route/#:~:text=The%20Western%20Balkans%20route%20refers,main%20migratory%20paths%20into%20Europe

D'Urso, Dario, *Vetrini, Lada,* Montenegro's Political Transition: from Djukanovikj to Where?, FEPS, Renner Institut, CeSPI, available at: https://feps-europe.eu/wp-content/uploads/2023/08/Montenegro-political-transition.pdf

Dayton Peace Agreement, OSCE, available at: https://www.osce.org/bih/126173

Deren, Jean-Arnault, Geslin Laurent, Balkans Are the New Front Line, Le Monde Diplomatique, available at: https://mondediplo.com/2015/07/04balkans

Dogovor za prijatelstvo, dobrososedstvo I sorabotka megju Republika Makedonija I Republika Bugarija, available at: https://mfa.gov.mk/en/document/1712/treaty-friendship

Enlargement, Accession criteria, European Commission, available at: https://neighbourhood-enlargement.ec.europa.eu/enlargement-policy/glossary/accession-criteria_en

Enlargement, Council Conclusions on North Macedonia and Albania, Council of the European Union, available at: https://data.consilium.europa.eu/doc/document/ST-11440-2022-INIT/en/pdf

EU and Bulgaria Unlikely to Accept VMRO's Proposal for Re-Negotiating Constitutional Change, European Western Balkans, available at: https://europeanwesternbalkans.com/2024/07/12/eu-and-bulgaria-unlikely-to-accept-vmros-proposal-for-re-negotiating-constitutional-change/

EU Sanctions Against Russia: Alignment of the EU Enlargement Countries, European Parliament, available at: https://www.europarl.europa.eu/RegData/etudes/IDAN/2022/639327/EXPO_IDA(2022)639327_EN.pdf

EU Strategic Autonomy (2013–2023), from Concept to Capacity, European Parliament, available at: https://www.europarl.europa.eu/RegData/etudes/BRIE/2022/733589/EPRS_BRI(2022)733589_EN.pdf

EU-Western Balkans Summit Thessaloniki, 21 June 2003, Declaration, available at: https://ec.europa.eu/commission/presscorner/detail/en/PRES_03_163

Final Agreement for the Settlement of the Differences as described in the United Nations Security Council Resolutions 817 (1993) and 845 (1993), the Termination of the Interim Accord of 1995, and the Establishment of the Strategic Partnership Between the Parties, available at: https://vlada.mk/sites/default/files/dokumenti/spogodba-en.pdf

Freedom in the World 2023, Bosnia and Herzegovina, Freedom House, available at: https://freedomhouse.org/country/bosnia-and-herzegovina/freedom-world/2023

General EU Position, Ministerial Meeting opening the Intergovernmental Conference on the Accession of Serbia in the European Union, 2014., available at: https://data.consilium.europa.eu/doc/document/AD%201%202014%20INIT/EN/pdf

Greek EU Law Maker to Remain in Albanian Prison, Politico Europe, available at: https://www.politico.eu/article/greece-mep-fredi-beleri-albania-politics-prison-crime-charges-judicial-outcome/

Kosovo, European Neighbourhood Policy and Enlargement Negotiations, European Commission, available at: https://neighbourhood-enlargement.ec.europa.eu/enlargement-policy/kosovo_en

McBride, James, Berman, Noah, Chatzky, Andrew, China's Massive Belt and Road Initiative, Council on Foreign Relations, available at: https://www.cfr.org/backgrounder/chinas-massive-belt-and-road-initiative

Michel: We Must Be ready, on Both Side, to Enlarge by 2030, European Western Balkans, available at: https://europeanwesternbalkans.com/2023/08/28/michel-we-must-be-ready-on-both-sides-to-enlarge-by-2030/

Moloney, Marita, Kosovo Monastery Siege Ends After Heavy Gun Battles, BBC News, available at: https://www.bbc.com/news/world-europe-66905091

Montenegro., European Neighbourhood Policy and Enlargement Negotiations, European Commission, available at: https://neighbourhood-enlargement.ec.europa.eu/enlargement-policy/montenegro_en

North Macedonia, European Neighbourhood Policy and Enlargement Negotiations, European Commission, available at: https://neighbourhood-enlargement.ec.europa.eu/enlargement-policy/north-macedonia_en

Open Strategic Autonomy for a Competitive and Resilient EU, Spanish Presidency, Council of the European Union, available at: https://spanish-presidency.consilium.europa.eu/en/programme/open-strategic-autonomy-spanish-presidency-eu-council-resilient-eu2030/

Petke, Sven, Petzke, Jan, Kalbe, Sebastian, Garcia Čaušević, Sharin, Demographic Development in Bosnia and Herzegovina, Konrad Adenauer Stiftung, available at: https://www.kas.de/en/country-reports/detail/-/content/demographische-entwicklung-in-bosnien-und-herzegowina

Revised Enlargement Methodology: Questions and Answers, European Commission, available at: https://ec.europa.eu/commission/presscorner/detail/sl/qanda_20_182

Rohan, Albert, Kosovo's Path to Independence, European Council on Foreign Relations, available at: https://ecfr.eu/article/commentary_kosovos_path_to_independence/

Serbia and Montenegro Union: Background and Pending Dissolution, Congressional Research Service, available at: https://crsreports.congress.gov/product/pdf/RS/RS21568/7

Serbia, European Neighbourhood Policy and Enlargement Negotiations, European Commission, available at: https://neighbourhood-enlargement.ec.europa.eu/enlargement-policy/serbia_en

Sorbonne Speech of Emmanuel Macron, Ouest France, available at: https://international.blogs.ouest-france.fr/archive/2017/09/29/macron-sorbonne-verbatim-europe-18583.html

Vulović, Marina, Crisis in Bosnia and Herzegovina: Years of Power Struggles Come to the Boil, Stiftung Wissenschaft und Politik, available at: https://www.swp-berlin.org/publikation/crisis-in-bosnia-and-herzegovina-years-of-power-struggles-come-to-the-boil

Western Balkans Regional Poll, February–March 2024, international Republican Institute, available at: https://www.iri.org/resources/western-balkans-regional-poll-february-march-2024-mini/

Western Balkans Route, European Council, Council of the European Union, available at: https://www.consilium.europa.eu/en/policies/eu-migration-policy/western-balkans-route/#:~:text=The%20Western%20Balkans%20route%20refers,main%20migratory%20paths%20into%20Europe

Stagnation in Western Balkans' Security Regionalization: The Problem of Competing Regional Cultures of Anarchy

Ana Bojinović Fenko and Marko Kovačević

Abstract

The problem in Western Balkans' unstable and growingly challenged security provision is identified by scholars and practitioners in too many actors with diverse (regional) interests and lack of local states' ownership in the regional security regime. This chapter's aim is to offer a more comprehensive reading of the regionalization process—defining the Western Balkans as a regional complex advancing towards regional society. Focusing on the content of security regionalism, we answer "How can we explain the stagnation of security regionalisation in the Western Balkans?" Based on the conceptual linkage between levels of regionness and culture of anarchy, we make an empirical investigation of all 40 regional security institutions in operation mapped by MIND research project. The results show that that the Western Balkan countries are currently practicing divergent cultures of anarchy, moving from Hobbesian to Lockean culture of regional anarchy and at the same time being strongly incentivized to accelerate regional dynamics towards Kantian culture. The endogenous initiatives by Western Balkan states expose countries' interest to functionally cooperate on the basis of interdependence needs (energy, environmental security, disaster prevention, and crisis management) (strengthening Lockean culture of anarchy) but lack willingness in cooperation in security areas that demand relaxed inward orientation of states and would lead to trust and collective identity-building (elements of Kantian culture of anarchy).

A. B. Fenko (✉)
Faculty of Social Sciences, University of Ljubljana, Ljubljana, Slovenia
e-mail: ana.bojinovic@fdv.uni-lj.si

M. Kovačević
Faculty of Political Science, University of Belgrade, Belgrade, Serbia

A. Stojkov, T. Warin (eds.), *Western Balkans and the Future of Europe*, The Future of Europe, https://doi.org/10.1007/978-3-031-86465-0_4

Keywords

Regionalisation · Security · Western Balkans · Levels of regionness · Regional culture of anarchy

1 Introduction

In the quarter century past the post-Yugoslav wars of the 1990s, the policies of peacebuilding and externally driven forms of regional security cooperation in the Western Balkans produced mixed results by putting an end to most of the conflict formations and establishing the security regime. Regional security organizations and initiatives have stabilized in what conceptually is called a regional security complex (Buzan and Wæver 2003). In the 2000s, one thus observed the period of enthusiasm and upswing in regional cooperation institutionalization, induced mostly by the European Union (EU) which lives as a mature tightly coupled pluralistic security community (Adler and Barnet 1998; Deutsch et al. 1957), in some policies already an amalgamated one (e.g. trade, migration, and monetary policy). All Western Balkan states have thus committed to a common priority foreign policy goal, namely regional integration into the EU. Yet during the last 23 years, the EU-set conditions for post-conflict membership-aspiring states have still not been met; Europeanization to normatively align the Western Balkan states to the functioning of the states in the EU has been weak and shallow (Elbasani 2013; Džankić et al. 2018).

Especially the period after 2010 was largely marked by stagnation and business-as-usual approach. An abundance of institutions with a regional cooperative mandate exists in the Western Balkans, and new initiatives keep being proposed, yet this does not seem to correlate with—let alone determine—the quality of regional interstate relations. A mix of regional processes and actors sustaining the established regional security regime has been largely based on the treaties guaranteed by the international community, i.e. external actors to Western Balkans region exposing weak endogenous regional ownership (Prezelj 2013). Moreso, several external powers have contested the EU's regional hegemony and have ever since contributed to a fierce competition for influence in the region (e.g. Russia, China, Turkey, UK, and the Gulf states) (Keil and Stahl 2022). Therefore, there exists a cognitively dissonant situation of strongly security interdependent states linked by collective memory of historical armed conflicts and recently re-manifesting disputes on the one side, and the stagnating aspiration of a mutual trust and peaceful cohabitation-based community of states as friends on the other side. In sum, the Western Balkans has stopped short of the desired idea to extend the EU-like security community model of regional integration (Ejdus and Kovačević 2019).

The problem in Western Balkans security regime identified by scholars and practitioners likewise is that there are too many actors with diverse (regional) interests that need to be coordinated: there is the lack of regional identity, "the escape syndrome", the lack of implementation and "rhetorical regionalism", the lack of coherence in the regional cooperation (Prezelj 2013, pp. 98–102, 104), as well as the problem of effectiveness of regional initiatives (Radoman 2007). The coherence problem in the region has been identified through external and internal dimensions. The external dimension refers to external countries' and international organizations' individual agendas that are implemented through various multilateral frameworks whereas the internal dimension of regional incoherence means diversity in individual agendas of regional countries and their limited ability of effective governance (Prezelj 2013, p. 104). Our aim in this chapter is to offer a more comprehensive reading of the regionalization process in the Western Balkans, focused more on the content and less on the form of security regionalism. The research question of this chapter thus is: How can we explain the stagnation of security regionalization in the Western Balkans?

To answer this question, we first apply New Regionalism Approach (NRA) which conceptualizes the various intensity and quality of cohesiveness in a region as levels of regionness (Hettne and Söderbaum 2000; Hettne 2003; Söderbaum 2016). To look beyond only regionalizing actors-based literature, we then conceptualize Western Balkans as one of the levels of regionness—a regional social complex—developing towards a regional society with the aim of reaching at minimum a regional community (in an effect of joining the EU). We link these levels of regionness to cultures of anarchy (Wendt 1999) to identify regional cultures of anarchy (enemy, rival, and friend). Empirically, we provide a systematic overview of the regional security-related initiatives especially in the decade from 2013 to 2023 and identify elements of growing regional cohesion and cultures of anarchy, respectively. By this we illustrate the regional cultures of anarchy the states in the region have been practicing. Our thesis is that the relative stagnation in security regionalization is due to several co-existing regional cultures of anarchy in the Western Balkans.

2 Levels of "Regionness" in the Western Balkans' Security Regionalization

In scientific analysis, several approaches have been applied and they offer abundant empirical investigation of such a patchy, or zig-zag, non-linear regional dynamics of the Western Balkan regional cooperation, yet they each focus on a specific aspect of this dynamics. These clusters of international relations (IR) literature are international governance focusing on type of actors (mostly international—external actors) or on type of governance (e.g. the EU's normative power and Europeanization), security dimension of regionalism or security governance, and understanding the post-conflict transformation of societal patterns of amity and enmity. Equally relevant are studies treating the Western Balkans simply as an interest sphere rather than an autonomous area of cooperation-willing states (e.g. Bechev 2019; Cruz 2021; Keil and Stahl 2022).

We offer a (re)theorization of the content of regional norms to enable understanding of regionalization's "movement along" the continuum between conflict, external governance, and indigenous regional cooperation towards integration. To understand this dynamic process, we propose to take off from a conceptual framework of the New Regionalism Approach (NRA) (Hettne and Söderbaum 1998, 2000; Hettne 2003; Söderbaum 2004, 2016). NRA focuses on the content of regionalism, not the form, questioning any type of regionalization in terms of "by whom, for whom and with what purpose/consequences it is being put into practice, consolidated or resisted" (Söderbaum 2004, pp. 4, 38). The approach departs from the Social Constructivist approach to IR and focuses on the *process* of becoming, rather than on being "a region"—it understands regions as constantly in the process of being constructed—acquiring *regionness*.

Levels of regionness are conceptualized as stages of the intensity and quality of the constructed regional cohesiveness and are applicable to analysis of regionalization in any observed region. NRA has defined individual levels of regionness upon an inspiration from phases of economic regional integration, thus depicting five levels: regional social space, regional social complex, regional society, regional community, and a regional institutionalized polity (Hettne 2003; Söderbaum 2016). Based on their definition, the Western Balkans can be identified as a regional social complex. In the regional dimension of security, this is conceptually identical to regional security complex (RSC) as defined by Buzan and Waever (2003, p. 44) as a cluster of states where "the major processes of securitization and desecuritization among states are so interlinked that their security problems cannot reasonably be analysed or resolved apart from one another". Elements of regional social complex are states and human groups as regionalizing actors and elements of cohesiveness are (Hettne and Söderbaum 2000, 462–468, Hettne 2003, 28–29, Söderbaum 2016, Chap. 10) (Table 1):

> little shared knowledge or mutual trust, anarchy, inward orientation of states, collective memory, possible temporary decline in level of regionness due to nation/state-building, state balance of power, unification through area's conflicts, exploitative rather than co-operative and mutually reinforcing economic interdependencies, states looking towards larger external system, rather than the region, coercive regionalisation process (territorial conquests, building empires).

Preconditions for a regional social complex to advance to regional society are: "states must relax their "inward-orientedness" and become more open to external relation, degree of transnational contact has to increase dramatically". In a regional society, regionalizing actors are states, regional intergovernmental organizations, non-state actors, social institutions, and micro-regions and elements of cohesiveness are: "multidimensional regionalisation,[1] variety of processes of

[1] NRA critically recognizes that level of regionness can both increase and decrease, literally meaning that a "/…/ region can be a region 'more or less'" (Hettne and Söderbaum 2000, 461). "Regionalisation process can also proceed unevenly along the various dimensions of regionalism" (i.e. economics, politics, culture, security, sustainable development, etc.) (Hettne 2005, 545). This can most certainly be observed not only in the Western Balkans but also in regions at the highest level of regionness, such as within the EU (e.g. supranationality and deepening vs. intergovernmentalism and diversification, Brexit and EU enlargement withdrawals and fatigue). In this study, we focus only on security regionalization.

Table 1 Conceptualization of levels of regionness

Regionalizing actors	Elements or regional cohesiveness	Level of regionness
States and external actors	• Strong inward orientation of states • Balance of power • Exploitative economic interdependencies • Looking towards larger external system • Ideas of territorial conquests	Regional social complex
States, regional intergovernmental organizations, non-state actors, social institutions, and micro-regions	• Relaxed "inward-orientation" of states • Multidimensional regionalization • Formal and "real" region • More rule-based pattern of relations • Increasing interdependence	Regional society
All above + regional society	• Enduring organizational framework • Convergence and compatibility of ideas, values, organizations, and processes • Social communication and social trust • Regional collective identity	Regional community

communication and interaction, anarchical society, formal and 'real' region, membership (in formal regions), more rule-based pattern of relations, increasing interdependence, relaxed 'inward-orientation', moving towards transcendence of national space" (ibid.). Yet, the next level of regionness—a regional community—displays a much stronger quality of regional cohesiveness: next to the previous regionalizing actors, regional society becomes active, and elements of this level of regionness are: "enduring organisational framework (formal or less formal), convergence and compatibility of ideas, values, organisations, and processes (actions), social communication, social trust at the regional level and regional collective identity" (ibid.).

We now upgrade the NRA by understanding the levels of regionness continuum as part of "three cultures of anarchy" (Wendt 1999, Chap. 6). We understand a typology of regional agency–structure dynamics in terms of anarchy in their region; how states identify their role as the central regional norm and how they practice this regional norm. In the empirical part, we identify above elements of preconditions for regional complex to advance to regional society in the case of the Western Balkans including the context of countries from the region trying to join the EU as a regional community.

3 Cultures of Anarchy as Levels of Regionness

The NRA presupposes—similarly to Acharya (2004)—that "/a/gents engage in regionalism not only on the basis of material resources (power capability, routine behaviour, economic man) but also ideational elements like ideas and identities" (Söderbaum 2004, p. 45). Paraphrasing Wendt (1992) "regionalism is what actors make of it"—reflective capacity of actors is seen as an important explanation for the emergence and quality of regionalism (Söderbaum 2004, p. 45). Since there are nearly always a multitude of strategies and ideas about a particular region, which merge, mingle, and clash, regions as such are also politically contested; in many cases, connectedness comes from influential actors from outside the region (e.g. in the Mediterranean as a historical region reinvented by the EU or the Western Balkans as an EU-constructed region).

We link the principal regional norm of states' role within individual levels of regionness, to three central roles in cultures of anarchy. Hobbesian culture is based on the role of enemy (regulating the states' right of to live), Lockean culture on the role of rival (regulating the states' right to sovereignty), and Kantian anarchy on the role of friend (regulating the states' right to avoid violence) (ibid.). The Hobbesian enemy-based anarchy functions in a regional social complex, the Lockean rival-based anarchy in a regional society, and the Kantian friend-based anarchy operates in a regional community. Such a conceptualization reorients the focus of the analysis onto the inherent regional cooperation properties built by the states in the region and then fully enables an assessment of the effects that the diverse forms of regional cooperation have on the level of regionness. This novel analytical model enables identification of regional institutions and initiatives by diverse regionalizing actors (internal/external and state/non-state) which contribute to the practice of regional states' role of enemy, rival, or friend and eventually determining their contribution to advancement or stagnation in the regionalization process.

Wendt (1999, pp. 251, 311–312) assesses that in the international community, even though there is no guarantee that the Lockean culture of anarchy, which has at the beginning of the twenty-first century been practised by many states as legitimate, and by others due to a good price or due to fear, will move forward towards a Kantian culture. Yet, he believes it is at least unlikely to move backward unless there is a big exogenous shock (ibid.). But he (Wendt 1999, p. 282) does recognize a possibility of temporary regressions of the logic of culture due to asymmetry in roles' perception (e.g. enmity instead of rivalry).

4 Empirical Findings on Regional Cultures of Anarchy in Western Balkans Security Regionalization

The regional security complex level includes most of all the official discourses of institutions and their representatives where the cooperation may occur but still being short of the full state-to-state or societal trust. In the language of the Regional Security Complex Theory (Buzan and Wæver 2003), it is still valid to say the

Western Balkans is a sub-complex of the wider EU-Europe regional security complex, since its security dynamic is not fully distinct but connected to the dominant influences of the European and other external powers.

The cooperation was more dispersed and less formalized until 2008, because the transformation of the Stability Pact for Southeastern Europe into the Regional Cooperation Council (RCC) has promised a greater organizational coherence in terms of political and technical cooperation. In fact, regional cooperation and the drive towards regional society are largely connected to two distinct nodes that can improve comprehensive security: Regional Cooperation Council (since 2008) and EU-bound Justice and Home Affairs policies (Prezelj 2013, p. 88). Bechev, Ejdus, and Taleski propose the typology of the regional security initiatives per two criteria (top-down/bottom-up and external/local). These top-down initiatives come from the governments, whereas bottom-up initiatives acknowledge the cooperation between the governments or the workings of the civil society. Also, based on challenges and perspectives, they divide regional cooperation into several policy areas, such as: justice and security, energy and infrastructure, and social development (Bechev et al. 2015, pp. 15–31). More recently, Džananović et al. (2021, pp. 58–61), following the EU agenda for the Western Balkans, provided the classification of the regional initiatives based on the following areas of work: competitiveness, connectivity, fight against organized crime, good governance, security, labour and social mobility, and multiple. The areas of security and fight against organized crime can be labelled in this classification as instances of hard and soft security, which is similar to the classification provided by Dehnert and Taleski (2013).

In this section, we identify empirical reality of the Western Balkan region as moving from regional security complex to regional society (Table 3), in a rather uneven and often protracted manner. For this purpose, we broadly organize regional security themes (Radoman 2007, pp. 18–21) into three clusters based on NRA's elements of growing regional cohesiveness identified in Table 2: (a) interdependence issues (energy, environmental security, disaster prevention, crisis management, fight against terrorism, and organized crime); (b) rule-based relations (police and cross-border cooperation, migration, and fight against corruption); and (c) issues demanding a relaxed inward orientation (national military security, security sector reform, control of small arms and light weapons, and post-conflict reconciliation). In the final step, we then synthesize these elements and identify logics of anarchy they uphold. Since we are putting content of regionalism to the forefront instead of regionalizing actors, we have organized empirical data according to geographical areas of security. Security, however, is also viewed comprehensively as political, military, economic, societal, and environmental (Buzan et al. 1998). Regional institutions are identified according to their ownership as external, Southeast European (SEE), or Western Balkan (WB). External regional institutions are foreign policy initiatives by non-Southeast European states (e.g. the USA, UK, China, Russia, Turkey, and Norway) or international organizations' programmes for the region (e.g. the UN system, EU, NATO, IOM, OSCE, EBRD, and EIB). Southeast European regional institutions are regional institutions that include all Western Balkan states but are purposed for a larger—Southeastern European region. Western Balkan regional institutions are regional initiatives by Western Balkan states.

Table 2 Regional cultures of anarchy in level of regionness

Level of regionness	Regional culture of anarchy	Conceptual overlap
Regional social complex	Hobbesian culture of enemy (right to live)	States are the main regionalizing actors, use of force is legitimate, and inward state orientation combined with external powers linkages
Regional society	Lockean culture of rival (right to sovereignty)	States regulate behaviour via rules in regional institutions, use of force is highly limited, and sovereignty against aggressors is guaranteed via a collective security
Regional community	Kantian culture of friend (right to avoid violence)	States form trust-based regional institutions (supranationality), regional rules and norms based on collective identity, and use of force among them is unimaginable and never applied

4.1 Interdependence Issues

Regional cooperation initiatives in the Western Balkans are related to what we call interdependence issues—that can be observed at three levels: strategic stability (military and political), regional cooperation initiatives, and regional projects. Firstly, in the realm of military security, this interdependence is strategic—for example, the externally supported and partly regionally-guaranteed Dayton Peace Agreement, as well as the subregional arms control regime presents the very foundation of the still fragile neighbourly relations that are short of war, but still holding potential for occasional political crises spurred by heightened ethnonationalist rhetoric. Shortly, the processes of securitization within the region are highly interdependent, so that the (in)securities among the states cannot be observed separately from one another (cf. Buzan and Wæver 2003; Ejdus and Kovačević 2019; Kovačević 2018). This strategic level of cooperation has proven resistant and too costly to be abandoned, so all the states abide by it by their own design and the role expectations of the external powers that value regional stability.

Secondly, the interdependence is exhibited at the level of regional cooperation initiatives that tackle political and technical cooperation among the governmental and other levels of institutions.[2] This can be seen most notably within the RCC and its associated sub-institutions, initiatives, and projects that are funded by the international donors. The initiatives ranging between fighting terrorism and organized crime within the police cooperation are also indicators of relative success, as well as the control of small and light weapons (e.g. SEESAC and RACVIAC). Although the setting up of the RCC has been connected for more than a decade with the problem of regional ownership—and one can ask is this now more than a "mantra?" As Prezelj notes, "Regional ownership has also become one of the key principles and mantras of the RCC. Regional countries have been taking on extra responsibilities in directing, managing, and financing the existing initiatives. However, these

[2] We offer a map of regional security institutions in the Appendix.

countries do not have as many financial and human resources as richer external players" (cf. Prezelj 2013, p. 98). Related to this is the issue of financing by the states.

Thirdly, at the level of regional projects, most recently, the cooperation was extended to the securitized realm of public health during the Covid-19 pandemic, including some elements of regional solidarity in the vaccine provision. There are also various fora, networks, and projects ranging from women in police (WPON) to addressing the challenges of migration within the cooperation with the EU (including EUROPOL and FRONTEX), as well as intra-regionally under MARRI, and they are strongly needs-based and functional in their aims.

4.2 Rule-Based Relations

When it comes to rule-based relations, those cooperation initiatives are related to the matters of rule of law and may deal most notably with the matters such as police and cross-border cooperation, migration, and fight against corruption. Although some of these issues may also appear within the regional interdependence, they are more strongly regulated within the framework of the dominant cooperation with the EU, under the Stabilization and Association Process. As of January 2024, Albania, Bosnia and Herzegovina, Montenegro, North Macedonia, and Serbia are all candidates for EU membership, whereas Kosovo* is a potential candidate.[3]

Furthermore, there have been several initiatives that have been developed in line with EU or NATO accession processes. Successful regional cooperation is one of the prerequisites for all candidate countries on their integration path in the EU. However, the crisis of EU enlargement for much of the 2010s has caused disillusionment in the region, and some auxiliary plans had to be drawn in the meantime. For example, in 2014, the Berlin Process was promoted by Germany and other EU states interested in the region, which appeared at a time when the discourse of the "enlargement fatigue" obscured the membership perspective for the countries in the region (cf. Đukanović and Krstić 2021). The Berlin Process is focusing on resolving the bilateral issues and reconciliation within the region, promoting the idea of a common regional market and providing support for the sustainable economic development. The goal of this initiative is to keep the region on the track of EU perspective in the years when the enlargement policy was undergoing crisis (Kovačević et al. 2023). Also, as part of the Berlin Process, the youth regional cooperation has been put under the mandate of the new international organization called Regional Youth Cooperation Office (RYCO). EU rule-based approach is also present within the Energy Community that helps the countries in the region harmonize their legislation and work towards fulfilling the relevant standards of energy security. The

[3] Kosovo applied for EU membership in December 2022. It is designated in EU enlargement policy with the following footnote (Kosovo* 2023 Report, p. 1): "Kosovo*; *This designation is without prejudice to positions on status, and is in line with UNSCR 1244/1999 and the ICJ Opinion on the Kosovo Declaration of Independence."

recently adopted Growth Plan for the Western Balkans for the period of 2024–2027 aims to support reforms in the function of the preparation for the economic integration in the EU according to merits (European Commission 2023).

As Bechev finds, "intra-Balkan functional demands for cooperation, though visible in the ministerial conferences under SEECP, have not been a sufficient condition for cooperation to advance. Security agendas and perceptions differ across wider Southeast Europe, which has constrained *a priori* the formation of a truly multilateral regime on a regional scale", with a particular role for identity politics preventing a more genuine defence cooperation within the region (Bechev 2011, pp. 127–128). As noted in one of the analyses, "No resources beyond the contribution fees were allocated to support regional cooperation. Agenda setting processes are institutionalized and top-down. Ministers make most of the decisions about regional initiatives at national level. The countries are eager to push regional cooperation forward when they are chairing initiatives—or rather they see an opportunity to put their interests forward within the framework of regional cooperation" (Dehnert and Taleski 2013, pp. 24–25).

4.3 Issues Demanding a Relaxed Inward Orientation

The inward orientation of the countries was most visible in the 1990s during the Yugoslav wars, and this orientation mostly depends on the push and pull of the EU-integration process. This can be said most of all for Slovenia and Croatia, whereas other states of the region have had more problems in giving precedence to integration and supranationalism due to the problems related to state weakness (political, security, economic, or societal). Given that the Western Balkans is a region of small and relatively weak states in terms of their intra-state sociopolitical cohesion, the problems of functioning of institutions, economic development, corruption, and societal stress are making it difficult to focus on developing externally trust-based policies in a region still heavily burdened by post-conflict logic. The questions of national security, security sector reform, and post-conflict reconciliation were considered progressive agenda in line with the EU enlargement in the 2000s, but the 2010s have unravelled the problems of democratic backsliding and unravelling of the non-consolidated democratic institutions (Stojanović Gajić and Pavlović 2021). The initiatives such as RECOM Reconciliation Network are CSO-led but never got the support from the governments to pursue a regional approach to transitional justice, but depend on international donors (Bojicic-Dzelilovic et al. 2016). All of this makes it still not possible to imagine the transcendence of national space in the realm of politics and defence.

Despite the presence of still unresolved issues related to post-Yugoslav identities (ethno-national or pluralist), and orders, bilateral relations are mostly functional but carrying the potential for occasional crises and disruptions. Currently, the biggest regional hotspot is related to the problem of the status of Kosovo and the highly securitized context of the interaction between Belgrade and Pristina. The main external determinants and initiators of the regional cooperation in the post-conflict period of the security regime development have been the EU and NATO, and particularly in the area of security and defence. The cornerstone of this security regime most notably includes the Agreement on Sub-Regional Arms Control (the Florence Agreement) from 1996 that established the caps on the quantity of weapons for the states in the region, and all the signatories have been operating within this regional norm (Ejdus et al. 2022). The use of force in the region is limited by the fact of the EU and NATO presence, whereas several incidents involving dissatisfied local Serbs and Kosovo police in the north of Kosovo during 2023 that raised the tensions between Belgrade and Pristina demonstrate that the security dilemma can be further escalated only to be de-escalated by the diplomatic engagement of the international community.

Also, the arms-race rhetoric characteristic for the late 2010s and early 2020s (Ejdus et al. 2022) now is also showing new concerns with the restored security dilemma in the relations between Belgrade and Pristina. In the recent years, the process of formation and arming of the Kosovo Security Forces indirectly approved by the Western partners and Serbia's responses by its modernization of armed forces and the latest calls for reintroducing conscription may raise an alarm. Although the military conflict in the region is unlikely, the collective security norm is still not available because the states of the region largely observe their national interests in the realm of military security. The latter primarily relates to Serbia whose defence policy is geared towards military neutrality, whereas other countries of the region are either members of NATO or have the presence of NATO troops on its territory. The regional cooperation may give some effects when it comes to communication and occasional meetings of the army chiefs or regarding the police cooperation, together with the regular communication with NATO, including the periodical military exercises. This may be a case of what Kulkova (2022) terms as "routinisation" in the communication among the state officials engaging in or working at various levels of regional cooperation.

When it comes to the possibility of the use of force among the actors in the region, it is considered too costly and unreasonable (but not unimaginable as in the security communities) due to the troop presence or membership in NATO for most of the region's countries (with the exception of Serbia due to its proclaimed military neutrality and Kosovo—a non-recognized state). The effects of external security shocks and geopolitical implications of the ongoing regional wars such as those in Ukraine and the Middle East may affect the concentration of authority for regional cooperation in the hands of governments. This does not mean that the citizens and civil society organizations (CSOs) are not making impact in fostering cooperation—the key premise is that the locus of decision-making and agenda setting still remains in the hands of governments that mostly seek to harmonize their national legislation in line with the requirements of the EU Acquis to varying degrees of success in actual implementation of the rule of law. In this sense, the status of regional cooperation as one of the key prerequisites of the EU accession process is somewhere between the conditionality and simple functionalism. Therefore, the full internalization of regional cooperation norms is something that needs to be further worked on across the region.

Table 3 Elements of cohesiveness in Western Balkans' security regionalization

Elements of growing regional cohesiveness	Area of security	Regional institutions		Regional culture of anarchy
		Sum	Ownership	
Increasing interdependence	1_Energy, environmental security, disaster prevention, and crisis management	21	External: 6 SEE: 12 WB: 3	*From regional complex to regional society*
More rule-based pattern of relations	2_Police and cross-border cooperation, migration, fight against corruption, fight against terrorism and organized crime	11	External: 1 SEE: 8 WB: 2	
Towards transcendence of national space and relaxed inward orientation	3_National military security, security sector reform, control of small arms and light weapons, and post-conflict reconciliation	8	External: 3 SEE: 3 WB: 2	
Building regional identity and trust	4_Accession to the EU security community	5	External: 4 SEE: 1 WB: 0	*Regional community*

As shown in Table 3, we establish that out of some 40 existing regional initiatives aimed for the Western Balkans as a political region of Southeastern Europe, ownership of these initiatives is predominantly regional, namely Southeast European (23). Yet very compellingly, there is still more externally driven security fora (10) compared to Western Balkan ones (7). Very indicatively, there is no hegemon in externally owned regional initiatives; the latter are predominantly driven by the EU and enable presence of the USA and Turkey equally (each in 3 regional institutions).

As for the content of security regionalism, one could say there is evidence of growing elements of regional society. There exist 21 regional initiatives in the fields of energy security, environmental security, disaster prevention, and crisis management (recognition of the need to functionally cooperate on the basis of interdependence) and 11 initiatives on police and cross-border cooperation, migration, fight against corruption, fight against terrorism and organized crime (proof of a drive towards a more rule-based pattern of relations). The most demanding security issues for cooperation remain national military security, security sector reform, control of small arms and light weapons, and post-conflict reconciliation, where we found 8 existing institutions. Finally, only 5 institutions already promote Kantian culture-grounded trust-based cooperation and regional identity building, yet these are all EU-lead (4) initiatives and one framework in which EU includes Southeast European states, thus externalizing its demands for a security community. Regional cooperation remains a key part of the EU criteria for membership, together with good neighbourly relations, etc (Klemenc et al. 2021). As part of its enlargement approach towards the Western Balkans, the EU supports the Berlin Process (established in 2014) and regional cooperation organizations and initiatives (The EU and the Western Balkans n.d.).

5 Conclusion

After two decades of post-conflict regional cooperation, there is a rather complex map of initiatives and institutions of regional cooperation which largely depends on whether the region is socially constructed or imagined as "Southeast Europe", "the Balkans", or "'the Western Balkans". As described in the Introduction, in the past 25 years of the post-war regional security cooperation in the Western Balkans, the dominant conception of the culture of anarchy has been moving from the Hobbesian to the Lockean type. This corresponds to moving from hostile to cooperative regional relations and including some degree of their institutionalization. The Western Balkans is a Western a regional complex, and we studied how come the advancement towards regional society has been going so slowly in the context of promotion of regional integration by the EU and all Western Balkans states aiming for such security-community aim. We have focused on the security dimension of regionalism.

Researchers at the MIND project have compiled the database of 40 regional initiatives (both active and passive), that we draw from in this paper (Appendix) to identify empirical reality of the Western Balkan region as moving from regional security complex to regional society (Table 3) and thus determine current presence of culture of anarchy in the region. A critical observation of these findings indicates that the Western Balkans countries are currently practicing divergent cultures of anarchy, moving from Hobbesian to Lockean culture of regional anarchy and at the same time being strongly incentivized to accelerate regional dynamics towards Kantian culture. Should we observe only the endogenous initiatives by Western Balkan states, these initiatives still expose countries' interest to functionally cooperate on the basis of independence needs (energy, environmental security, disaster prevention, and crisis management). Yet two initiatives show rule-based cooperation and two indicate a relaxed inward orientation of Western Balkan countries, clearly exposing their capability and willingness for interest-based regional security cooperation. Trust and regional identity-based security cooperation are not yet present in governments' initiatives; it still demands some time, yet functional regional cooperation has historically already shown transformative power for closer regionalization of post-conflict countries in Europe.

One would expect that dozens of regional initiatives across different areas would mean greater institutionalization and possibly internalization of the purpose of regional cooperation in the Western Balkans, this is not always the case. The push of the Euro-Atlantic integration imperatives in the first decade of this century marked the rise of regional cooperation, whereas a relative stagnation started around the mid-2010s, lasting up to the present day. One could interpret stagnation not only in the lesser number of newly founded initiatives compared to the previous decades, but also in problems of duplication, lack or ownership and their eventual passivity.

For us it seems as if the region is currently stuck between interest-based cooperation and externally driven governance. The dominant form of regional (security) complex is still driven by the national level of decision-making that is not willing to take transformative risks in a distrustful environment, whereas the governance structures such as RCC are functional but lacking greater agenda setting capacity and authority to make regional rules that regulate state behaviour under a prospective regional society. Although the reawakened Berlin Process and the newly announced Growth Plan for the Western Balkans may provide a better "carrot" to the interest-based governments and politicians in the regional complex, this process would also benefit from clear expectations regarding good/better governance standards replacing the damning mix of stabilitocracy, democratic backsliding, and state capture. The whole setup of regional initiatives could then re-discover its purpose and give boost to any future process that would strongly follow a re-energized EU-integration path and drive the region to consolidate itself as regional society looking towards a regional community. Until then, the EU and the Western Balkans shall work to jointly re-negotiate the relative stagnation of the regional integration and work out the credible transformation of the regional security complex to a regional society/community in this decade. This idea is difficult but not impossible—and regional cooperation initiatives can be the key facilitators of undoing old enmities and building new common interests and trust in an EU-integrated Western Balkans.

Acknowledgments Marko Kovačević would like to acknowledge that his research was supported by the Science Fund of the Republic of Serbia, grant no. 7744512, Monitoring and Indexing Peace and Security in the Western Balkans—MIND. The contribution by Ana Bojinović Fenko has been supported by the Slovenian Research and Innovation Agency, programme P5-0177.

Appendix: Regional Institutions by Ownership and Area of Security in the Western Balkans

Ownership	Name of the Institution	Area of Security[a]	Sum
External	The Berlin Process	1, 4	10 Area 1 = 6 Area 2 = 1 Area 3 = 3 Area 4 = 4 UN-lead: 1 EU-lead: 3 Incl. USA: 3 Incl. Turkey: 3
	South-East European Cooperation Initiative (SECI)	1	
	Energy Community	1, 4	
	South Eastern and Eastern Europe Clearinghouse for the Control of Small Arms and Light Weapons (SEESAC)	3	
	South East Europe Defense Ministerial (SEDM) Process	3	
	Forum for Western Balkans Defense Cooperation (SEEC)	3	
	The United States Adriatic Charter	1	
	Western Balkans Prosecutors' Network	2	
	Conference of the European Integration Parliamentary Committees of States participating in the Stabilization and Association Process (Western Balkans COSAP)	1, 4	
	Brdo-Brijuni Process	1, 4	

Ownership	Name of the Institution	Area of Security[a]	Sum
Southeast European	The South East European Cooperation Process (SEECP)	1	23 Area 1 = 12 Area 2 = 8 Area 3 = 3 Area 4 = 1
	Regional Cooperation Council (RCC)	1	
	The Black Sea Economic Cooperation (BSEC)	1	
	Central European Initiative (CEI)	1	
	EU Strategy for the Danube Region	1, 4	
	The Adriatic Ionian Initiative (AII)	1	
	Central European Free Trade Agreement (CEFTA II)	1	
	Disaster Preparedness and Prevention Initiative for SEE (DPPI)	1	
	Centre for Security Cooperation (formerly Regional Arms Control Verification and Assistance Centre—RACVIAC)	3	
	Women Police Officers Network in SEE (WPON)	2	
	Southeast Europe Police Chiefs Association (SEPCA)	2	
	Regional Anti-Corruption Initiative (RAI)	2	
	Southeast European Law Enforcement Center (SELEC)	2	
	Southeast Europe Police Cooperation Convention Secretariat	2	
	Southeast European Prosecutors Advisory Group (SEEPAG)	2	
	Regional Secretariat for Parliamentary Cooperation in Southeast Europe (RSPC SEE)	1	
	Cetinje Parliamentary Forum (CPF)	1	
	Regional Working Group on Justice	2	
	Regional Housing Programme (RHP)	1	
	Southeast Europe Military Intelligence Chiefs' Forum (SEEMIC)	3	
	Southeast Europe National Security Authorities' Forum (SEENSA)	3	
	Igman Initiative	1	
	Southeast Europe Coalition on Whistleblower Protection	2	

Ownership	Name of the Institution	Area of Security[a]	Sum
Western Balkans	Migration, Asylum and Refugees Regional Initiative (MARRI)	2	7 Area 1 = 3 Area 2 = 2 Area 3 = 2 Area 4 = 0
	Western Balkans Fund (WBF)	1	
	Open Balkan Initiative	1	
	Regional Working Group on Justice	2	
	Regional Youth Cooperation Office (RYCO)	1	
	RECOM Reconciliation Network	3	
	The Agreement on Sub-Regional Arms Control (established 1996, regional ownership since 2015)	3	

Source: Compiled by the authors based on the MIND WP3 database (available at https://rsi.mind-project.ac.rs)

[a]Areas of security:

1. Energy, environmental security, disaster prevention, and crisis management;
2. Police and cross-border cooperation, migration, fight against corruption, fight against terrorism and organized crime;
3. National military security, security sector reform, control of small arms and light weapons, post-conflict reconciliation;
4. Accession to the EU security community

References

Acharya A (2004) Ideas, norms and regional orders. In: Paul TV (ed) International relations theory and regional transformation. Cambridge University Press, Cambridge, pp 183–209

Adler E, Barnet M (eds) (1998) Security communities. Cambridge University Press, Cambridge

Bechev D (2011) Constructing South East Europe: the politics of Balkan regional cooperation. Palgrave Macmillan, Hampshire

Bechev D (2019) Russia's strategic interests and tools of influence in the Western Balkans. NATO Strategic Communications Centre of Excellence

Bechev D, Ejdus F, Taleski D (2015) Culture of regional cooperation in Southeast Europe. Balkans in Europe Policy Advisory Group, Belgrade

Bojicic-Dzelilovic V, Kostovicova D, Randazzo E (2016) EU in the Western Balkans: hybrid development, hybrid security and hybrid justice. SiT/WP/03/16. Friedrich Ebert Stiftung and LSE International Development, London

Buzan B, Wæver O (2003) Regions and powers. The structure of international security. Cambridge University Press, London

Buzan B, Wæver O, de Wilde J (1998) Security: a new framework for analysis. Lynne Rienner Publishers, Boulder

Cruz M (2021) Russia in the Western Balkans: interests and tools of influence. In: Mölder H, Sazonov V, Chochia A, Kerikmäe T (eds) The Russian Federation in global knowledge warfare. Contributions to international relations. Springer, Cham. https://doi.org/10.1007/978-3-030-73955-3_16

Dehnert S, Taleski D (eds) (2013) Monitoring regional cooperation in South East Europe. Friedrich Ebert Stiftung, Berlin

Deutsch KW et al (1957) Political community and the North Atlantic state. Princeton University Press, Princeton

Đukanović D, Krstić M (2021) Regionalna saradnja na Zapadnom Balkanu: dugoročno čekanje na članstvo u Evropskoj uniji i/ili 'Balkanska unija'. Srpska politička misao 28(71):9–26

Džananović N, Emini D, Krisafi L, Nikolovski I, Velinovska A (2021) The impact of regional organizations and initiatives in the Western Balkans. Institute for Democracy "Societas Civilis", Skopje

Džankić J, Keil S, Kmezić M (eds) (2018) The Europeanisation of the Western Balkans: a failure of EU conditionality? Palgrave Macmillan, Basingstoke

Ejdus F, Kovačević M (2019) Penetration, overlay, governmentality: the evolving role of NATO in the Western Balkan security dynamics. J Interv Statebuild 13(5):566–580. https://doi.org/10.1080/17502977.2019.1660032

Ejdus F, Rečević T, Kovačević M (2022) Military dynamics, conventional arms control, and regional security in the Western Balkans. In: Džuverović N, Stojarová V (eds) Peace and security in the Western Balkans: a local perspective. Routledge, Abingdon, pp 129–155

Elbasani E (2013) European integration and transformation in the Western Balkans: Europeanization or business as usual? Routledge, London

EU and the Western Balkans (n.d.). https://www.eeas.europa.eu/eeas/eu-and-western-balkans-towards-common-future_en. Accessed 6 Mar 2023

European Commission (2023) Commission presents a new Growth Plan for the Western Balkans including €6 billion in grants and loans to accelerate economic convergence with the EU. https://neighbourhood-enlargement.ec.europa.eu/news/commission-presents-new-growth-plan-western-balkans-including-eu6-billion-grants-and-loans-2023-11-08_en. Accessed 27 Jan 2023

Hettne B (2003) The new regionalism revisited. In: Söderbaum F, Shaw TM (eds) Theories of new regionalism. A Palgrave reader. Palgrave Macmillan, Houndmills, pp 22–42

Hettne B (2005) Regionalism and world order. In: Farrell M, Hettne B, van Langenhove L (eds) Global politics of regionalism: theory and practice. Pluto Press, London, pp 269–286

Hettne B, Söderbaum F (1998) The new regionalism approach. Politeia 17(3):6–21

Hettne B, Söderbaum F (2000) Theorising the rise of regionness. New Polit Econ 5(3):457–472

Keil S, Stahl B (eds) (2022) A new eastern question? Great powers and the post-Yugoslav states. Ibidem, Stuttgart

Klemenc J, Hrabálek M, Đorđević V (2021) Regional security cooperation revisited: the Western Balkans as the future security provider, European security. Eur Secur 30(2):285–304. https://doi.org/10.1080/09662839.2021.1872545

Kosovo* 2023 Report, issued by European Commission on 8 November 2023, SWD(2023) 692 final. https://neighbourhood-enlargement.ec.europa.eu/system/files/2023-11/SWD_2023_692%20Kosovo%20report_0.pdf

Kovačević M (2018) Bringing in Bibó: understanding identities and reality of small post-Yugoslav states. In: Pudar Draško G, Pavlović A, Meka E (eds) Politics of enmity. Institute for Philosophy and Social Theory, Beograd, pp 184–210

Kovačević M, Milošević A, Rečević T, Varda M (2023) Old wine in new bottles? Good governance, misgovernance and three scenarios for the future of open Balkan-Berlin process relationship. MIND Project Publications. University of Belgrade—Faculty of Political Science

Kulkova M (2022). (online first)) We speak over the phone almost daily': routinisation as an overlooked source of pacification in the Western Balkans. J Int Relat Dev 26(1):111–130. https://doi.org/10.1057/s41268-022-00281-z

Prezelj I (2013) Challenges of multilateral regional security and defence cooperation in South East Europe. J Eur Persp West Balkans 5(2):83–112

Radoman J (2007) Regional initiatives in Southeast Europe. Western Balkans Security Observer 6(July–September):18–24

Söderbaum F (2004) The political economy of regionalism. The case of Southern Africa. Palgrave, Houndmills

Söderbaum F (2016) Rethinking regionalism. Palgrave Macmillan, Houndmills

Stojanović Gajić S, Pavlović D (2021) State capture, hybrid regimes, and security sector reform. J Reg Secur 16(2):89–126

Wendt A (1992) Anarchy is what states make of it: the social construction of power politics. Int Organ 46(2):391–424

Wendt A (1999) Social theory of international politics. Cambridge University Press, Cambridge

The Future Relations Between the European Union and Albania

Erjon Luçi

Abstract

Albania's path towards European Union (EU) membership has been a lengthy and arduous journey. Despite this, public support for joining EU remains strong. The EU integration process provides Albania with a unique opportunity for boosting economic growth and accelerating income convergence, as it pushes the country to undertake a series of challenging reforms. These reforms, although demanding, are essential for fostering long-term development, ultimately helping to bridge the gap between Albania and more developed EU nations.

Keywords

EU membership · Market economy transition · Stabilization and Association Agreement · Public support · Judicial reform

1 Introduction

Albania's aspirations to join the EU started with its transition to the market economy in early 1990s that put an end to a long period of centralized planning under the communist regime. Albania was associated to the EU initially in 1992, when it signed a trade and cooperation agreement. It took a while before moving to the next stage of pre-accession with the singing of Stabilization and Association Agreement (SAA) in 2006. This was followed by another long period to get to the candidate status in 2014 for the Accession Conference taking place much later in 2022. As of 2023, Albania still has to open any of the chapters, waiting for the Greece consent for opening of the first five chapters under the fundamentals cluster.

E. Luçi (✉)
Independent Researcher, Tirana, Albania

A. Stojkov, T. Warin (eds.), *Western Balkans and the Future of Europe*, The Future of Europe, https://doi.org/10.1007/978-3-031-86465-0_5

To many this feels a very long process, caught in-between the sluggish progress of reforms, the enlargement fatigue among some EU member states, and the geopolitical tensions in the region, risking eroding the initial drive of joining the Union and the appetite for reforms. There are cases of this vicious circle already, but Albania so far has avoided falling into this trap. It still enjoys a strong public support for the EU membership. According to the latest Eurobarometer survey (https://europa.eu/eurobarometer/surveys/detail/3215) (Autum 2024), more than 80% of Albanians are in favour of joining the EU, which is the highest percentage among Western Balkan countries. Albanians still see the EU as an anchor of stability, prosperity, and security, and are broadly supportive of the reforms necessary for the accession process. Albania has aligned many of its laws and policies with the EU's acquis and has made progress in several areas; more recently, the judiciary reform. It still needs to implement a few more reforms and in particular demonstrate concrete results in particular for the rule of law and anti-corruption but early signs show it is moving in the right direction.

While Albania's commitment and determination to join the EU remains strong it is important for its efforts to be recognized and rewarded by opening of the chapters and adopting a more flexible approach to EU accession funds and markets. The visa liberalization agreement signed in 2010 is a good example of how to keep the momentum of reforms. The more recent Economic and Investment Plan for the Western Balkans launched as the New Growth Plan for Western Balkan is another opportunity to boost the level of EU funds available to support reforms and the income convergence of Albania and Western Balkan countries.

The income convergence for new members was faster prior to membership. The advantage offered by EU integration process is within reach for countries like Albania. The challenge is how to fully utilize these benefits despite potential delays and frictions. Enhancing absorption capacity of EU funds and of other European donors is now more critical that EU is committing larger contributions for Western Balkans. Exports to EU can be further boosted as they are still a fraction of what new members managed to achieve. In the meantime, EU accession remains a critical leverage to influence the reform agenda. These are all opportunities that could help future growth and income convergence. Eventually, the speed of convergence depends on many factors beyond Albania-EU relationship. The road to membership is not a guarantee for the convergence but certainly an opportunity that not many developing economies have.

2 The Current Status of Albania's EU Membership Bid

Albania is a small country in Southeast Europe that has been pursuing its European integration since the early 1990s but has been on the agenda for EU enlargement since 2000, when it was recognized as a "potential candidate country". It applied for EU membership in April 2009. Since then, the accession process has been slow and challenging. The European Commission recommended granting Albania candidate status in October 2012, subject to completion of key measures in the areas of judicial and public administration reform and revision of the parliamentary rules of procedures. The candidate status was granted in June 2014. The recommendation from the European Commission to open accession negotiations came in April 2018. The Council of the European Union decided in March 2020 to open accession negotiations with Albania. This was a historic decision that recognized Albania's efforts and reforms, especially in the areas of judicial reform and fight against corruption and organized crime.

However, accession negotiations did not start until 2022. One of the reasons for the delay was the revision of the enlargement methodology with more rigorous and reversible conditions for the candidates, following the scepticism of some member states about further enlargement. Another reason for the delay was the linkage of Albania's candidacy with that of North Macedonia. The two countries were treated jointly, according to some member states, for avoiding instability and frustration in the region. This meant that Albania's progress was held back by factors beyond its control, because its candidacy was linked to that of North Macedonia, which was vetoed by Bulgaria, over historical and linguistic disputes. Bulgaria's lifted its veto in June 2022, opening the way for starting accession negotiations.

In July 2022, Albania held its first intergovernmental conference with the EU, which marked the official start of accession negotiations. This was another significant step that opened a new phase in Albania's relations with the EU. The conference adopted a general framework for negotiations and agreed on an indicative timetable for opening and closing chapters. The conference also confirmed that Albania's negotiations would be based on its own merits and performance.

The screening process to evaluate Albania's readiness for implementing EU legislation and policies and setting the framework and targets for the next steps of negotiation has been completed in 2023. The formal opening of the five chapters under the fundamental cluster faced further delays due to a dispute over a Greek minority leader arrested ahead of local elections of April 2023. The first Cluster of chapters was finally opened at the second intergovernmental meeting on 15 October 2024, followed by the opening of negotiations for Cluster 6 on External relations in December of the same year.

The opening of accession negotiations is not an end goal, but rather a more advanced phase for Albania's EU integration process. Now Albania faces higher expectations and challenges from both the EU and its own citizens. It will have to demonstrate commitment and capacity to implement deep and comprehensive reforms in all areas covered by the negotiation chapters.

The EU integration process is a transformative opportunity for Albania. It offers a chance to build an economic model that stimulates growth, job creation, and knowledge transfer. By providing access to the world's largest single market, EU membership offers businesses a larger customer base and greater opportunities for trade and investment. It also provides a framework for enhancing its security, stability, and prosperity in a changing regional and global context. It is therefore a pragmatic approach for Albania to adapt its economic model to this opportunity, implementing all reforms to be prepared for making most of it.

3 Challenges and Opportunities of EU Integration

Albania occupies a strategic position at the juncture of Europe and Asia with direct access to the Adriatic and Ionian seas, which connect it to the Mediterranean and beyond. It also shares borders with four other candidate or potential candidate countries (Montenegro, Kosovo, North Macedonia, and Serbia), which creates opportunities for regional cooperation and integration. Being the only country in Western Balkans not part of former-Yugoslavia puts Albania in the unique position to play a constructive role in promoting peace, stability, and development in the Western Balkans, as well as in enhancing the dialogue and partnership between the EU and other actors in the region.

Albania's economic transition since the early 1990s has been marked by significant progress and challenges. The country has moved from a centrally planned economy to a market-based economy and has experienced periods of both rapid growth and economic instability.

In the early stage of transition, Albania saw a sharp decline in GDP, widespread unemployment leading to mass migration, and high inflation. In the meantime, a number of reforms were implemented including price liberalization, privatization, and trade liberalization. This led to a period of strong economic growth that lasted until 1997 when the collapse of a number of pyramid schemes led to widespread protests and violence. The turmoil resulted in the loss of many lives and a significant damage to the country's economy.

In the 2000s, the Albanian economy began to recover and grow again. The government continued to implement reforms, and the country attracted foreign investment. GDP growth averaged over 6% per year, and unemployment fell. Albania also made progress in reducing poverty and improving living standards. Global financial crisis of 2008 did not lead up to a recession, but real growth rates halved at about 3%. Albania's economy proved relatively resilient to the COVID-19 crisis, thanks to its strong fundamentals and policy support. The country's economic growth rebounded strongly in 2021, driven by a recovery in tourism, construction, and extractive industries.

The shift of the resources from agriculture to services, construction, and other activities helped Albania going from a low-income to upper income country. The gap between Albania's income level and that of the EU has narrowed from just 9% of the EU average in 1991 to a third (27%) in 2022. However, the convergence has slowed down since the global financial crisis of 2008–09, also because the intersectoral shift cannot sustain the high growth rates experienced at the beginning of the transition. At the current growth rates of 3–4%, it will take a long time for Albania to achieve EU living standards.

In order to accelerate growth rates and the convergence, Albania needs to enable an economic model that boosts firm level productivity and promotes economic diversification, particularly by expanding the variety of goods in its export portfolio. Currently, the country faces a significant challenge as its export composition remains concentrated in a limited range of products. This concentration underscores the imperative for Albania to strategically address this issue by implementing measures that promote investment in education and training, improves the backbone infrastructure, access to finance, easy of doing business, trade facilitation, enables a fair and competitive environment particularly for public procurement.

Maintaining strong growth rates has become more challenging considering the environmental upheavals like droughts, floods, and earthquakes. Albania's economy faces heightened vulnerability due to its heavy reliance on agriculture, tourism, and hydropower in the energy sector, amplifying exposure to weather-related shocks. Adaptation to climate change adds another important reform needed to sustain high growth rates and protect the most vulnerable.

Growth also needs to be inclusive to create a more cohesive and resilient social fabric by ensuring that the benefits of economic development are distributed equitably across various segments of society. In the context of Albania, embracing inclusive growth implies a commitment to narrowing socio-economic disparities and fostering an environment where every individual has equal access to opportunities. This encompasses not only economic opportunities but also extends to education, healthcare, and other essential services.

Albeit ageing fast, Albania still has one of the youngest populations in Europe. This means that Albania has a pool of human capital that can contribute to its economic growth, social development, and innovation potential. However, this also poses some challenges, such as high unemployment, low education levels, brain drain, and emigration. Investment in education, training, employment, and social inclusion of its youth remain critical to mitigate these problems. The early mass migration of the labour force is now taking the form of migration of highly skilled workers depleting the country of valuable resources. Addressing the brain drain or migration of workforce generally falls under policy reforms to be pursued by Albania's government in improving the economy, education, and creating more job opportunities with competitive salaries. But there is another aspect of proactive recruiting policies by more advanced economies that require some coordination at least in terms of sharing the burden of education costs and pensions.

All these reforms are important for any developing country that wants to accelerate economic growth. The EU integration process can act as a catalyzer for these reforms through a combination of incentives, requirements, and shared objectives (Gill et al., 2012; World Bank, 2012). The prospect of EU membership provides a powerful motivation to undertake significant political, economic, and institutional reforms. Following this path hopefully will enable the convergence windfall EU accession brings for countries like Albania.

Albania has several opportunities that facilitate its EU integration process. First of all, it enjoys a strong support of the Albanian people for EU membership. According to the latest Eurobarometer survey, 93% of Albanians are in favour of joining the EU, which is the highest level among all candidate countries. This shows that Albanians see the EU as a source of stability, prosperity, and democracy, and are willing to support the necessary reforms for EU integration.

EU membership would lead to an improved quality of life for Albanians. By adopting EU standards in areas such as environmental protection, food safety, and consumer protection, it would lead to a cleaner environment, safer food, and better products for consumers.

A critical benefit of EU membership is the access to the single market, which would boost the Albania's economy and create jobs. EU is already the largest trading partner of Albania and a major source of tourists visiting the country. EU membership prospect would help Albania to attract foreign investment, which would further boost the economy.

Albania's NATO membership has achieved in terms of security and stability many of the objectives that EU membership would aim to address. The EU membership is still an added value in fostering security and stability in the Western Balkans region.

The positive momentum created by the launch of accession negotiations in 2020, creates a new dynamic and incentive for Albania to accelerate its reforms and alignment with the EU acquis.

There is also an increased EU engagement and support for the Western Balkans. In particular, Berlin Process has helped to raise the profile of the Western Balkans in the EU. This has led to an increased EU engagement with the region and to a greater understanding of the Western Balkans' EU accession aspirations.

The Berlin Process has played a key role in enhancing Albania's diplomatic ties with neighbouring countries like North Macedonia and Serbia. Additionally, it has facilitated the attraction of investments from the EU and other global partners. Furthermore, the process has been instrumental in raising awareness of Albania's aspirations for EU accession, aiming to garner support both within the Albanian population and among EU member states. The EU provided significant financial and medical assistance to Albania and the region, during the Covid-19 crisis as well as facilitated the access to vaccines. The EU has proposed and is now implementing a new EUR 6 billion Economic and Investment Plan for the Western Balkans, on top of the IPA funds, to boost economic growth, create jobs, and improve connectivity and infrastructure in the region.

3.1 Trade Agreements and Economic Integration

The EU is Albania's largest trading partner, a major source of foreign investment, and a provider of financial assistance. The Stabilization and Association Agreement (SAA) with the EU provides for a gradual liberalization of trade between Albania and the EU. Albania's trade with the EU has also increased [significantly] in recent years (Figs. 1 and 2).

Since 2011, Albania's trade with EU has been consistently three quarters of its total exports and more than half of its total imports. Albania has ample space to further increase its volume of exports to EU given its relatively low ratio of exports to GDP, expanding in more sophisticated categories of goods and services. Tourism has been particularly strong in the last few years with the number of tourists

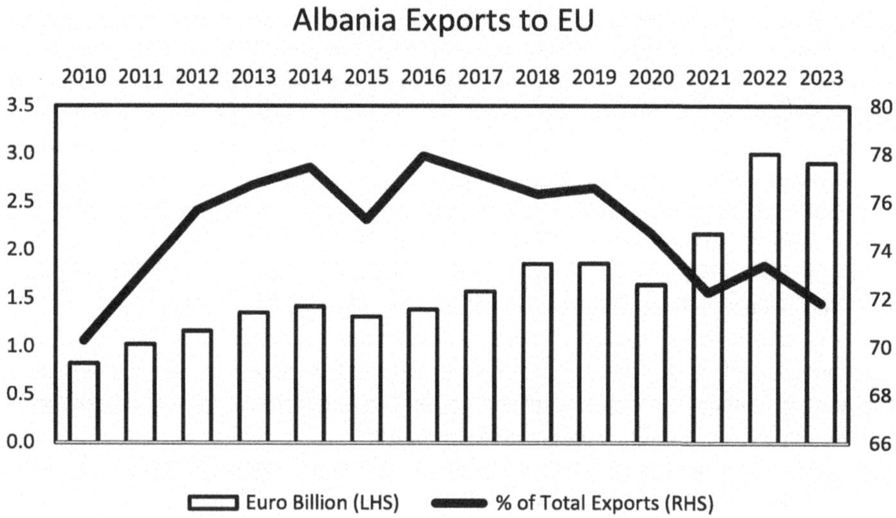

Fig. 1 Albania's exports to the European Union, 2010–2022 (In billions of euros and in percent of total exports). Source: State Statistical Office of Albania (2024)

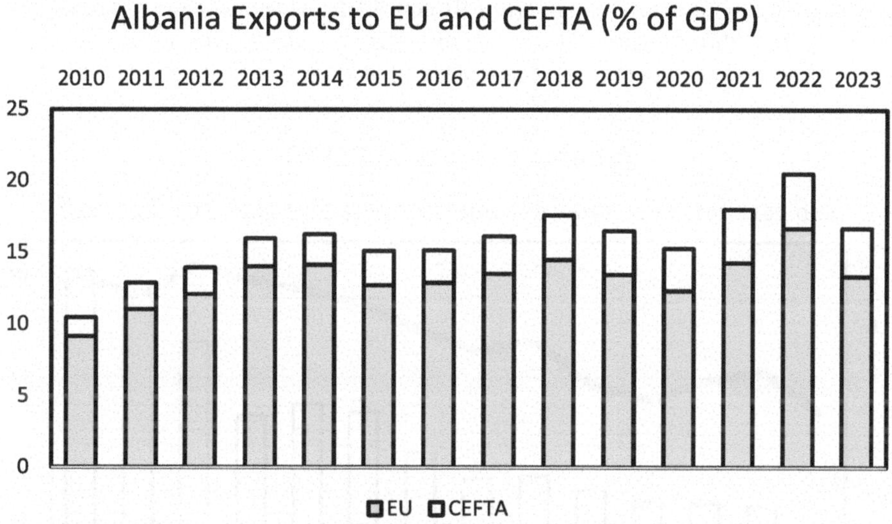

Fig. 2 Albania's exports to Central European Free Trade Agreement (CEFTA) countries, 2010–2022 (In percent of country's GDP). Source: State Statistical Office of Albania (2024)

exceeding by a factor of three Albanian population and still raising. A large number of tourists, 92% in 2022, come from European countries given the proximity and the favourable prices.

The EU has been instrumental for deepening the regional economic integration and harmonization of Western Balkans countries through CEFTA. This alignment contributes to the creation of a more seamless and integrated economic space in the Western Balkans, facilitating trade with EU member states. Albania has been a member of CEFTA since 2006. Under CEFTA it has eliminated tariffs on most goods traded with its member states, and it has also simplified customs procedures. Regional trade of Albania with CEFTA partners has quadrupled in the last decade mostly with Kosovo (Fig. 3). Albania also has a free trade agreement with the European Free Trade Association (EFTA). Albania's trade with CEFTA member states has been steady at roughly 20% of total exports.

EU is also a major source of foreign investment in Albania. In 2022, the EU accounted for 60% of all foreign direct investment in Albania. The EU has also provided Albania with visa-free travel to the Schengen Area, which has boosted tourism and economic ties between the two parties.

EU provides financial assistance to Albania through various programmes, such as the Instrument for Pre-Accession Assistance (IPA) and Rural Development Funding (IPARD). This financial assistance helps Albania to improve its infrastructure, education, and healthcare systems and modernize its agriculture sector. It also helps Albania to implement reforms necessary for EU accession.

The EU has been financing the construction of new roads, railways, and airports in Albania through its investment arm EIB and WBIF. This has improved transport connectivity within Albania and with neighbouring countries. This has made it easier for businesses to operate and has improved trade and investment. The EU has

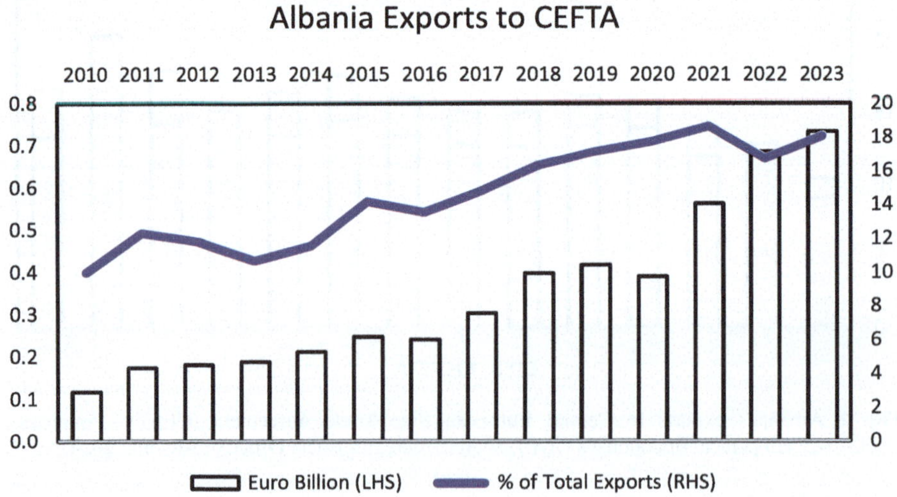

Fig. 3 Albania's exports to Central European Free Trade Agreement (CEFTA) countries, 2010–2022 (In billions of euros and in percent of total exports). Source: State Statistical Office of Albania (2024)

also helped to finance the development of Albania's energy sector. This has led to better energy security and reliability in Albania.

The EU has also contributed to the development of Albania's education and healthcare systems. The intervention has aimed improving the skills of the Albanian workforce to make Albania more competitive. The EU has also provided financial assistance to Albanian businesses to help them to innovate and become more competitive.

All these have made Albania more attractive to foreign investors. Foreign direct investments have gone from lows of 3% of GDP during the initial phase of transition to 6.5% of GDP currently.

3.2 Other Challenges

The country's divisive political climate has been a long-standing challenge for Albania. The lingering effects of authoritarian past, coupled with the challenges of transitioning to a democratic system, have made it difficult to shed the perception of instability. The political parties are often divided along ideological and personal lines and have difficulty cooperating on key reforms and policies. This could affect the timely adoption of laws and regulations that Albania has to approve and enforce as part of its accession process.

The regional and international context poses both opportunities and threats for Albania's EU integration. On one hand, Albania benefits from the support and cooperation of its neighbours, especially those that are already members or candidates of the EU, such as Greece, Italy, Croatia, Montenegro, and North Macedonia. These countries share common interests and values with Albania and can help and expertise in its accession process. On the other hand, Albania faces some external pressures and uncertainties that could complicate or delay its integration. These include the unresolved status of Kosovo, which is claimed by Serbia but recognized by most EU countries; the rise of nationalism and populism in some EU member states, which could affect their willingness to accept new members; and the impact of the recent conflicts, which could change the dynamics and priorities of the EU.

The war in Ukraine has raised concerns about Russia's intentions in the Western Balkans, and it has also led to increased tensions between the EU and Russia. Albania is well aligned with the EU and NATO countries in its policies and has little ties to Russia politically and economically.

Despite China's growing investments in the region, Albania has not been a significant recipient of substantial investments. Even a major Chinese investor involvement in the takeover of the main airport in Albania was eventually sold to a local investor.

3.3 Addressing the Key Challenges

Albania has been implementing a series of reforms to align its legislation and policies with the EU acquis. According to the European Commission's 2022 Progress Report on Albania, the country has aligned its legislation with 65% of the acquis with particularly good progress in areas of judiciary, public administration, and the environment.

The EU agenda encompasses a wide range of reforms that are crucial for developing countries like Albania to achieve sustainable economic growth and advance to a higher income group. These reforms span various sectors, including: Implementing the comprehensive judicial reform, which aims to strengthen the rule of law, fight corruption and ensure the independence and efficiency of the judiciary; Enhancing the capacity and coordination of the public administration, especially regarding EU integration, integrated planning, public consultations, e-services, and payroll automation; Improving the quality and relevance of education and skills, both at basic and tertiary levels, to meet the needs of the labour market and foster innovation and entrepreneurship—Diversifying the sources of growth and increasing productivity, by investing in energy and transport infrastructure, digital communication, research and development, and supporting key sectors such as tourism, agriculture, and manufacturing; Strengthening local government capabilities and fiscal autonomy, by consolidating the territorial administrative reform, improving intergovernmental relations, enhancing public financial management, and delivering quality public services to all citizens; Broadening the revenue base and ensuring fiscal sustainability, by improving tax compliance, reducing informality, rationalizing public expenditure, strengthening debt management, and enhancing transparency and accountability; Addressing air pollution and environmental challenges, by implementing the green agenda for the Western Balkans, promoting renewable energy sources, improving waste management, enhancing climate resilience, and protecting natural resources; Respecting diversity and fostering social inclusion, by promoting human rights, gender equality, non-discrimination, cultural heritage, civic participation, and dialogue with civil society.

In this section, we review some of those reforms where Albania has made notable progress as part of the EU integration process.

3.4 Justice Reform and Human Rights

One of the key areas where Albania has made significant progress is the justice reform, which aims to ensure the independence, impartiality, accountability, and efficiency of the judiciary and the prosecution.

Justice reform is probably the most remarkable example of the crucial role that EU can play on pushing the reform agenda. The reform of the judiciary and the fight against corruption and organized crime are crucial issues for the EU, as they affect the rule of law, democracy, and human rights in Albania. Albania's justice system has been plagued by corruption, inefficiency, and a lack of accountability for many years. The EU has been supporting Albania in these areas since the beginning of the integration process, but the results have been mixed. Albania adopted some important laws and established new institutions, but their implementation and effectiveness was questionable. Corruption and crime remained widespread and undermined public trust in these institutions.

In 2014, the Albanian government launched a comprehensive justice reform programme in an effort to address these issues and strengthen the rule of law. The reform has been ambitious and far-reaching, and it has had a significant impact on the Albanian justice system.

One of the key components of the reform was the establishment of new institutions to oversee the judiciary. The High Judicial Council (HJC) was created to appoint judges and prosecutors, and the High Prosecutorial Council (HPC) was created to oversee the prosecution service. These institutions were designed to be independent of the executive and legislative branches of government, and they were given the power to discipline judges and prosecutors for misconduct.

Another important component of the reform was the introduction of a vetting process for judges and prosecutors. The vetting process was designed to identify and remove corrupt or incompetent judges and prosecutors from the judiciary. The process was overseen by an independent commission, and it involved a thorough review of judges' and prosecutors' assets, professional records, and links to organized crime.

The vetting process has been controversial, but it has also been successful in removing a number of corrupt judges and prosecutors from the judiciary. As of October 2024, the vetting commission had dismissed 283 judges and prosecutors with 167 opting out of the vetting process and resigning, out of 798 cases representing 99% of the total (European Commission, 2024).

In addition to the establishment of new institutions and the introduction of a vetting process, the justice reform also included a number of other measures to improve the Albanian justice system. These measures included: (1) Reforming the court system to make it more efficient and transparent; (2) Improving the training and education of judges and prosecutors; (3) Strengthening the independence of the judiciary; and (4) Increasing access to justice for ordinary citizens.

Organizations such as the Council of Europe, the Venice Commission, and the Group of States against Corruption (GRECO) have provided Albania with guidance and assistance on how to conduct the vetting process, how to ensure the independence and accountability of the judicial bodies, and how to strengthen the legal framework and the institutional capacity for combating corruption. Another important aspect of the reform has been the involvement of the civil society and the media in the monitoring and evaluation of the justice reform, as well as in raising public awareness and trust in the judiciary.

3.5 Public Administration Reform

Another area where EU assistance has focused its efforts is the public administration reform, with the aim to improve the efficiency, effectiveness, accountability, and transparency of the public sector. The reform includes measures to enhance the merit-based recruitment and promotion of civil servants, to strengthen the policy-making and coordination capacities of the government, to improve the delivery of public services to citizens and businesses, and to increase the openness and participation of civil society in decision-making processes.

The reform also involves the implementation of a comprehensive public financial management strategy, which aims to ensure fiscal sustainability, budget credibility, fiscal transparency and accountability. Effective public finance management (PFM) systems are essential for EU membership, as they underpin sound fiscal management, ensure efficient allocation of public resources, and promote transparency and accountability. These principles are cornerstone values of the EU and are crucial for the successful functioning of the EU's internal market and economic governance framework.

Albania's PFM reform efforts are aligned with the EU's broader enlargement agenda, which emphasizes the importance of strengthening public institutions and fostering good governance. Albania has adopted EU principles for good public finance management and fiscal prudence as expressed in the EU 2011 directive on budgeting. Albania's Public Finance Management Reform aims to comply with this directive currently such that its provisions will be met upon Albania's accession to the EU. The EU has provided substantial financial and technical assistance to Albania to support its PFM reform efforts.

Albania has made considerable progress in implementing PFM reforms in recent years. In particular, it has strengthening budgetary planning and execution framework. The government has introduced a medium-term budget framework and improved the budget preparation process. The General Directorate of Taxes has implemented reforms to streamline tax collection and improve compliance. The Public Procurement Agency has implemented measures to increase transparency and competition in public procurement. Some progress can be reported with regard to internal control and audit. The Supreme State Audit Institution has enhanced its capacity to conduct independent audits of public finances.

PFM reform is an ongoing process that requires continuous commitment and effort. Despite the significant strides in strengthening its PFM systems, further work is needed to fully align its practices with EU standards. There is the need to strengthen the control and oversight mechanisms over budget execution to ensure that funds are used as intended. Corruption remains a significant challenge in Albania, and there is a need to further strengthen anti-corruption measures. Public participation in the budget process is still limited, and there is a need to improve transparency and accountability. The EU's support for Albania's PFM reform efforts is crucial in addressing the remaining challenges and ensuring that Albania's public finances are managed effectively and transparently.

3.6 Energy Reform

The alignment of legislation and standards with the EU acquis is a complex and demanding task that requires substantial technical and administrative capacities, as well as political will and consensus. Albania has to adopt and implement thousands of EU laws and regulations in various sectors, such as agriculture, environment, energy, transport, competition, consumer protection, etc. The EU provides financial and technical assistance to support Albania's alignment process, but the country still faces many gaps and challenges in meeting the EU requirements and expectations.

The energy reform is a telling case of a process that is well aligned with the EU legislation and its market framework.

Albania's energy sector is undergoing significant reform as the country prepares for accession to the European Union (EU). The goal of this reform is to align Albania's energy sector with the EU's energy acquis, which is the body of EU legislation that governs the energy sector.

Some of the key objectives of energy sector reform in Albania are to:

1. Increase the security of energy supply: Albania is heavily reliant on imported energy, which makes it vulnerable to disruptions in supply. The reform process aims to diversify energy sources and reduce reliance on imports.
2. The EU has ambitious targets for renewable energy, and Albania is committed to meeting these targets. The reform process aims to encourage the development of renewable energy projects.
3. Albania's energy sector is inefficient, which contributes to high energy costs and greenhouse gas emissions. The reform process aims to improve energy efficiency by upgrading infrastructure and promoting energy-efficient technologies.
4. Albania's energy market is not fully competitive, which can lead to higher prices and lower quality services. The reform process aims to create a more competitive market, which will benefit consumers and businesses.

Albania has made significant progress in energy sector reform in recent years. The government has implemented a number of measures to improve the security, efficiency, and competitiveness of the energy sector. These measures include:

1. Diversifying energy sources: Albania has expanded fruther its renewable capacity exploring in particular by tapping its potential for geothermal and solar energy.
2. The government has introduced a number of incentives for renewable energy development, including feed-in tariffs and tax breaks.
3. The government has implemented a number of energy efficiency programmes, including energy audits and financial incentives for retrofits.
4. Liberalizing the energy market: The government has taken steps to liberalize the energy market, including unbundling the state-owned power company and opening up the market to new entrants.

There are still many challenges to fully meet EU energy standards. More investment is needed in new energy infrastructure, such as transmission lines and distribution networks, to support the development of renewable energy and energy efficiency. Also, Albania's energy regulatory framework needs to be strengthened to ensure that the market is competitive and that consumers are protected.

The EU has provided significant financial and technical assistance to Albania to support energy sector reform. This assistance has been provided through a variety of instruments, including the Instrument for Pre-Accession Assistance (IPA) and the Technical Assistance and Information Exchange instrument (TAIEX).

4 Conclusions

Albania's accession to the European Union is a transformative opportunity that has the potential to accelerate its development and bring it in line with the standards of a modern European democracy and economy. By aligning its legal and institutional framework with EU norms, Albania will gain access to several opportunities. It will open up new markets for Albanian goods and services, leading to increased trade and investment. This influx of capital will create more jobs and boost economic growth. The EU is an important source of funding for infrastructure projects which will improve Albania's connectivity and reduce transportation costs, making it more attractive to businesses and tourists.

Human capital exchanges will encourage Albania to invest in education and training, leading to a more skilled and productive workforce. This will enhance Albania's competitiveness in the global economy.

The relationship between the EU and Albania has been one of the gradual progresses. Albania has made significant reforms in recent years, and the EU external pressure has helped Albania to strengthen its institutions and fight corruption.

Albania's accession to the EU will also send a strong signal to the international community that the country is committed to democratic values and good governance. This will attract foreign investment and make Albania a more attractive destination for tourism and trade.

Albania's accession to the European Union is a unique opportunity to embark on a path of sustainable development. By embracing the principles of European integration, Albania can achieve its full potential as a prosperous and democratic nation.

References

European Commission (2022) Albania 2022 Progress Report, COM(2022) 528 final

European Comission (2024), SWD(2024) 690 final

Gill I, Raiser M, Richter A (2012) Restoring the lustre of the European economic model. World Bank

World Bank (2012) Golden Growth in Southeast Europe: Key Implications for Policy Reforms. South East Europe Regular Economic Report, June 5

The Future Relations Between the European Union and Kosovo

Gazmend Qorraj

Abstract

This paper examines the European Union's (EU) strategy towards the Western Balkan countries, with a particular focus on Kosovo's relationship with the EU. The analysis begins with the inception of the regional integration process through the Stability Pact, followed by various EU instruments such as Free Trade Agreements, CEFTA 2006, the Regional Economic Area, and the Common Regional Market. Highlighting the significance of Albania and North Macedonia commencing EU accession negotiations in 2022, the paper addresses the impact of the Russian invasion of Ukraine on the EU enlargement process. It also evaluates the EU's absorption capacity and the influence of regional initiatives like the Common Regional Market and the Stabilization and Association Agreement on Kosovo's EU integration. The concluding sections explore future challenges in Kosovo-EU relations, emphasizing the need for reforms and regional cooperation to overcome political and economic hurdles.

Keywords

EU integration · Western Balkans · Kosovo · Regional integration · Common regional market

G. Qorraj (✉)
University of Prishtina, Prishtina, Kosovo

Uninettuno University, Rome, Italy

A. Stojkov, T. Warin (eds.), *Western Balkans and the Future of Europe*, The Future of Europe, https://doi.org/10.1007/978-3-031-86465-0_6

1 Introduction

This chapter analyses the European Union's (EU) relationship with the Western Balkan (WB) countries with a special focus on Kosovo's relationship with the European Union.

The regional integration process as an important part of European integration initially started with the Stability Pact, as the first serious initiative after a decade of conflicts in the Western Balkans, followed by different EU instruments such as Free Trade Agreements, CEFTA 2006, Regional Economic Area, and Common Regional Market for the Western Balkans.

Last year, respectively, July 2022, Albania and North Macedonia opened the accession negotiations to the European Union, which was considered a historic event for the WB countries, despite the EU's limited absorption capacity, BREXIT, political party landscape, COVID-19, and other EU challenges.

This article also addresses whether the recent EU enlargement process of the WB is affected by the Russian invasion of Ukraine, or whether the EU's recent support for the WB resulted from EU standards that these countries have fulfilled. Furthermore, there will also be analysed the EU Absorption Capacity as well as for the Western Balkans and the EU.

In addition, analyzing the future relations between Kosovo and the European Union it is also affected by the EU initiatives in the Western Balkans such as the implementation of the Common Regional Market (CRM) followed by the implementation of the Stabilization and Association Agreement (SAA), and other EU instruments.

This chapter is structured into six sections. After the introduction, section two offers an overview of the EU enlargement towards the WB countries, followed by three other sections on regional ownership and absorption capacities in the region and the EU, followed by SAA and Common Regional Market. The last section concludes with the main findings of the article.

2 Regional Integration

Given the lack of cooperation in the Western Balkans, the intensification of regional cooperation by the EU is welcomed, as the Western Balkan region needs a European agenda—for many reasons, but especially because of the political challenges, as the changes of the geopolitical environment could have the potential to drag the region in other conflicts in future. In addition, the regional integration process is crucial for the Western Balkan countries from the economic approach in order to increase economic prosperity, investments, and growth. The European Union and the International community initiated the Stability Pact for South East Europe as the first initiative aiming for regional reconciliation. The Stability Pact supported the region's political, economic, and security issues for many years. Later in 2008, the Stability Pact was transformed into RCC (Regional Cooperation Council) as the local initiative aiming to give priority to the countries of the region, respectively, introducing the process of regional ownership.

In addition, regional integration increases cooperation between Western Balkan countries and stimulates foreign investments; therefore, companies are able to exploit the economies of scale. Further macroeconomic policy coordination stimulates growth, increases competitiveness, and reduces the cost of adjustments of an economy in the face of globalization. While all of the countries in the region aim to join the EU and its single market, enhancing regional trade integration prior to EU membership would help their economies better prepare to face the competitive pressures of the EU's market.

Within the regional integration framework, the EU introduced the Stabilization and Association Process (SAP), which process ensured different instruments for the Western Balkan countries such as:

- Free Trade (Bilateral Free trade Agreements between the countries).
- CEFTA 2006, as a Multilateral Free Trade, between the countries.
- Financial Assistance (IPA—Instrument for Pre-Accession Assistance).
- SAA (Stabilization and Association Agreement).
- EU programmes such as Tempus, Erasmus+, Horizon 2020, Horizon Europe, etc.
- Regional Economic Area (REA).
- Common Regional Market (CRM), etc.

Some of the above-mentioned initiatives will be explained in the paper considering the current relevance of these instruments and their implementation for the Western Balkan countries.

3 Stabilization and Association Agreement in the Western Balkans and Kosovo

The SAA constitutes the relationship between the EU and the West Balkans for implementing the Stabilization and Association Process. According to the European Commission, 2020, these agreements are designed according to each partner country's specific situation. Furthermore, in this framework, the agreements provide institutional support for implementing the integration path and have brought the WB countries closer to the EU by strengthening economic and institutional relations with EU institutions. Among the key points of the agreement, it has to do with the commitment of the WB countries to accelerate the reforms and, therefore, approximation with the EU *acquis* and continuously the market reforms. The EU is the leading trading partner and by far the largest investor in the Western Balkans. The EU concluded the SAA-s with all WB countries between 2001 and 2016. In addition to providing the legal instrument for aligning these countries' laws with those of the EU, and supporting these countries in undertaking necessary reforms, the SAA supports trade flows and the political stabilization of the region. Furthermore, the EU created the Interim Agreements between the EU and WB countries, by eliminating restrictions, with a few exceptions (European Commission 2021). The following sections will describe the impact of the SAA agreement on Kosovo. However, the EU offered an additional trade framework for Kosovo and the opportunity for further cooperation with the EU, Kosovo was the last country in the Balkans to begin implementing the agreement in 2016. Compared to other Western Balkan countries Kosovo started an adopted Stabilization and Association Process, namely Stabilization and Association Tracking Mechanism (STM). It then proceeded to fulfil its obligations stemming from the SAA, such as the approximation of legislation and trade issues (Council of Europe, 2015). Regarding economic benefits, different analyses applied in Kosovo confirmed that: due to the firm performance, lack of institutional support, and lack of experience with international markets, local firms could not derive sustainable positive effects from trade liberalization, namely SAA (Qorraj and Jusufi 2019). Consequently, the SAA was not a sufficient instrument for improving the trade deficits of the WB countries as many of these economies are infant industries, due to the deindustrialization process in the region. According to Kosovo Customs statistics in 2022, Kosovo's main trade partners are the European Union countries, with around 44% of imports and around 30% of exports. Kosovo's exports to the European Union, to Germany are around 8.2%, Italy 8%, and the Netherlands 2.7%. While with its Western Balkans neighbouring countries, Kosovo trades tariff-free under the terms of the Central European Free Trade Agreement (CEFTA 2006). These countries are the source of approximately 19% of imports and the destination for 38% of exports. Although Kosovo foreign trade continues to be oriented mainly towards the European Union it is recorded a large trade deficit, with exports covering only about 15.3% of imports.

4 Common Regional Market

The Leaders' Declaration on the Common Regional Market (CRM) and its Action Plan were endorsed at the Berlin Process Summit in November 2020, establishing a fundamentally new framework for regional cooperation in the Western Balkans that prioritizes regional cooperation and EU standards. They introduced the Common Regional Market project, which is built around the four freedoms (free movement of goods, services, capital, and people) and includes elements of digital, investment, innovation, and industry policy. Due to this, it is the Western Balkans' most ambitious attempt at regional integration to date. Prior to admission, the region could be more fully integrated into the EU Single Market by using the Common Regional Market as a stepping stone. To maximize the benefits of its special relationship with the EU, the region must do this. Western Balkans' progress towards membership will be aided by regional economic integration based on EU regulations and deeper ties to the EU Single Market. The process of joining the EU and gradually adopting its acquis will strengthen this at the same time (DG NEAR, n.n). The main components introduced by the CRM are as follows:

(a) Regional Trade Area, by including four freedoms.

(b) Regional Investments Area, by promoting investments and changing the perception of the investors about Western Balkans.
(c) Regional Digital Area, by supporting the further digitalization of the Western Balkans and connecting with the EU.
(d) Regional Industrial and Innovation Area by supporting the transformation of the Western Balkan economic sectors from trade to industrial sectors. It includes involvement in innovation activities as a precondition for the competitive abilities of these economies (Regional Cooperation Council 2020).

The main expected challenges of the Common Regional Market implementation are as follows: Political challenges of the region; Inefficient institutions in the Western Balkans and the capability of the Regional Cooperation Council to monitor the process.

Regarding the challenges to the implementation, the RCC (Regional Cooperation Council) reported that progress has been made towards achieving key deliverables in 2021, particularly having in mind the post-pandemic environment, which continues to impose serious restrictions in terms of fully-fledged implementation of regional agendas. Nonetheless, the majority of regional actions planned for 2021 have either been concluded or progressed significantly, with some challenges identified as important to consider for the next year (RCC, 2022).

Apart from political and regional cooperation, it is projected that, if the CRM would be implemented successfully, it could bring an additional 6.7% GDP growth to the region, which makes investment to this regional agenda cost-effective. The RCC and CEFTA Secretariats continue to seek ways to align the needs of CRM agendas and match them with existing financial opportunities through CRM Donor Coordination meetings.

5 The EU Enlargement

The EU enlargement is considered a process that could generate different benefits for the countries such as political, economic, and institutional. The effects of the internal market are significant followed by the economic impact of removing formal trade barriers and other obstacles (Lejour et al. 2021). Trade structure and reciprocal liberalization can force sectors to expand in both regions due to improved exploitation of scale economies (Baldwin et al. 1997). According to Schimmelfennig and Sedelmeier (2005), European governments and Western and Eastern countries calculated the expected economic and geopolitical consequences of enlargement for their domestic societies and acted accordingly. Other scholars such as Rapacki and Prochniak (2009) by analyzing the EU enlargement and economic growth in CEE new member countries reported that most current EU countries will experience slight increases in welfare from the EU enlargement process. In addition, (Brülhart et al. 2004) in their study found that a future Balkans enlargement could be effective in reducing economic inequalities among the EU periphery, due to positive impact on relative market access of Greek regions.

The EU integration process of the WB has geopolitical benefits for the EU, including regional cooperation and democratic reforms. Meanwhile, for the candidate countries, great geopolitical and economic benefits of membership remain, which motivate these countries for unequal democratic reform, but sometimes also falter because the EU fights with expertise, consistency, and legitimacy in the pre-accession process. However, an illiberal turnaround within the EU could shape enlargement moving forward (Vachudova 2019).

The current conflict between Russia and Ukraine accelerated the need to analyse and monitor the situation and think about new instruments and new ideas within the EU. This conflict apart from security and cohesion spillover effects was a good message for the individual small countries that the best opportunity for them regarding security but also social issues are being part of the EU, NATO, and other mechanisms rather than acting on an individual basis. Analysing the reaction of Finland and Baltic States, due to the current conflict there was an immediate interest of different EU member states for deepening integration within the EU. While other non-EU member states, despite Serbia, are interested in being part of the EU.

The delay in the EU accession process of the WB countries, as well as the disappointment of these countries regarding their European perspective, enabled more significant external influences. According to Panagiotou 2021, Russia and China (re-) activate their impact and strengthen their roles in the WB region. Russia's economic presence is weaker than the EU; however, Russia has successfully gained its soft power and cultivated the perception that it is an important strategic partner that cares more about interests in the WB than the EU.

6 Future Challenges in Kosovo–EU Relationship

Based on the current experience and geopolitical trends could be noted that the future relationship between Kosovo and the EU depends on three main factors.

First is a technical component based on the fulfilment of the EU criteria and reforms from Kosovo required by the European Union. This component also includes Kosovo's absorption capacity, opportunities from the regional market, and other additional components.

Second, the negotiating process with Serbia is among the complex challenges for both countries, but also these political disputes are creating a negative spillover effect for the whole region of the Western Balkans.

The third issue has to do with the EU absorption capacity, EU institutional setting, and geopolitical issues from which the EU could be threatened and consequently the European perspective of the Western Balkans.

6.1 Absorption Capacity

Several scholars agreed that the Absorption capacity of the Western Balkans countries is essential for further steps towards EU integration. Currently, as Western

Balkan countries are benefiting from similar instruments from 2007, namely IPA I (2007–2013), IPAII (2014–2020), and IPA III (2021–2027), the local institutions are better informed and prepared to benefit from it. One of the key features of this evolution is that (IPA II) and (IPA III) are created in full coordination and cooperation of the EU and beneficiaries, therefore the beneficiary countries have ownership in the process of designing and implementing it. Regarding the relevance of the absorption capacity, it is extremely important for the Western Balkans to increase absorption capacities, as these countries face their own limited financial resources therefore the EU financial assistance will support them in developing different crucial sectors.

Given that Western Balkans, namely Kosovo face various budgetary problems, high unemployment rates, and trade and external debts, there is a substantial need for financial support from the European Union, but also other international donors (Qorraj, 2016).

Furthermore, Qorraj et al. (2023) in their study analysed the (i) Western Balkans Absorption capacity, (ii) EU Absorption capacity which is described in Table 1. To ensure appropriate regional inclusiveness the data were collected through interviews with 15 respondents ($N = 15$) included at three Western Balkans countries, but this paper represents only findings for Kosovo.

6.2 Political Tensions in the Region

The EU-facilitated dialogue between the Kosovo and Serbian leaderships, first with the objective to overcome the political challenges and conflict of the region and second supporting process aimed at assisting Serbia and Kosovo towards accession to the EU. Despite these complexities, there still seem to exist other opportunities and important instruments for the normalization of relations between the two countries, promoted by the Brussels administration, hopefully resulting in reconciliation between the two countries. According to (Lehne 2012), the EU should take the lead,

Table 1 Absorption Capacity of Kosovo

Themes	Detailed Findings
(1) Western Balkans absorption capacity	• Kosovo faces difficulties in coordinating activities to benefit from IPA and EU programmes, resulting in missed opportunities and inefficient resources.
	• Kosovo has weak institutions, insufficient capacity, and a lack of political will frequently results in ineffective implementation of EU-funded projects.
	• Corruption and a lack of transparency are major barriers to accessing and benefiting from EU funding in Kosovo.
	• Political instability and inconsistent policies are major barriers to accessing and benefiting from EU funding.
	• The Kosovo's weak private sector makes it difficult to benefit from EU programmes and promote the private sector.

Source: Absorption capacity and the European integration of the Western Balkans; RSPP 2023

Table 2 EU institutional and absorption capacity challenges

Themes	Detailed findings
EU institutional and absorption capacity	• The administrative capacity of the EU and its member states to accommodate new member states is also critical to its institutional setting development.
	• A lack of coordination between EU institutions and member states might have an influence on the EU's enlargement absorption capability
	• Financial and budgetary considerations are also important to the EU's institutional setting development.

Source: Absorption capacity and the European integration of the Western Balkans; RSPP 2023

but an active engagement of the United States is essential; Washington is still perceived by the Kosovo Albanian population as the principal international backer, and its support for the EU's efforts will be crucial for the overall success of negotiations. As the EU and the United States worked well together during the technical dialogue, there is a good basis for tackling other challenges jointly. The EU framework and appropriate actions and policies in Western Balkans could overcome the political challenges in the region and prevent further increase of Russian influence in the region especially in Serbia and Montenegro—a kind of influence capable of generating additional challenges to cooperation efforts among Western Balkans.

6.3 EU Challenges and Other Geopolitical Issues

First, regarding the EU institutional setting, it is crucial to note the trade-off between EU Institutions and EU Member states. In the case of the Kosovo–Serbia negotiations, there was proposed a French German plan instead of offering an EU plan for the resolution of political disputes between the countries. The paper presents Table 2 the findings from the previous study regarding EU institutional setting and absorption capacity.

Second, the Russia–Ukraine conflict accelerated the need to analyse and monitor the situation and think about new instruments and new ideas within the EU. The conflict between Russia- and Ukraine apart from security and cohesion spillover effects was a good message for the individual small countries that the best opportunity for them regarding security but also social issues are being part of the EU, NATO, and other mechanisms rather than acting on an individual basis. Analysing the reaction of Finland and the Baltic States, due to the current conflict currently there is a huge interest of different EU member states for deepening integration within the EU. While other non-EU member states, despite Serbia, are interested in being part of the EU.

7 Conclusions

Considering the challenges ahead for Kosovo to fulfil the EU standards on their path towards the EU the current political disputes between Kosovo and Serbia within the dialogue will postpone the institutional reforms in these countries, but also in the whole region. The practical example of this scenario is the delay in SAA—Stabilization and Association Agreement implementation in Kosovo as most of the political leaders as well as the government are focused on negotiations instead of being committed to institutional reforms, namely economic and business environment promotion. In addition, from an institutional point of view, these disputes between Kosovo and Serbia will hamper the economic perspective of the region, which could destabilize the regional market by increasing political austerity and security which will create a negative effect for the foreign investment in the region. Knowing that the countries of the Balkans are small therefore they represent individual small markets, the unification of these individual markets is crucial for the investment promotion as a region.

From the EU integration perspective, the EU institutional setting and EU external challenges could postpone the reforms in the Western Balkans. Furthermore, these challenges could delay the EU perspective, respectively Kosovo integration at the EU.

References

Baldwin RE, Francois JF, Portes R (1997) The costs and benefits of eastern enlargement: the impact on the EU and Central Europe. Econ Policy 24. https://doi.org/10.1111/1468-0327.00018

Brülhart M, Crozet M, Koenig P (2004) Enlargement and the EU periphery: the impact of changing market potential. World Econ 27(6). https://doi.org/10.1111/j.1467-9701.2004.00632.x

European Commission (2021) EU enlargement policy and the 2021 enlargement package for the Western Balkans. European Neighbourhood Policy and Enlargement Negotiations. Available at: https://neighbourhood-enlargement.ec.europa.eu/2021-communication-eu-enlargement-policy_en

Lehne S (2012) Kosovo and Serbia: toward a normal relationship. Carnegie Endowment for International Peace, Policy Outlook

Lejour AM, De Mooij RA, Nahuis R (2021) EU enlargement: economic implications for countries and industries. SSRN Electron J. https://doi.org/10.2139/ssrn.287847

Panagiotou R (2021) The Western Balkans between Russia and the European Union: perceptions, reality, and impact on enlargement. J Contemp Eur Stud 29(2). https://doi.org/10.1080/14782804.2020.1798218

Qorraj G (2016) Economic cooperation as a way toward reconciliation and EU integration for Kosovo and Serbia. In: Kosovo and Serbia: contested options and shared consequences. https://doi.org/10.2307/j.ctt1qv5n21.16

Qorraj G, Jusufi G (2019) EU vs. local market orientation: Western Balkan entrepreneurs' challenge. Entrep Bus Econ Rev 7(4) Available at: https://eber.uek.krakow.pl/index.php/eber/issue/archiv

Qorraj G, Hajrullahu A, Qehaja D (2023) Absorption capacity and the European integration of the Western Balkans. Reg Sci Policy Pract 16(8):100043

Rapacki R, Próchniak M (2009) The EU enlargement and economic growth in the CEE's new member countries. Econ Pap 367:1–21

Regional Cooperation Council (RCC) (2020) Western Balkans leaders' declaration on the common regional market 2021–2024. Available at: https://www.rcc.int/docs/544/declaration-on-common-regional-market

Regional Cooperation Council (RCC) (2022) Common regional market implementation report for the year 2021, April

Schimmelfennig F, Sedelmeier U (2005) The politics of European Union enlargement: theoretical approaches. In: The politics of European Union enlargement: theoretical approaches. https://doi.org/10.4324/9780203008720

Vachudova MA (2019) EU enlargement and state capture in the Western Balkans. In: The Europeanisation of the Western Balkans. https://doi.org/10.1007/978-3-319-91412-1_4

Bosnia and Herzegovina on the Way to the European Union: Past, Present, and Future

Snježana Brkić

Abstract

This chapter explores the past, present, and future of Bosnia and Herzegovina (BiH) in the context of its European path. For the last 20 years, BiH has been trying to reform its economic and political system with a view of becoming a member of the European Union (EU) one day. The country's long journey towards the EU began within the so-called EU regional approach to the countries of Southeast Europe (SEE), continued through the Stabilization and Association Process (SAP) and, after acquiring candidate status, finally reached the opening of negotiations with the EU in March 2024. Thus, BiH became the last SEE country that opened negotiations with the EU—after 25 years from the beginning of the process together with others in the region. However, the latest improvements in BiH's relations with the largest economic integration of the modern world are more caused by the current geopolitical situation in Europe than by the country's actual achievements in political and economic reforms. In the future, this should not be the case—the ultimate goal of BiH should not be only a formal membership in the EU but reaching a level of economic and institutional development that enables full use of advantages the EU membership can bring. The challenges, both economic and non-economic, for BiH but the EU as well, are numerous.

Keywords

Stabilization and association process (SAP) · Candidate status · Negotiation process · Bosnia and Herzegovina (BiH) · European Union (EU)

S. Brkić (✉)
School of Economics and Business, University of Sarajevo,
Sarajevo, Bosnia and Herzegovina
e-mail: snjezana.brkic@efsa.unsa.ba

A. Stojkov, T. Warin (eds.), *Western Balkans and the Future of Europe*, The Future of Europe, https://doi.org/10.1007/978-3-031-86465-0_7

1 Introduction

Although Bosnia and Herzegovina (BiH) is significantly politically, economically, historically and culturally connected with the region of Southeast Europe (SEE), the country has always prioritized membership in the European Union (EU). In numerous official documents of BiH[1] from the early post-war period until today, membership in the EU has been stated as a strategic goal of the country. In this respect, the country does not differ from other countries in the region, or from other transition countries that have already gained EU membership. The attractiveness of the EU for all these countries stems from the success of its members in improving their economic performance and position in international relations, which is attributed to integration.

Official relations between BiH and the EU began to develop after the international recognition of the Republic BiH as an independent and sovereign state in the spring 1992. During the war 1992–1995, political support and humanitarian aid from the EU were of a particular importance for BiH. Since the signing of the Dayton Peace Agreement in 1995, the EU has been deeply involved in BiH much more than in other countries of the Western Balkans (WB), with regard to the establishment of the Office of the High Representative (OHR)[2] in 1995 and, later, since 2004, the EU military mission EUFOR Althea.[3]

In the economic sense, there is a significant functional orientation of BiH to the EU which is its most important trading partner and investor. Bosnia and Herzegovina carries out two-thirds of its trade with the EU (MoFTER 2023). The situation is the same in terms of investments—the EU is the main investor with more than 5 billion euros invested in BiH so far (FIPA 2024). Importance of the EU as an economic partner will also continue to increase with each new member which will be "recruited" from the region.

Functional economic ties always strengthen when accompanied by establishing and developing institutional ties as well. In the case of BiH, an institutional (contractual) component in relations with the EU was missing for years after the war, but mutual economic flows and cooperation continued to gain intensity even in those circumstances. The turning point in the relations with the EU occurred in 2008, when the Stabilization and Association Agreement (SAA) was concluded. Since

[1] Declaration on Special Relations with the EU (1998); Decision of the BiH Council of Ministers on launching the initiative for the accession of BiH to the EU (1999); Resolution of the BiH Parliamentary Assembly on European integration and the Stability Pact for Southeastern Europe (1999); Conclusions of the Parliamentary Assembly of BiH No. 01–02-661/03 (April 2003); Statement of the presidents of political parties No. 01–50–3-180/04 (February 2004).

[2] "OHR is ad hoc international institution responsible for overseeing implementation of civilian aspects of the Dayton Peace Agreement. OHR has the status of a diplomatic mission to BiH" (OHR 2024). (See: https://www.ohr.int/about-ohr/general-information/)

[3] EUFOR Althea has "an executive mandate of the UN Security Council to support the local authorities in maintaining a stable and secure environment in the country" (EC 2024c). (See: https://neighbourhood-enlargement.ec.europa.eu/enlargement-policy/bosnia-and-herzegovina_en)

then, 15 years have passed before BiH received candidate status and then opened accession negotiations, as the last country in the region. Although other SEE countries also were not remarkably fast in this process, it was especially demanding and challenging for BiH for many reasons.

The chapter provides a chronological insight into economic and institutional aspects of relations between BiH and the EU during the period 1995–2024. It also aims to discuss possible further developments in the "European" future of BiH.

The structure of the chapter is as follows. After the introduction, the next section analyses economic motives as well as trade and capital flows between BiH and the EU. The very beginning of institutionalization of relations of BiH with the EU and Stabilization and Association Process (SAP) are described in the third section. The fourth section presents the main steps taken in order to achieve the candidate status and start negotiations. The fifth section discusses what is expected to be done in order to achieve EU membership and possible challenges along the way. In final section, some concluding comments and related predictions are presented.

2 Economic Motives and Flows in Relations with the European Union

The EU has proven to be a successful long-term project for its members. Membership in the EU has brought significant benefits, both economic and non-economic, to many European countries, which leads to the so-called demonstration effect—motivation of other countries to join this integration. Among these advantages, the following stand out in particular (Bitzenis and Andronikidis 2006): increase in (intra- and extra-EU) trade, increase in the inflow of foreign direct investments (FDI), greater mobility of labour and capital, improvement of competitiveness through increased productivity, improvement of the business environment, use of structural and other funds, significant common bargaining power, growth in living standard due to overall economic growth, stabilization and strengthening of institutions, and strengthening of the rule of law.

The motives of BiH to join the EU are, as with other economies of the WB, multiple and diverse—political, economic, legal, social, etc. When it comes to economic motives, they primarily stem from the needs for a wider market, attracting investment and using various EU funds and favourable loans.

Before the war, in 1991, BiH realized ¾ of its exports to the European Community's market (MoFTER 1998) which is even more than today. A few years after the war, in 2003, the EU share in BiH's exports amounted to only 40% (Brkić 2012), although the integration was increased by three new members (from 12 to 15). At the same time, BiH exported 46% of its total exports to the countries of the WB (Brkić 2012). Since 2003, the EU's share in BiH's exports has been continuously growing and reached 74% in 2022 (Table 1).

In relative terms, the EU is more important for BiH as an export market than the market of origin of imports. Since the beginning of the implementation of the SAA in 2008, the participation of the EU in BiH imports ranges between 50 and 61%

Table 1 EU shares in exports and imports of BiH (in selected years)

Shares	1991	2003	2008	2013	2018	2022
EU share in BiH's exports (%)	75	40	55	66	73	74
EU share in BiH's imports (%)	45	37	49	54	61	57

Notes: 2003—the year when BiH finished the process of concluding bilateral free trade areas (FTAs) with all SEE countries; 2008—several years after Slovenia, an important BiH's trade partner, joined the EU; the year when SAA was signed and Interim Agreement on Trade with the EU came into the force; 2013—the year when Croatia, the first BiH's trade partner, joined the EU. Source: MoFTER (2024)

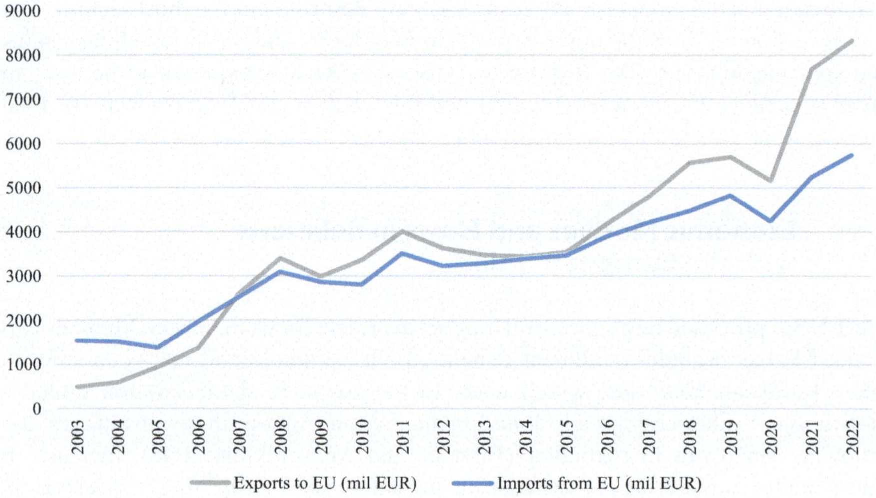

Fig. 1 Bosnia and Herzegovina's exports to and imports from the EU (2003–2022). Source: Based on data of the Agency for Statistics of BiH (BHAS 2013, 2019, 2023)

(57% in 2022). However, in nominal terms, BiH imports more than it exports to the EU which results in continuous trade deficit of BiH in trade with the EU. In 2022, BiH's imports reached 8.33 billion euros while exports reached 6.76 billion euros (BHAS 2023).

In any case, the importance of the EU for BiH total trade is growing both in absolute and relative terms, especially with each new enlargement of the EU (Fig. 1), of which the most significant for BiH was the enlargement to Slovenia in 2004, and then to Croatia in 2013.

Trade of BiH with the EU mostly takes place with several EU members—Croatia, Germany, Italy, and Austria, which have been on the list of BiH's top trading partners for years.

On the other hand, BiH is not of such great economic importance for the EU: BiH is on the 38th place on the list of EU export destinations (the share of BiH in EU exports is 0.3%) and on the 47th place as the country of origin of imports into the EU (the share of BiH in EU imports is 0.2%). The share of all WB countries amounts to only 1.9% in EU exports and only 1.1% in EU imports (EC Directorate General for Trade 2023).

The EU is not only the most important trade partner of BiH but also the principal investor in the country as well as its main creditor and donor. The total stock of FDI in BiH amounts to 8.9 billion euros (December 2022) of which investment from the EU amounts to 5.3 billion euros or 59.4% (FIPA 2024). Among the 10 largest individual investors in BiH are six EU members: Austria—which is the biggest individual investor in BiH with almost 1.4 billion euros invested, Croatia, Slovenia, Germany, the Netherlands, and Italy (Fig. 2).

The EU also provides continuous financial support to BiH in form of loans and grants. Since 1999, the EU has provided 3.2 billion euros in loans through the European Investment Bank (EC 2023b). From 1996 until now, the Union has also implemented grants in amount of 3.7 billion euros for projects in various areas key to development, such as follows: reconstruction, rule of law, education, employment, transport, agriculture, rural development, etc. (EEAS 2023).

Previously, the EU provided financial support to BiH in the form of various financial instruments and programmes: The European Commission's Civil Protection and Humanitarian Aid Operations Department—ECHO, Poland and Hungary: Assistance for the Restructuring of the Economy—PHARE (for BiH since 1996), and Community Assistance for Reconstruction, Development and Stabilization—CARDS (for BiH since 2001).[4]

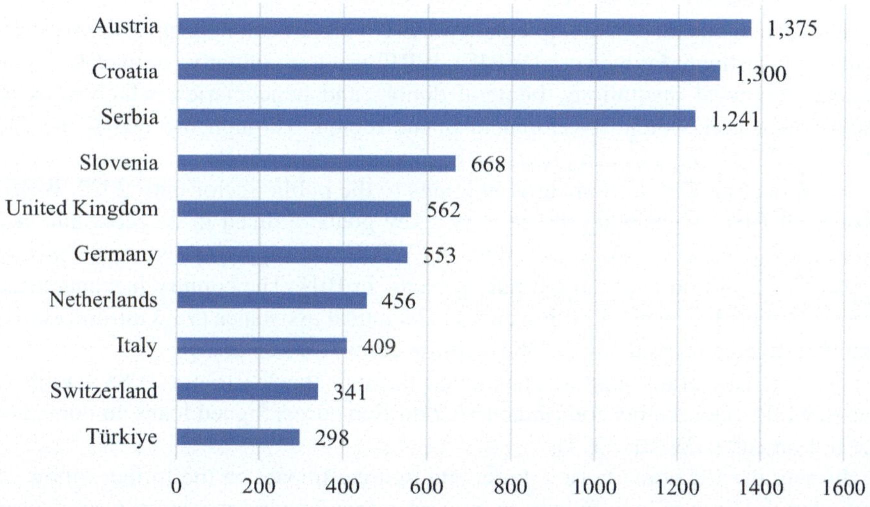

Fig. 2 FDI stock in BiH, by main investor countries (in million EUR, 1994–2022). Source: Based on data of the Foreign Investment Promotion Agency (FIPA)

[4] EU pre-accession funds are intended for public sector of countries that are preparing for future membership. These funds provide financial resources for the implementation of numerous, long-term, and demanding economic and political reforms in the EU accession process.

In the period 1991–2000 within the framework of the ECHO, PHARE, and OBNOVA programmes in BiH, 2 billion euros was allocated for various purposes. In the period 2001–2006, the amount of 412 million euros was used within the CARDS programme.

Since 2007, meanwhile, the European Commission (EC) has replaced the mentioned pre-accession funds with a new unique aid instrument for potential candidate and candidate countries—Instrument for Pre-Accession Assistance (IPA). Funds within the framework of the IPA are allocated in the form of grants. In the period 2007–2013, BiH received about 615 million euros as part of "IPA I" (EU Delegation 2024).

In the period 2014–2020, funds for allocation within "IPA II" amounted to 552.1 million euros (EC 2024b). For 2021–2023, the "IPA III" funding for BiH amounted to over 256 million euros (EC 2023b). In 2021, 73 million euros were allocated, and in 2022, 45.5 million euros (EEAS 2023).

The additional new instrument of financial support was launched in 2020—Economic and Investment Plan (EIP) for the WB. The Plan aims "to spur the long-term recovery, accelerate the green and digital transition, and foster regional cooperation" identifying 10 investment flagships and aims. Under the EIP for BiH, the EU has already mobilized 3 billion euros in investments, out of which 934 million euros in grants (EC 2023b).

EIP will mobilize up to 30 billion euros in cooperation with international financial institutions by 2027. The EU has so far approved funding of 4.29 billion euros in grants, expected to mobilize 15.9 billion euros in overall investments (EU 2023).

The main financial tool to implement the EIP's investment flagship is the Western Balkans Investment Framework (WBIF). WBIF is a joint initiative of the EU, international financial institutions, bilateral donors and beneficiaries, which aims to improve socio-economic development of the region. Through the WBIF, the EU allocated 2.6 billion euros in grants to the countries of the WB.

By allocating 736 million euros in grants to the public sector until 2022, WBIF supported BiH in achieving the country's key goals outlined in its economic and investment plans (Fig. 3). Since 2009, the WBIF has supported estimated investments of 6.5 billion euros in the public sector in BiH. The country has benefitted from 82 grants for over 1.1 billion euros in technical assistance (73.3 million euros) and investment co-financing (1030.6 million euros) (WBIF 2023).

The EU IPA grant support channelled through the WBIF for 1085.2 million euros, while other donors contributed 18.7 million euros. Signed loans amounted to 2.1 billion euros (WBIF 2024).

Joining the EU could have a direct and indirect impact on the further inflow of capital in the form of investments, loans, and grants. The indirect impact is reflected in the creation of a more favourable and safer investment environment in general, which would act as an incentive for investors from other countries that are not members of the EU. It also could provide a higher credit rating and a better position of the country in international borrowing.

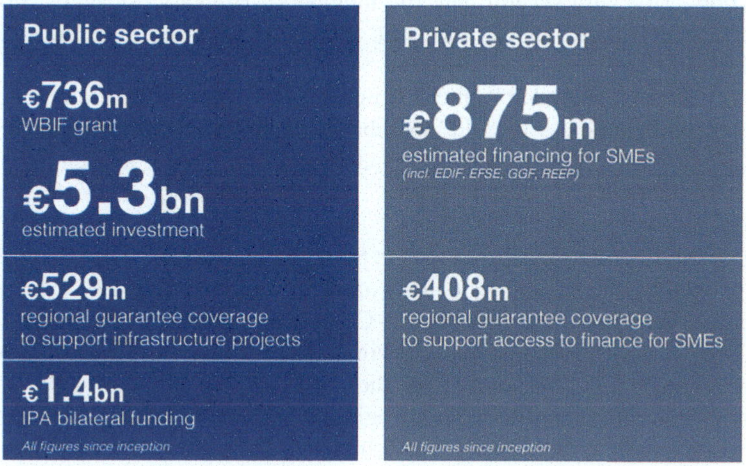

Fig. 3 The financial package of growth plan for Western Balkans for Bosnia and Herzegovina

3 How It Started: Stabilization and Association Process

Although BiH's economic flows with the EU became increasingly intense after the war, for a number of years (until the conclusion of the SAA in 2008) they took place without an appropriate long-term institutional framework. Namely, at the beginning of the war on the territory of the former Yugoslavia, in 1992, the EU unilaterally suspended the Agreement on Cooperation between the European Economic Community (EEC) and the Socialist Federal Republic of Yugoslavia (SFRY).

Given the need to regulate and further develop economic flows with the EU, and the fact that at that moment it was impossible to do so with a comprehensive agreement, BiH tried to conclude many bilateral agreements in various economic areas with individual EU members. But it was not possible to conclude bilateral agreements on one of the most important issues—mutual trade. The trade policy that determines the trade relations of the Union with third countries and multilateral organizations is one of the common policies of the EU and as such is within the competence of the Union as a whole.

In an effort to attract investments from the EU to the country, a series of agreements on the improvement and protection of investments were signed, first with many "old" EU members, and later with new members. The first such agreement was signed with the Netherlands in 1998. This was followed by agreements with Italy, Austria, Finland, Greece, and Sweden which were signed in 2000, then Germany in 2021, Portugal, Spain, and Great Britain in 2002, France in 2003, and Belgium, Luxembourg, and Denmark in 2004. Agreements with some new members—Slovenia, Slovakia, Hungary, the Czech Republic, Lithuania, and Croatia—were signed either before or after they joined the EU (MoFTER 2024).

Agreements on economic cooperation, excluding trade issues, were signed in the period 2006–2014 with several new EU members—Hungary, Slovakia, Slovenia, the Czech Republic, Romania, Bulgaria, and with one "old" member—Greece (MoFTER 2024).

BiH has so far concluded numerous agreements on avoiding double taxation with many EU members—12 "old" members (Austria, Belgium, Finland, France, Greece, Netherlands, Ireland, Italy, Germany, Spain, Sweden, and Great Britain) and 7 new members (Czech Republic, Slovakia, Hungary, Poland, Slovenia, Romania, and Croatia) (MFT 2024).

In the period before the signing of the SAA, intensive trade flows with the EU were regulated by the trade laws of BiH and trade policy of the EU accompanied with the short-term decisions made by the Council of the EU for the countries of the former Yugoslavia. Bosnia and Herzegovina applied tariffs on the most-favoured-nation principle (MFN) for goods from the EU. The EU, starting in 1996, applied preferential trade treatment (duty-free regime) for 95% of the products that BiH could export, based on the Generalized Scheme of Preferences (GSP).[5] Since 2000, the EU has started to apply even greater trade preferences to trade with BiH—the so-called Autonomous Trade Measures (ATM). The condition is to have a proof of origin for BiH's products, and that they meet EU technical and technological standards, and product quality and safety conditions. At first, these measures for BiH were valid until 2005, but their validity was later extended. In addition, in 2001, the EU signed a bilateral agreement with BiH on trade in textile products, which abolished all restrictions on the import of textile products from BiH.

In parallel with the signing of various agreements that treated only certain areas of economic cooperation and with the adoption of unilateral decisions by the Council of the EU on the regulation of mutual trade, processes were underway that led to the signing of a comprehensive agreement—SAA which would finally provide an appropriate institutional framework for BiH's relations with the EU.

It should be emphasized that the EU's policy towards the countries of the region, and therefore also towards BiH, changed depending on the regional and global political and economic circumstances, and the interests of the Union itself. During the 1990s, three phases can be distinguished in the relationship between the EU and the region (Brkić 2020):

- Until the mid-1990s—the practice of an exclusively bilateral approach.
- From 1996 to 1999 (after the Dayton Peace Agreement and the Royaumont process)—the so-called regional approach.
- Since 1999—the evolution of the regional approach through the Stability Pact for Southeast Europe as a regional instrument and the Stabilization and Association Process as a bilateral instrument created for individual countries of the WB.

[5] There are three types of preferential schemes approved by the EU: standard GSP, "GSP plus", and "Everything but Arms" (EBA) (EC 2024d).

The focus of all these concepts was, on the one hand, EU support[6] for establishment and improvement of the cooperation among the SEE countries and opening the perspective of their inclusion in European integrations, and, on the other hand, the conditionality policy. The EU has set numerous political and economic conditions—the degree of development of relations with the Union depended on their fulfilment. Those conditions mainly related to internal reforms and regional cooperation and integration. Political conditions included the development of democracy, respect for human rights, basic freedoms, and minority rights. Economic and legal conditions included, among other things, the establishment of a market economy, the construction of a modern legal system, stabilizing of macroeconomic situation, etc. Additional conditions were established for individual WB countries. The specific conditions for BiH included the establishment of a single foreign trade policy and customs policy at the state level, the creation of a single economic area, and cooperation with the OHR (MoFTER 1998).

At the initiative of BiH, the EU adopted the Declaration on Special Relations with BiH in June 1998. Thereafter the EU-BiH Consultative Task Force (CTF) was formed, which would provide technical and professional assistance in the fields of governance, regulatory framework, and policy.

The SAP began in May 1999, while the Stability Pact was established in June. In the same year, in BiH, the Decision of the Council of Ministers of BiH on the initiation of the initiative for the accession of BiH to the EU and the Resolution of the Parliamentary Assembly of BiH on European integration and the Pact on Stability for Southeastern Europe were adopted. Thus, BiH officially started a long-term process, the final goal of which is full membership in the EU.

The next step was the announcement of the so-called Road Map in March 2000, with 18 essential political, legal, and economic conditions that BiH had to fulfil, in order to start work on the Feasibility Study of SAA negotiations. In September 2002, the EC announced that the conditions of the roadmap were "substantially fulfilled". However, complete fulfilment of these conditions remained an integral part of the requirements set in the Feasibility Study. The European Council also decided about a regime of asymmetric trade liberalization for BiH and other WB countries[7]—more favourable trade treatment for potential candidate countries than for candidate countries for which a symmetrical free trade agreement with the EU was foreseen.

In March 2003, work on the Feasibility Study began. The EC handed the Council of Ministers of BiH a questionnaire with 346 questions on the economic and political organization of BiH, and other areas relevant to the conclusion of the SAA. A few months later, in November 2003, the EC presented the Study in which it identified 16 priority areas of reform, progress in which would enable the opening of SAA negotiations. In this regard, BiH prepared a programme of priorities in 2004, which

[6] The support was in the form of political, financial, and technical assistance.

[7] Council Regulation No 2007/2000 of 18 September 2000 introducing exceptional trade measures for countries and territories participating in or linked to the SAP.

obliged the country to undertake 44 activities, adopt 46 laws, and establish or restructure 27 institutions (DEI 2004).

At the summit in Thessaloniki held on 19–20 June 2003, the European perspective of the countries of the region was confirmed and the European Partnership was established for each of them. Within the framework of the European partnership, short-term and medium-term priorities were determined, which served as a list of obligations according to which the progress of countries on the way to European integration would be measured (DEI 2004). The EU Council adopted the first European partnership with BiH in June 2004, identifying 23 short-term priorities (with a deadline of 1–2 years) and 30 medium-term priorities (with a deadline of 3–4 years) (DEI 2006). The second European Partnership for BiH was adopted by the Council of the EU in January 2006, and the third in February 2008.

In the meantime, in order to support ongoing processes on the path to the EU, in December 2002, the Directorate for European Integration of BiH (DEI) was established as a permanent, autonomous, and professional body of the Council of Ministers of BiH, whose responsibility is the coordination and supervision of processes and activities required in the integration of BiH into the EU.[8]

After the EC assessed that BiH had made significant progress in implementing the reforms from the Feasibility Study, negotiations on the SAA were opened on 25 November 2005 in Sarajevo. They were completed after 2 years, and the signing of the SAA was initialed on 4 December 2007.

4 The Path to the Candidate Status

The Stabilization and Association Agreement is a standardized agreement that regulates political and economic relations between the EU and the WB countries that intend to join the Union. The basic areas covered by the Agreement are political dialogue, regional cooperation, "four freedoms"—freedom of movement of goods, services, people, and capital, adoption of the *Acquis* of the EU, entrepreneurship, financial aid, cooperation in justice and internal affairs, and financial cooperation. Before signing the SAA, the WB countries were in the phase of the so-called voluntary rather than binding harmonization of their legislation with the EU *Acquis*. The SAA represents the third generation of European association agreements. It is adapted to the circumstances of each country. Although it is concluded for an indefinite period, actually it depends on the dynamics with which a country fulfils the set conditions (Brkić 2020).

The SAA between BiH and the EU was signed on 16 June 2008, in Luxembourg. It was one of the key steps on the way towards European integration, because BiH finally established a formal contractual relationship with the EU and received the status of a potential candidate country. Simultaneously with the signing of the SAA, the Interim Agreement on Trade and Trade Issues was signed, which was applied

[8] DEI took over the responsibilities of the former Ministry for European Integration of BiH, which was formed by the Decision of the Parliamentary Assembly of BiH from 22 June 2000.

from 1 July 2008, until the end of the SAA ratification procedure in all signatory countries.

The SAA ratification process by all EU member states ended in 2011. In April 2015, the Council of the EU adopted the Decision on the Conclusion of the SAA between BiH and the EU. Seven years after it was signed, the SAA finally entered into force on 1 June 2015 and joint bodies for the implementation of the Agreement were formed.

After the ratification, the trade part of the SAA came into force instead of the Interim Trade Agreement, which continued the process of trade liberalization. In the meantime, BiH also succeeded to solve problems related to the establishment of an accreditation body and verification of compliance of its industrial products with technical standards of the EU, as well as problems with exports of agricultural products to the EU market. Institute for Accreditation of BiH (BATA) has been participating in the work of European and international accreditation organizations since 2013, facilitating foreign trade of BiH through the removal of technical barriers for exports of its products (BATA 2024).[9] Before that, exporters from BiH had to test their products in laboratories of other countries, with significant additional costs. When it comes to the export of agricultural products from BiH, progress has been achieved by adopting the so-called hygiene package in 2012, which enabled the exports of certain types of agricultural products to the EU. Export of milk and milk products by a large number of BiH's producers to the EU was allowed in 2015.

In the period between the signing and entry into force of the SAA, one of the most significant events in relations between BiH and the EU was the abolition of the visa regime for BiH citizens in December 2010. New regime enabled them to travel freely to the signatory countries of the Schengen Agreement, which was especially important for the business community. This was preceded by the fulfilment of a series of requirements by the EU—more precisely, 174 technical conditions (the most important of which was the introduction of biometric passports for citizens of BiH), determined by the roadmap for the liberalization of the visa regime, which was handed over to BiH in 2008.

In June 2013, another road map—the Road Map for BiH's application for EU membership—was delivered to BiH. However, excluding the existence of a high level of integration in the area of trade with the EU,[10] regional cooperation and maintenance of macroeconomic stability, the progress that BiH achieved in the reforms necessary to achieve the Copenhagen political and economic criteria was assessed as insignificant or limited in many other areas (EC 2010). Therefore, in November 2014, the Reform Agenda ("British-German initiative for Bosnia and Herzegovina") was presented. It called on the authorities in BiH to commit to implementing institutional reforms at all levels, and to the development of a reform plan in cooperation with the EU, which will advance BiH in the integration process. During 2015, BiH authorities adopted necessary documents such as the Declaration

[9] http://www.bata.gov.ba/O_nama/Medunarodna_saradnja/default.aspx?id=43&langTag=en-US

[10] https://archive.europa.ba/?page_id=484

on Commitment of Government Institutions in BiH, the Reform Agenda for BiH for the period 2015–2018, and Action plan for its implementation.

In February 2016, BiH applied for the EU membership. The request was accepted by the Council on General Affairs of the EU which gave an order to the EC to prepare a questionnaire for BiH. Next 2 years BiH was preparing answers to the questionnaire (to 3242 questions in total), which were submitted in February 2018, and then answers to 655 additional questions, which were submitted in March 2019. However, the opinion of the EC from May 2019 on BiH's request for membership was disappointing: "Bosnia and Herzegovina does not yet sufficiently fulfil the criteria related to the stability of institutions guaranteeing democracy, the rule of law, human rights and respect for and protection of minorities, set by the Copenhagen European Council in 1993… Bosnia and Herzegovina is overall at an early stage regarding its level of preparedness to take on the obligations of EU membership and needs to significantly step up the process to align with the EU acquis and implement and enforce related legislation…" (EC 2019).

According to the assesment of the EC in 2019, along with Kosovo*, BiH was ranked the lowest in key areas of preparedness in the EU accession process (Fig. 4).

The opinion of the EC included a new comprehensive roadmap for reforms in the areas of democracy/functionality, the rule of law, fundamental rights, and public administration identifying 14 priorities that BiH needs to fulfil in order to open accession negotiations with the EU. However, 2 years later, only one out of key 14 priorities was fully implemented, but in such a way that formal prerequisites were created for its fulfilment—it is about ensuring the proper functioning of the Parliamentary Committee for Stabilization and Association. No other priority from the Opinion has been implemented as a whole. A five of them were realized partially. The lack of progress in the implementation of priorities in the area of

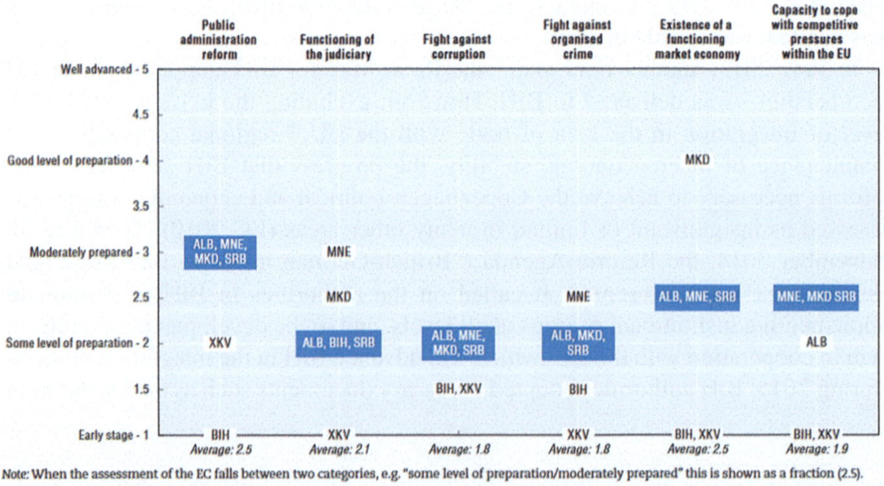

Fig. 4 The EC's assessment of preparedness for Western Balkans (2019). Source: OECD (2020)

democracy/functionality and the rule of law, which are made up of several units, was of particular concern (Transparency International BiH 2021).

Despite the fact that the process of integration of BiH into the EU seemed to be essentially stopped, in October 2022, the EC recommended BiH for candidate status, "on the understanding that a number of steps are taken". The decision on granting status of candidate country to BiH was made on 15 December 2022.[11]

Not long after the granting candidate status, some other decisions concerning BiH were made, which were also more politically motivated than based on the real progress of BiH. On 8 November 2023, the EC recommended to open accession negotiations with BiH, "once the necessary degree of compliance with the membership criteria is achieved; the country needs to apply further efforts to fulfil the key priorities set out in the Commission Opinion on its EU membership application" (EC 2023c). In December 2023, the European Council announced its intention to open accession negotiations with BiH (Table 2). Although the required degree of compliance with the membership criteria was not achieved, on 21 March 2024, the Council made the decision of a historical importance—to open accession negotiations with the BiH.[12]

The other countries of the WB region did not progress quickly in the process of approaching the EU either. However, the period from the beginning of SAA negotiations to the granting of candidate status for most of them was more than two or three times shorter than for BiH—it lasted from 4 years (North Macedonia) to

Table 2 The status of WB Countries on their way to the EU

WB country	Status	SAA (signed/entered into the force)	Application for membership
Albania	Candidate	22/05/2006 12/06/2006	28/04/2009 (accepted 24/06/2014)
BiH	Candidate	16/06/2008 01/06/2015	15/02/2016 (accepted 20/09/2016)
Croatia	Member	29/10/2001 01/02/2005	21/02/2003 (accepted 01/06/2004) Accession 01/07/2013
Kosovo*	Potential candidate	27/10/2015 01/04/2016	15/12/2022
North Macedonia	Candidate	09/04/2001 01/04/2004	22/03/2004 (accepted 17/12/2005)
Montenegro	Candidate	15/10/2007	15/12/2008 (accepted 17/12/2010)
Serbia	Candidate	01/03/2012	22/12/2009 (accepted 28/06/2013)

Source: Author, based on data of the EC

[11] https://www.parlament.ba/Content/Read/126?title=Klju%C4%8Dni-doga%C4%91aji-u-odnosima-EU-i-Bosne-i-Hercegovine&lang=en

[12] https://neighbourhood-enlargement.ec.europa.eu/enlargement-policy/bosnia-and-herzegovina_en

Table 3 From application until achieving EU candidate status

WB country	Period	Number of years for achieving EU candidate status
North Macedonia	2000–2004	4 years
Croatia	2000–2005	5 years
Montenegro	2005–2010	5 years
Albania	2003–2009	6 years
Serbia	2005–2013	8 years
Bosnia and Herzegovina	2005–2023	18 years

Source: Author

8 years (Serbia), while BiH needed more than twice or three times as long, even 18 years (Table 3).

According to the ESI report from 2022, Montenegro leaded the way in the formal sense, having opened all 33 chapters in the negotiations and managed to close 3 so far. Serbia followed with 21 chapters opened and 2 closed, while Albania and North Macedonia have not yet opened any chapters in negotiations with the EU. However, a paradox appeared in practice—in terms of success in the implementation of requests per chapter, the EC gave almost the same average rating to a country that formally did not open any chapter but was better prepared in 23 out of 33 chapters—North Macedonia 3.0, as well as the country that opened all chapters—Montenegro 2.9. BiH has the lowest score with 4.4 which means that country achieved only "some level of preparation".

5 Future Challenges

There is an evident trend of increasingly complex criteria, requirements, and procedures within the EU accession process. Something similar is visible in the accession to some other international organizations such as the World Trade Organization (the so-called WTO plus). Within that context, for BiH, as for all acceding countries of the WB, the opening of negotiations means very demanding tasks and significant challenges—political, legal, administrative, financial, and others. Challenges are related to the improvement and adjustment of legal system (adoption of the *Acquis*), adaptation to the requirements of the EU single market, increasing competition in the country's own market, and partial transfer of sovereignty.

The adoption of the *Acquis* is considered the longest and most complex process within the framework of EU accession, especially considering the fact that the *Acquis* itself changes and develops. Additionally, what put BiH apart from other candidate countries is its complicated state structure (Box 1)[13] and the role of the

[13] Sources: DEI (2012). *Schematic Overview of Levels of Governance in Bosnia and Herzegovina, 2012* (https://bih-parliamentary-twinning.eu/uimages/documents/schematic_overview_of_the_levels_of_governance_in_BiH.pdf); Association of Municipalities and Cities of the FBiH (https://

OHR—this will make the adoption of the *Acquis* and the coordination of that process at all levels to be an additional challenge.[14] It is necessary to take significant steps both in the direction of harmonization with the EU *Acquis* and the implementation of the legislation. In most chapters of the *Acquis*, there was no or limited progress in 2023 in BiH.

Box 1 State structure of Bosnia and Herzegovina
BiH has three main administrative units: two entities—the Federation of BiH and the Republic of Srpska, and Brčko District. BiH has 14 constitutions, 14 assemblies, and 14 governments.

The executive power of the state is exercised by the Council of Ministers of BiH which includes 9 ministries and 8 permanent bodies, governments at the entity level with 16 ministries each, and the Brčko District government with 11 departments.

The Federation of BiH is divided into 10 cantons; each of them has its own government with 7–12 ministries, depending on the canton. There are 81 units of local self-government in the Federation of BiH (81 municipalities, 22 of which are also cities; the city of Sarajevo has 4 municipalities).

The Republic of Srpska is administratively divided into regions and 64 local self-government units, of which 54 are municipalities and 10 cities (East Sarajevo has 6 municipalities).

After acquiring candidate status, despite negative legislative changes at the entity level, certain results were achieved in terms of fulfilling 14 key priorities, such as the adoption of some strategic documents and laws. The Directorate for European Integration has finalized the programme for EU integration as a key step towards developing the national programme for the adoption of the EU *Acquis* (EC 2024a). Some other strategic documents have also been adopted, as follows: strategy on public procurement, migration strategy, strategy on fight against corruption and organized crime, strategy for preventive of conflict on interests, strategy on border control, on foreigners, etc. (EC 2023a). However, the adoption of sectoral strategies at the state level remains a key requirement to fully use the IPA funds. Authorities are also preparing some new laws such as laws in the field of judicial system (on High Judicial and Prosecutorial Council, on courts, etc.).

Regarding the political criterion, the conclusion is that institutional and electoral reforms are still missing. The High Representative intervened several times in electoral matters—especially during 2022 when the OHR introduced several changes in the electoral framework. The problem still exists, as well as problems regarding

www.sogfbih.ba/clanice); Association of Municipalities and Cities of the RS (https://www.alvrs.com/lat/)

[14] Council of Ministers of BiH and Directorate for European Integration of BiH (2010). *Development Strategy of BiH—Proposal* (See: http://www.dep.gov.ba/razvojni_dokumenti/razvojna_strategija/Archive.aspx?langTag=bs-BA&template_id=140&pageIndex=1)

functioning of the Constitutional Court and implementing its decisions. However, the situation is better regarding foreign policy as BiH reached almost full alignment with the EU Common Foreign and Security Policy in the new European geopolitical context determined by the war in Ukraine, and sanctions towards Russia.

Trade aspects of economic integration with the EU are at a respectable level, but despite preferences given by the EU (asymmetric trade liberalization), BiH has not realized its trade potentials. Regarding implementation of the trade part of the SAA, the EC reported some problems related to protectionist measures, mostly export restrictions, unilaterally introduced by BiH. The special challenges for the future will be creation of full free trade area with the EU as well as joining to the WTO.[15] One of the final steps to finish bilateral negotiations with all WTO members—the Decision on the quality of liquid fuels—was adopted by the Council of Ministers of BiH in December 2023.

When it comes to other economic criteria, BiH is still in the early stage of developing a functional market economy (Table 4). Due to differences in procedures and legislation, and insufficient cooperation and coordination when creating economic policy at the state and entity level, the internal market is still fragmented, and the business environment is insufficiently stimulating. The programme of economic reforms in the country is still of poor quality, and the implementation of reforms is limited, especially in terms of the business environment, public companies, green and digital transition, and employment. BiH is between an early stage and some level of preparedness when it comes to its capacity to deal with competitive pressure of the EU market (EC 2023a). Most of the costs caused by the EU membership come down to the costs of adapting to the EU single market, both on a macro and micro level, such as: costs of accepting EU norms and standards, migration problem, possibility of experts going to other countries within integration ("brain drain" and losing potential for new idea and innovation), possibility of unemployment growth and income reduction, costs of modernization of industrial facilities, loss of market share of local companies, existence of bureaucracy within the EU (centralized system), etc. (Bitzenis and Andronikidis 2006).

Generally speaking, BiH is between an early stage and some level of preparedness in its ability to assume the obligations entailed by EU membership (Table 4).

Bosnia and Herzegovina lags behind in institutional convergence towards the EU in relation to WB countries that much earlier acquired candidate status and started negotiations, as well as in real economic convergence. A study from 2008 (Hodžić 2008) showed that in that year the gross domestic product per capita (GDP p/c) of BiH was only about a quarter of the average GDP p/c of the EU. Even with a growth rate of about 6% in BiH and with slower growth in the EU of about 2.6%, it would take 32 years to reach 75% of the average GDP p/c of the EU. Achieving macroeconomic convergence of BiH towards the EU requires significantly higher economic growth. However, in the years since, the growth rate has ranged from (−) 2.8% to 3.1%.

[15] BiH has the observer status in the WTO since 1999—almost 25 years.

Table 4 Levels of assessment for BiH (2023)

	Assessment of progress				
State of play	No progress	No progress or limited progress	Some/limited progress	Good progress	Significant progress
Early stage of preparation	– Socio-economic reforms; – Functional market economy; – Internal market (free movement of goods, workers, services, and capital, company law, intellectual property, competition policy, financial services, and consumer and health protection); – Resources, agriculture, and cohesion (agriculture and rural development, food safety, veterinary and phytosanitary policy, fisheries and aquaculture, and financial and budgetary provisions);	/	– Public administration reform; – Judiciary; – Green agenda and sustainable connectivity; – Energy, environment, and climate change;	/	/
Between early stage and some level of preparation	– Fight against corruption and organized crime; – Capacity to cope with competitive pressure and market forces of the EU; – Economic and monetary policy;	– Competitiveness and inclusive growth (taxation, digital transformation and media, social policy and employment, enterprise and industrial policy, science and research, education and culture, and customs);	/	/	/

(continued)

Table 4 (continued)

State of play	Assessment of progress No progress	No progress or limited progress	Some/limited progress	Good progress	Significant progress
Some level of preparation	/	/	– Public procurement; – Statistics; – Financial control; – Sustainable connectivity–Transport and trans-European network;	/	External relations (EU Common Foreign and Security Policy and regional cooperation within CEFTA);
Moderately prepared	/	/	/	/	/
Good level of preparation	/	/	/	/	/
Well advanced	/	/	/	/	/

Note: Similar results as in 2021 (See: https://www.esiweb.org/publications/balkan-turtle-race-warning-ukraine). *Source*: Author, based on the EC's "Report on Progress in BiH, 2023" (The scale of assessment to describe current status—"state of play"—and progress of the country during the reporting period have been taken from the mentioned EC report)

According to Eurostat data (2023),[16] 14 years later BiH reached one third of the average EU27 GDP p/c—only 35%, which placed BiH at the bottom (together with Albania 34%) among other candidate countries in the WB region. The best result was achieved by Montenegro, whose GDP p/c was 50% of the EU average, followed by Serbia with 44%, and North Macedonia with 42%. All the mentioned countries had significantly lower GDP p/c than the least developed EU member—Bulgaria (62% of the average EU27 GDP per capita) (Fig. 5).

The gap in economic performance is too large for BiH to expect the so-called smooth adjustment in the process of accession, and especially after a potential admission to the EU membership.

Even if BiH is at an approximate level of economic development compared to EU members, different countries have different economic needs and priorities. The loss or limitation of autonomy in the creation of economic policies (as a result of joining the EU) makes it difficult to achieve those priorities, which can be particularly pronounced in areas where the EU has exclusive competence, such as common policies. For example, BiH's trade with the EU will be completely liberalized, with the obligation of BiH to apply the EU's common trade policy towards "third"

[16] See: https://ec.europa.eu/eurostat/statistics-explained/index.php?title=GDP_per_capita,_consumption_per_capita_and_price_level_indices#Relative_volumes_of_GDP_per_capita

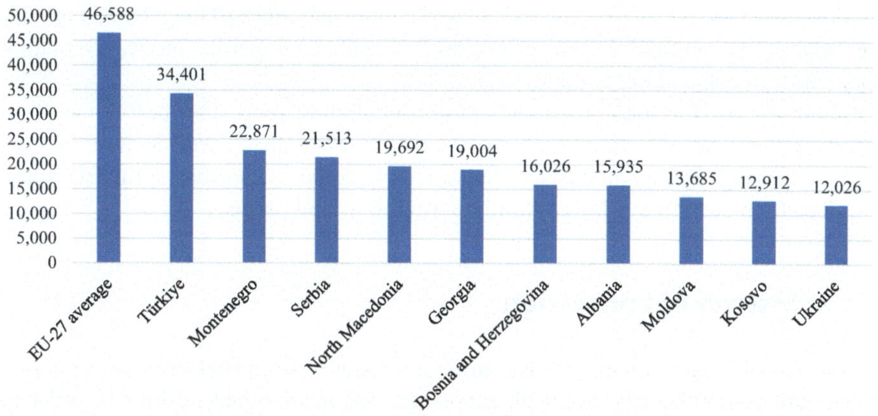

Fig. 5 GDP per capita of EU27 and EU potential candidate and candidate countries in 2023 (purchasing power parity; 2017 international dollar). Source: International Monetary Fund, World Economic Outlook Database, April 2024

countries. The EU customs tariff is adapted to its members, mainly to countries that are far more developed than BiH and to countries with a different production structure than BiH. The common trade policy also implies the acceptance of preferential agreements with numerous countries of the world. This will further open up BiH's market, and it is questionable whether BiH will benefit from the markets of those countries. In addition, by joining the Eurozone, members lose the possibility to conduct independent monetary policy—one of the main government instruments for stimulating economic activity when needed.

However, it is not only about costs of the acceding process and possible membership, but also potential high (direct and indirect) costs of "staying out". Namely, expansion of the EU will confront outsiders with competition from new members, especially when it comes to countries with a similar export structure—outsiders could lose a part of the large and growing EU market. The EU single market is now the largest market in the world—it presently includes a population of 448.4 million[17] and has the nominal GDP of over 16,962 billion euros[18] (2023), with around 15% of world total imports[19] (WTO 2023). For all the WB countries, the EU is a market of strategic importance and the leading trade partner, with more than 70% share in total regional trade.[20] It is obvious that remaining an outsider to this expanding market can only lead to retardation of development. In addition, a country that lags behind in adapting to the standards and requirements of the EU market would also face a decrease in participation in the markets of countries that are at

[17] https://ec.europa.eu/eurostat/statistics-explained/index.php?title=Population_and_population_change_statistics

[18] https://ec.europa.eu/eurostat/databrowser/view/tec00001/default/table?lang=en

[19] Excluding intra-EU trade.

[20] See: https://webgate.ec.europa.eu/isdb_results/factsheets/country/details_bosnia-herzegovina_en.pdf; https://webgate.ec.europa.eu/isdb_results/factsheets/country/details_montenegro_en.pdf; https://webgate.ec.europa.eu/isdb_results/factsheets/country/details_albania_en.pdf; https://webgate.ec.europa.eu/isdb_results/factsheets/country/details_north-macedonia_en.pdf

the forefront of the accession process and apply more and more EU regulations in relations with third countries. "Defensive reaction" is really an important motive for putting more efforts to come closer to the EU.

Obviously, BiH is facing a much more demanding road than before, with an uncertain end. The only thing that is clear is that this path, as well as its final outcome, will bring significant costs, whether BiH becomes a member of the EU in the next decade, or whether it lags behind the region in that process.

6 Instead of Conclusion

The process of integration into the EU structures requires from BiH stronger economic growth and comprehensive political, economic, and institutional reforms in order to "catch up" with EU requirements. It will continue to be a long-term, demanding, and expensive process. BiH can only hope that one day, the benefits of the EU membership will outweigh the costs of adjusting the state, economy, and society as a whole.

However, the European way of BiH has no alternative. Commitment to European integration has been no longer a matter of the will and desire of the country and its constitutive and other nations, but an imperative. In a situation where a few European countries that do not yet belong to the Union are trying to join,[21] staying outside this integration would turn BiH into an "enclave", making it even more vulnerable economically and politically.

But despite the declarative support at all levels of government, the reports of the EC have emphasized for years that there is no political consensus on the main priorities of the reform. The lack of political consensus leads to BiH progressing very slowly towards European integration.

The fact is that two extremely important developments in the relations between BiH and the EU—the acquisition of candidate status and the opening of negotiations—happened thanks to the new political circumstances in Europe, and not because of the achieved progress of BiH. However, BiH would not be the only one that advances in the process of joining the EU thanks primarily to the political circumstances and interests of the Union. It used to be the case with Greece, Bulgaria, and Romania, as well as today with Moldova and Ukraine.

In the future, BiH can also "count" on political circumstances, i.e. the geopolitical interest of the Euro-Atlantic integration. The political moment for BiH is favourable, primarily due to the West's fear of an increasing influence of countries such as Russia and China in the Balkans, and the significant decrease in the enthusiasm of certain countries (Türkiye, North Macedonia, and Serbia) for joining the EU. On the one hand, there is primarily geopolitical interest in the Union itself for another enlargement, and on the other hand, there is a certain fatigue from enlargement, as well as some political disagreements between old and new EU members. The EU consists of a very large number of countries with different economic performances, different political and economic interests, as well as different problems.

[21] Except members of the European Free Trade Association (EFTA) who have a special privileged relationship with the EU.

Political relations and interests in general have always been of great importance for the EU—both for its establishment and for its enlargement. In the case of BiH, the development of relations with the EU will significantly depend on a number of political factors and processes in the national, regional, and global context—on political relations within BiH, especially between the entities (and in that context, Serbia's relations with the EU due to that country's special relations with the Republic of Srpska), mutual political relations of the countries in the region, as well as the political situation in Europe and the world. However, the political and economic interest of the EU itself is of crucial importance. We can say that the dynamics of enlargement depends, on the one hand, on the dynamics with which the candidate country fulfils the criteria from Copenhagen and Madrid, and, incomparably more, on the interests of the EU, on the other hand. The EU determines the conditions and assesses their fulfilment in the context of its own interests.

It is realistic to assume that the process of accession of BiH to the Union will continue to take place slowly, with numerous delays. The key issue is to change the attitude towards EU membership in BiH—to stop looking at EU membership as a goal for which it is not important how it will be achieved (thanks to real progress or favourable political circumstances), but to understand it as an opportunity for faster achievement of economic and social prosperity of the country and its citizens.

References

Agency for Statistics of BiH – BHAS (2013) Robna razmjena BiH sa inostranstvom 2012 (BiH's Foreign Trade, 2012). Tematski bilten TB 06, Sarajevo. Available at: https://bhas.gov.ba/data/Publikacije/Bilteni/2013/ETR_00_2012_TB_1_BS.pdf. Accessed 25 Apr 2024

Agency for Statistics of BiH – BHAS (2019) Robna razmjena BiH sa inostranstvom 2018 (BiH's Foreign Trade, 2018). Tematski bilten TB 06, Sarajevo. Available at: https://bhas.gov.ba/data/Publikacije/Bilteni/2019/ETR_00_2018_TB_0_BS.pdf. Accessed 25 Apr 2024

Agency for Statistics of BiH – BHAS (2023) Robna razmjena BiH sa inostranstvom 2022 (BiH's Foreign Trade, 2022). Tematski bilten TB 06, Sarajevo. Available at: https://bhas.gov.ba/data/Publikacije/Bilteni/2023/ETR_00_2022_TB_1_BS.pdf. Accessed 25 Apr 2024

Association of Municipalities and Cities of the FBiH (2024) Web site. Available at: https://www.sogfbih.ba/clanice. Accessed 23 May 2024

Association of Municipalities and Cities of the RS (2024) Web site. Available at: https://www.alvrs.com/lat/. Accessed 23 May 2024

Bitzenis AP, Andronikidis A (2006) Cost and benefits of integration in the European Union and in the Economic Monetary Union (EMU). Econ Manag Financ Mark J 1(2) Available at: https://www.researchgate.net/publication/26451561_COST_AND_BENEFITS_OF_INTEGRATION_IN_THE_EUROPEAN_UNION_AND_IN_THE_ECONOMIC_MONETARY_UNION_EMU. Accessed 17 May 2024

Brkić S (2012) Intra-industrijska trgovina: Teorijski i empirijski aspekti (Intra-industry trade: theoretical and empirical aspects). School of Economics and Business University of Sarajevo, Sarajevo

Brkić S (2020) Integracija Bosne i Hercegovine u međunarodni trgovinski sistem (Integration of Bosnia and Herzegovina into the international trading system). School of Economics and Business University of Sarajevo, Sarajevo

Council of Ministers of BiH and Directorate for European Integration of BiH (2010) Development Strategy of BiH—Proposal. Available at: http://www.dep.gov.ba/razvojni_dokumenti/razvojna_strategija/Archive.aspx?langTag=bs-BA&template_id=140&pageIndex=1. Accessed 19 May 2024

Directorate for European Integration of BiH – DEI (2004) Bulletin 1. DEI, Sarajevo
Directorate for European Integration of BiH – DEI (2006) Strategy of integration of BiH into the European Union. DEI, Sarajevo
Directorate for European Integration of BiH – DEI (2012) Schematic overview of levels of governance in Bosnia and Herzegovina, 2012. Available at: https://bih-parliamentary-twinning.eu/uimages/documents/schematic_overview_of_the_levels_of_governance_in_BiH.pdf. Accessed 23 May 2024
Directorate for European Integration of BiH – DEI (2024) Who we are. Available at: https://www.dei.gov.ba/en/o-nama. Accessed 7 May 2024
EU Delegation in BiH and EU Special Representative in BiH (2024) BiH and the European Union: financial aid and trade relations. Available at: https://archive.europa.ba/?page_id=484. Accessed 3 May 2024
European Commission (2010) Communication from the Commission to the European Parliament and the Council: Enlargement Strategy and Main Challenges 2010–2011, Brussels, COM(2010)660, 09 November. Available at: https://eur-lex.europa.eu/legal-content/EN/TXT/?uri=CELEX:52010DC0660. Accessed 8 May 2024
European Commission (2019) Communication from the Commission to the European Parliament and the Council: Commission Opinion on Bosnia and Herzegovina's application for membership of the European Union, Brussels, 29 May 2019, COM(2019) 261 final. Available at: https://ec.europa.eu/neighbourhood-enlargement/sites/near/files/20190529-bosnia-and-herzegovina-opinion_hr.pdf. Accessed 12 May 2024
European Commission (2023a) Commission Staff Working Document: Bosnia and Herzegovina 2023 Report (Accompanying the document Communication from the Commission to the European Parliament, the Council, the European Economic and Social Committee and the Committee of the Regions 2023 Communication on EU Enlargement policy), Brussels, 8 November 2023, SWD(2023) 691 final. Available at: https://neighbourhood-enlargement.ec.europa.eu/system/files/2023-11/SWD_2023_691%20Bosnia%20and%20Herzegovina%20report.pdf. Accessed 22 May 2024
European Commission (2023b) EU Enlargement—Bosnia and Herzegovina on its European path. Available at: https://neighbourhood-enlargement.ec.europa.eu/document/download/c9f70a09-5a77-42b6-88fb-e82d798f0c9e_en?filename=factograph_BIH_Dec_2023.pdf. Accessed 2 May 2024
European Commission (2023c) Press release—Brussels 8 November 2023. Available at: https://neighbourhood-enlargement.ec.europa.eu/news/commission-adopts-2023-enlargement-package-recommends-open-negotiations-ukraine-and-moldova-grant-2023-11-08_en. Accessed 22 May 2024
European Commission (2024a) Communication from the Commission to the Council and the European Parliament: Report on progress in Bosnia and Herzegovina—March 2024. Available at: https://neighbourhood-enlargement.ec.europa.eu/document/download/fa9da504-4ecb-4317-b583-c9fff0b833b2_en. Accessed 22 May 2024
European Commission (2024b) European Neighbourhood Policy and Enlargement Negotiations (DG NEAR): Bosnia and Herzegovina—financial assistance under IPA. Available at: https://neighbourhood-enlargement.ec.europa.eu/enlargement-policy/overview-instrument-pre-accession-assistance/bosnia-and-herzegovina-financial-assistance-under-ipa_en. Accessed 5 May 2024
European Commission (2024c) Home—enlargement: Bosnia and Herzegovina. Available at: https://neighbourhood-enlargement.ec.europa.eu/enlargement-policy/bosnia-and-herzegovina_en. Accessed 26 May 2024
European Commission (2024d) Trade topics: generalised scheme of preferences. Available at: https://policy.trade.ec.europa.eu/development-and-sustainability/generalised-scheme-preferences_en. Accessed 6 May 2024
European Commission – Directorate General for Trade (2023) Trade in Goods with Bosnia-Herzegovina. Available at: https://webgate.ec.europa.eu/isdb_results/factsheets/country/details_bosnia-herzegovina_en.pdf. Accessed 2 May 2024)

European Commission – Directorate General for Trade (2024a) Trade in goods with Albania. Available at: https://webgate.ec.europa.eu/isdb_results/factsheets/country/details_albania_en.pdf. Accessed 2 May 2024
European Commission – Directorate General for Trade (2024b) Trade in goods with Bosnia-Herzegovina. Available at: https://webgate.ec.europa.eu/isdb_results/factsheets/country/details_bosnia-herzegovina_en.pdf. Accessed 2 May 2024
European Commission – Directorate General for Trade (2024c) Trade in goods with Montenegro. Available at: https://webgate.ec.europa.eu/isdb_results/factsheets/country/details_montenegro_en.pdf. Accessed 2 May 2024
European Commission – Directorate General for Trade (2024d) Trade in goods with North Macedonia. Available at: https://webgate.ec.europa.eu/isdb_results/factsheets/country/details_north-macedonia_en.pdf. Accessed 2 May 2024
European Commission – Directorate General for Trade (2024e) Trade in goods with Serbia. Available at: https://webgate.ec.europa.eu/isdb_results/factsheets/country/details_serbia_en.pdf. Accessed 2 May 2024
European External Action Service – EEAS (2023) EU4BiH financial assistance—EU projects in BiH. Available at: https://www.eeas.europa.eu/delegations/bosnia-and-herzegovina/eu-projekti-u-bih-0_bs?s=219. Accessed 2 May 2024
European Stability Initiative – ESI (2022) The Balkan Turtle Race: a warning for Ukraine, ESI report. Available at: https://www.esiweb.org/publications/balkan-turtle-race-warning-ukraine. Accessed 14 May 2024
European Union – Global Gateway (2023) Economic and investment plan for Western Balkans. Available at: https://neighbourhood-enlargement.ec.europa.eu/document/download/88af76e6-ab8e-4c96-966e-332528550af5_en?filename=EIP-WB-GG-October%202023.pdf. Accessed 2 May 2024
Eurostat (2023) GDP per capita, consumption per capita and price level indices. Available at: https://ec.europa.eu/eurostat/statistics-explained/index.php?title=GDP_per_capita,_consumption_per_capita_and_price_level_indices. Accessed 22 May 2024
Foreign Investment Promotion Agency of BiH – FIPA (2024) Information for investors—essential data and statistics: FDI position and performance, January 2024. Available at: http://www.fipa.gov.ba/informacije/statistike/investicije/default.aspx?id=180&langTag=en-US. Accessed 1 May 2024
Hodžić K (2008) Makroekonomsko konvergiranje Bosne i Hercegovine Evropskoj uniji: Neizvjesnost i dugotrajnost procesa (Macroeconomic convergence of Bosnia and Herzegovina to the European Union: uncertainty and long-term process). In: Papić Ž, Čaušević F (eds) Ekonomija ubrzanog razvoja (Economy of accelerated development). Forum Bosnae, 43/08. International Forum Bosna, Sarajevo
Institute for Accreditation of BiH – BATA (2024) About us—International Cooperation. Available at: http://www.bata.gov.ba/O_nama/Medunarodna_saradnja/default.aspx?id=43&langTag=en-US. Accessed 24 May 2024
Ministry of Finance and Treasury of BiH – MFT (2024) Fiscal affairs: double taxation avoidance—agreements in force. Available at: https://mft.gov.ba/Content/Read/sporazumi-u-primjeni. Accessed 5 May 2024
Ministry of Foreign Trade and Economic Relations of Bosnia and Herzegovina – MoFTER (1998) Strategy of economic relations of Bosnia and Herzegovina with the European Union, Sarajevo
Ministry of Foreign Trade and Economic Relations of Bosnia and Herzegovina – MoFTER (2023) Analysis of foreign trade exchange of Bosnia and Herzegovina for 2022, Sarajevo. Available at: http://www.mvteo.gov.ba/attachments/bs_Home/Ostale_stranice/Me%C4%91unarodni_trgovinski_odnosi_i_sporazumi/Me%C4%91unarodni_odnosi_-_Statistika/Analiza_vanjskotrgovinske_razmjene_BiH/Analiza_VTR_BIH_za_2022._godinu.pdf. Accessed 31 March 2024
Ministry of Foreign Trade and Economic Relations of Bosnia and Herzegovina – MoFTER (2024) Bilateral trade relations—Agreements. Available at: http://www.mvteo.gov.ba/Content/Read/bilateralni-trgovinski-odnosi-sporazumi. Accessed 4 May 2024

Office of the High Representative – OHR (2024) About OHR—general information. Available at: https://www.ohr.int/about-ohr/general-information/. Accessed 26 May 2024

Organization for Economic Cooperation and Development – OECD (2020) Public governance fundamentals and European integration: towards convergence for the Western Balkans? In: Government at a glance: Western Balkans. OECD Publishing, Paris. Available at: https://read.oecd-ilibrary.org/governance/government-at-a-glance-western-balkans_b2d01687-en. Accessed 12 May 2024

Parliamentary Assembly of Bosnia and Herzegovina (2024) Parliament and the EU: key events in the relation between BiH and European Union. Available at: https://www.parlament.ba/Content/Read/126?title=Klju%C4%8Dni-doga%C4%91aji-u-odnosima-EU-i-Bosne-i-Hercegovine&lang=en. Accessed 26 May 2024

Transparency International BiH (2021) The process of integration of BiH into the EU: 14 priorities from the opinion of the European Commission two years later. Available at: https://ti-bih.org/wp-content/uploads/2021/05/Analiza_14-prioriteta.pdf. Accessed 23 May 2024

Western Balkans Investment Fund – WBIF (2023) Economic and investment plan for Western Balkans—Bosnia and Herzegovina. Available at: https://www.wbif.eu/storage/app/media/Library/FactSheets/BIH/Beneficiary%20Factsheet%20BOSNIA%20ENG%20Mar%2030%202023.pdf. Accessed 3 May 2024

Western Balkans Investment Fund – WBIF (2024) Web site. Available at: https://www.wbif.eu/beneficiaries/bosnia-and-herzegovina. Accessed 3 May 2024

World Trade Organization – WTO (2023) Trade profiles 2023—European Union. Available at: https://www.wto.org/english/res_e/booksp_e/trade_profiles23_e.pdf. Accessed 24 May 2024

The Path of North Macedonia to the European Union Is the Only Way Forward

Fatmir Besimi

Abstract

This paper rigorously examines the comprehensive benefits of European integration, focusing on its profound impact on economic and social spheres. The discussion begins by emphasizing the need to revisit the integration discourse through economic, social, and geostrategic perspectives. It underscores the European Union's foundational role as a political peace project underpinned by economic union, illustrating the significant economic benefits such as enhanced GDP per capita, trade integration, economies of scale, and financial liberalization. Furthermore, the paper juxtaposes EU pre-accession assistance with cohesion funds, highlighting the substantial financial advantages conferred by full membership. The urgency of EU enlargement is discussed, particularly in the context of the geopolitical challenges precipitated by the conflict in Ukraine. The analysis concludes with a call for structural reforms in the Western Balkans to expedite convergence with the EU, emphasizing the importance of regional connectivity, economic resilience, and sustainable development. This integration is posited as a critical pathway to fostering a prosperous future within the European framework.

Keywords

European integration · Economic benefits · Structural reforms · Regional connectivity · Financial liberalization · Geopolitical challenges

F. Besimi (✉)
South East European University, Tetovo, North Macedonia
e-mail: f.besimi@seeu.edu.mk

A. Stojkov, T. Warin (eds.), *Western Balkans and the Future of Europe*, The Future of Europe, https://doi.org/10.1007/978-3-031-86465-0_8

1 Introduction

Today, when the narrative about European integration is mainly a political one, it is advisable to reopen the discussion for all aspects—economic, social, and geostrategic, so as for all of us to get the bigger picture. Clearly, we faced many ordeals in the past two decades, unsettling the confidence of part of the public that the European agenda will become a reality 1 day. Yet, there is a saying the darkest hour is just before dawn. For instance, in the case of Croatia, immediately before it joined the Union, the public was ambivalent about the EU integration process. I personally expect that Euroscepticism in our country will speedily decrease in the coming period, but we need to get to that point first.

The European Union, as a political peace project, is built upon the economic union. From the European Coal and Steel Community to the creation of a single currency monetary union, the countries on the European soil have always been motivated primarily by economic interests. However, all these countries also share common values, the urge for peace, democracy, security, and human rights. Altogether, nowadays, the 27 Member States represent a heterogeneous combination of culture, languages, and history, united with the aim of providing better living conditions for the citizens thereof.

Economists are inexhaustibly inspired by the European Union in view of their research, analyses, and papers, given its transformative power on society and the economy. The theory of comparative advantages, the achievement of economies of scale, the theories of financial and economic integration, as well as those related to endogenous growth, are applicable in the case of the EU. Single market, fiscal and financial integration, institutional connectivity, and harmonization with the EU Acquis, and overall, roughly speaking—symbiosis with the more developed and advanced countries, contribute to growth acceleration and development of the economies becoming part of the Union.

2 EU: The Whole is Greater than the Sum of its Parts

There are many macroeconomic indicators pointing to the positive effect of the EU in pre- and post-accession period. Even in the pre-accession process itself, positive trends are observed in the countries (by isolating the effects from the economic cycle phases). EU membership, above all, involves accessing a market of more than half a billion consumers. The EU's economic power is also reflected in both the trade and the foreign direct investments, accounting for 16% of the total global trade. North Macedonia's membership in the EU will provide for access to a 25 times larger market, five times higher nominal GDP per capita, whereby real GDP per capita of our economy is around 41% of EU's GDP in 2023 measured by volume indices of GDP per capita (Table 1), as well as bring about significantly lower unemployment rate.

Table 1 shows that economic convergence is faster in the New Member States compared to the candidate countries of the Western Balkans. Since the largest wave

Table 1 Volume indices of GDP per capita (EU27 = 100)

GDP per capita (EU27 = 100)	Status	1995	2004	2014	2023	2004–1995	2014–2004	2023–2014	2023–2004	2023–1995
European Union	*Member*	*100.0*	*100.0*	*100.0*	*100.0*	–	–	–	–	–
Belgium	1958	126.0	124.0	121.0	118.0	–	–	–	–	–
France	1958	117.0	112.0	108.0	101.0	–	–	–	–	–
Germany	1958	133.0	122.0	127.0	115.0	–	–	–	–	–
Italy	1958	126.0	114.0	98.0	97.0	–	–	–	–	–
Luxembourg	1958	215.0	249.0	283.0	239.0	–	–	–	–	–
Netherlands	1958	132.0	138.0	133.0	130.0	–	–	–	–	–
Denmark	1973	128.0	127.0	129.0	127.0	–	–	–	–	–
Ireland	1973	107.0	149.0	138.0	211.0	–	–	–	–	–
Greece	1981	87.0	98.0	72.0	67.0	–	–	–	–	–
Portugal	1986	81.0	83.0	77.0	83.0	–	–	–	–	–
Spain	1986	92.0	101.0	90.0	88.0	–	–	–	–	–
Austria	1995	133.0	130.0	132.0	123.0	–	–	–	–	–
Finland	1995	110.0	120.0	113.0	108.0	–	–	–	–	–
Sweden	1995	130.0	130.0	126.0	114.0	–	–	–	–	–
New Member States	*Member*	*53.5*	*61.9*	*72.4*	*82.2*	*8.5*	*10.5*	*9.8*	*20.3*	*28.8*
Cyprus	2004	96.0	100.0	81.0	95.0	4.0	−19.0	14.0	−5.0	−1.0
Czechia	2004	78.0	81.0	88.0	91.0	3.0	7.0	3.0	10.0	13.0
Estonia	2004	36.0	56.0	78.0	81.0	20.0	22.0	3.0	25.0	45.0
Hungary	2004	52.0	63.0	69.0	76.0	11.0	6.0	7.0	13.0	24.0
Latvia	2004	31.0	47.0	64.0	71.0	16.0	17.0	7.0	24.0	40.0

(continued)

Table 1 (continued)

GDP per capita (EU27 = 100)	Status	1995	2004	2014	2023	2004–1995	2014–2004	2023–2014	2023–2004	2023–1995
Lithuania	2004	33.0	50.0	76.0	86.0	17.0	26.0	10.0	36.0	53.0
Malta	2004	79.0	83.0	93.0	105.0	4.0	10.0	12.0	22.0	26.0
Poland	2004	44.0	51.0	67.0	80.0	7.0	16.0	13.0	29.0	36.0
Slovakia	2004	49.0	59.0	78.0	73.0	10.0	19.0	−5.0	14.0	24.0
Slovenia	2004	77.0	88.0	83.0	91.0	11.0	−5.0	8.0	3.0	14.0
Bulgaria	2007	44.0	35.0	47.0	64.0	−9.0	12.0	17.0	29.0	20.0
Romania	2007	31.0	35.0	56.0	80.0	4.0	21.0	24.0	45.0	49.0
Croatia	2013	45.0	57.0	61.0	76.0	12.0	4.0	15.0	19.0	31.0
Western Balkans	*Candidate*	–	*27.3*	*36.0*	*41.8*	*4.3*	*7.2*	*5.8*	*13.0*	*17.7*
Albania	2014	–	21.0	30.0	35.0	7.0	9.0	5.0	14.0	21.0
Bosnia and Herzegovina[a]	2022	–	26.0[a]	30.0	35.0	–	4.0	5.0	9.0	–
Montenegro[a]	2010	–	36.0[a]	41.0	52.0	–	5.0	11.0	16.0	–
North Macedonia	2005	–	28.0	39.0	41.0	0.0	11.0	2.0	13.0	13.0
Serbia	2010	–	33.0	40.0	46.0	6.0	7.0	6.0	13.0	19.0
Kosovo[a]	–	–	–	–	–	–	–	–	–	–

Source: Eurostat (2024). Available at: https://ec.europa.eu/eurostat/databrowser/view/prc_ppp_ind__custom_12478059/default/table?lang=en
[a]Data for B&H from 2005 and MNG from 2006. Not available data for Kosovo

of EU enlargement of 2004 to 2023, the New Member States have increased their GDP per capita from 61.9 to 82.2 of the EU average GDP per capita reaching a progress of about 20.3 percentage points towards economic convergence. On the other side, countries from the Western Balkans compared to New Member States showed slower progress in convergence from 27.3 to 41.8 of the EU average GDP per capita, which represents a convergence of 13 percentage points. This is an indication that New Member States have benefited more from joining the EU compared to candidate countries from the Western Balkans, which also benefited from the EU accession process (4.3, 7.2, 5.8 percentage points convergence in the last three decades, respectively) but with slower pace than the New Member States.

According to Campos et al. (2014), the results obtained by applying series of data from the 1980s and 2004 enlargement data show an increase of the existing GDP per capita by 12%. There are a number of studies dedicated to assessing the economic benefits from the European Union, with one of them showing that GDP per capita of the EU would be one fifth lower if no integration had taken place since 1950 (Badinger 2005). Other studies show high effects of membership on the growth, also warning of the heterogeneity of the economies as a factor. Moreover, studies about the European Commission (In 't Veld 2009; Freeman et al. 2022), referring to the benefits of the EU single market which, unlike any other free trade agreement, is open to all sectors and individuals. According to the studies, it is assessed that EU gross domestic product would be 9% lower if no full integration of the single market had taken place, which, on average, is around EUR 840 less annual income per capita. Observed by individual Member State, this number varies, ranging from EUR 193 per capita in Bulgaria to EUR 2834 in Luxembourg. Accordingly, viewed from this perspective, each Member State is better off in the EU rather than being out of it, pointing out to the fact that EU creates a new value, i.e. a value added with positive externalities. As Aristotle would say "The Whole is Greater than the Sum of its Parts".

Making a comparative analysis between the Member States which most recently joined the EU and the Western Balkan countries, according to World Development Indicators (World Bank 2024a), the new Member States register higher growth, approaching the EU standard of living with a much faster pace than the Western Balkan countries. Higher labour productivity is also observed in the new Member States. New Member State also show a greater progress in institutional democracy and good governance—freedom of expression, political stability, regulatory quality, government effectiveness, as well as rule of law and control of corruption, compared with the Worldwide Governance Indicators (World Bank 2024b) and structural reforms progress during the accession and joining the EU (Besimi and Monasitrioits 2010).

3 The Economic Benefits of the European Integration

Higher living standards in new Member States speak in favour of the Union's transformative power. According to the existing body of empirical literature of long-time series of statistical data, the impact of EU on the economy is estimated at additional 12%–20% of GDP per capita. As per certain studies, the effects of the European Single Market on trade and GDP are estimated at approximately 10% of EU GDP on average (European Commission 2020, 2023c). The improved business climate and progress as regards the structural reforms have also been recorded among the new Member States. If briefly summarized, the following benefits stand out.

Trade Integration The Single Market is an area of free trade without tariff or non-tariff barriers among its members. As I mentioned above, it provides for instigating labour specialization, growth and convergence among the Member States. For instance, trade between old and new grew Member States grew almost threefold in less than 10 years preceding the 2004 and 2007 enlargements and fivefold among the new members themselves. The benefits apply to both the business sector in view of its boosted competitiveness, and the citizens given access to more available high-quality products and services with less costs. For example, Internet and telephones services across the EU have the same costs, as a result of the abolition of roaming charges. It is also worth mentioning the protection of consumers' rights, being at a high level in the Union.

Economies of Scale Through the Single Market with half a billion consumers, from a microeconomic point of view, it is much easier to achieve an economy of scale, thus entailing lower costs via greater production volume. Moreover, the EU is the largest trade bloc in the world, as well as the world's largest exporter of manufactured goods and services, and the biggest import market. The EU accounts for around 15% of the world's trade in goods. Thanks to the joint actions, the common trade strategy, it is highly positioned on the global trade stage, whereby the bilateral trade agreements provide for opening up new opportunities for Unions' businesses to enter new markets.

Single Currency and Free Movement The adoption of a single currency, as well as the abolition of internal borders within the Union, is in support of further facilitation of trade, and thus boosting economic growth and development of the separate economies. Over 340 million EU citizens use the euro, thus protecting them against the risk of currency fluctuation and exchange costs, while also contributing to a strengthened Single Market. Free movement applies both to businesses, which are protected against globalization risks through the EU Rules supporting small businesses, and people, who can educate, practice, volunteer, and work in the Union.

Financial Integration European integration also implies financial openness, coupled with greater capital account liberalization. Economic literature also refers to the "spillover" effect of foreign direct investments, resulting from the integration, thus entailing new investments, jobs, transfer of technology and knowledge, up until economic development as a whole. The 2004 enlargement demonstrates that the inflows of foreign direct investments from EU-15 to the new Member States accounted for 30% of GDP from the new Member States in the next 2 years (European Commission 2006).

Solidarity and Common Funds The European Union provides structural and investment funds for the new Member States, as well as development funds for the candidate countries through the Pre-Accession Funds (IPA). These funds play a significant role in the regional equal development, development of the infrastructure, and boosting of the economic growth.

Institutional integration Improvements as regards rule of law, political stability, regulatory quality, fight against corruption, accountability, effectiveness in the public sector and services—these are the benefits of transposing European supranational legislation into the national legislation. Progress in the pre-accession period has been particularly evident, with the reform intensive dynamics yielding outstanding results as regards the institutional capacity building.

The other benefits cover integrated approach in resolving some essential issues of global significance, such as environment protection and tackling climate change, coupled with the international diplomacy, where the voice of all the EU Member States has a significantly stronger resonance and prominence internationally than in case they act separately. This also applies to safety as well as human rights, also governed by the supranational legislation.

4 Non-Economic Benefits from Joining the EU

The European Union has always been primarily an economic alliance throughout history. Economic and social well-being has always been the reason for integration, ever since the European Coal and Steel Community. It is one of the economic superpowers, with a market of over half a billion consumers and linked solid global value chains. For small economies (like ours), just gaining access to new consumers in the European Single Market is quite promising in view of growth acceleration. Accordingly, we can easily conclude that the economic benefits therefrom are abundant and there are non-economic benefits as well.

As regards the economic benefits, initially we may stress the increased living standard as a positive impact of EU membership. The impact of the EU on the economy is estimated at an additional 12%–20% of GDP per capita. The effects of the European Single Market on trade and GDP are rated at approximately 10% of EU GDP on average. Improved business climate and progress as regards the structural reforms have also been recorded among the new Member States. Access to the European Funds, being available as we advance on our road to the EU, is yet another benefit. Total EU budget for the period 2021–2027 is estimated at around EUR 2000 billion as funds aimed at supporting diverse areas of interest for the Member States. The support that EU extended to our country during the past 30 years is estimated at over EUR 3.3 billion (via grants and macro-financial support).

When talking about the non-economic benefits from the EU membership, we could forthwith highlight the strengthening of democracy and good governance—freedom of expression, political stability, regulation quality, effectiveness of governance, rule of law, and corruption control. Moreover, many of the significant global issues in the EU are addressed in a coordinated manner, which is particularly significant for a small economy like ours. This is illustrated with climate change and soil and water pollution, whereby the coordinated approach provides for increasing the efficiency and effectiveness of the joint actions compared to the steps taken by each of the nation, separately. This also covers the joint fight against corruption, smuggling, and prevention of money laundering, followed by the cross-border exchange of information, geared towards protecting the rights of both the citizens and the consumers. The last and most important is the security the EU offers, particularly in times of global safety challenges posed by hybrid attacks and geostrategic turmoil, bringing plenty of uncertainties.

5 EU Pre-accession Assistance vs. EU Cohesion Funds

As the country approaches the Union, more Funds, both development and structural, are unlocked, available for usage thereby, which are complementary to sustainable development goals (Stojkov and Besimi 2024). Members, have at their disposal Funds that are multiply higher than those available to the candidate countries. I will hereby make a comparison between the Cohesion Fund and the EU IPA Pre-Accession Funds.

The Cohesion Fund provides support to EU Member States with a Gross National Income per capita below 90% of the EU-27 average. This Fund aims to support the economically less developed Member States, the ultimate goal of which is economic and social cohesion of the EU. The Cohesion Fund will be used for providing financial contributions in the fields of environment and trans-European networks in the area of transport infrastructure. In the period 2021–2027, the Cohesion Fund concerns Bulgaria, the Czech Republic, Estonia, Greece, Croatia, Cyprus, Latvia, Lithuania, Hungary, Malta, Poland, Portugal, Romania, Slovakia, and Slovenia or around 128 million inhabitants of the Union. In the period 2021–2027, EUR 392 million was made available thereto via this Fund, or as per the rough estimates, approximately EUR 3000 per capita at these countries (with total population of 128 million inhabitants).

During the same period, Pre-Accession Fund—IPA III (2021–2027) is made available to the candidates or the potential candidate countries, amounting to total of EUR 14.2 billion. The purpose of this Fund, based on the principle of solidarity, is to support the candidate countries in implementing the political, institutional, legal, administrative, social, and economic reforms, being required so as to get harmonized with the rules, standards, policies, and practices of the European Union, all to the end of further ensuring its stability, security, and prosperity. As per the approximate estimates, under IPA III, around EUR 140 per capita are provided for the citizens of Albania, Bosnia and Herzegovina, Kosovo, North Macedonia, Montenegro, Serbia, and Turkey (with a total population of 103 million inhabitants).

To sum up, the difference between the status as an EU candidate country and a Member State thereof is EUR 2868 per capita, i.e. 21.8 times more resources under the Funds (3006/138 = 21.8). This means that, as per the approximate calculations, the EU membership will generate an additional EUR 2868 per capita in the country, i.e., an additional EUR 5.2 billion in 5 years, equaling the amount of our 2023 State Budget. These funds will provide for improved infrastructure, better living conditions, more operating assets for our businesses, and a higher living standard for our workers. I would like to hereby stress that this is only an approximate estimate, whereby the benefits from the EU membership are multiple, covering plenty of areas as mentioned above. Costs are unquestionably incurred, pertaining to the production adaptation and the observance of the stringent environmental standards, which must inevitably be implemented in support of boosted competitiveness and resilience of our economy, striving to integrate into the European and the global value chain.

6 Why Europe Now?

Upon the outbreak of the war in Ukraine, there is growing focus on the fact that now is the right time for EU enlargement, as well as for the Western Balkans to get close to and access the Union (European Commission 2023a). After the European Parliament elections held in 2024, it is increasingly likely that further enlargement will be a top priority on the agenda. The statements and those who stand for further integration and EU enlargement are becoming increasingly prevalent.

In May 2023, the President of the European Commission, Ursula Von der Leyen, announced the new plan for getting Western Balkans closer to the European Union, as well as the economic support therefor. This plan may be perceived as a helping hand lent to the Western Balkans. As Ursula von der Leyen herself pointed out, "We do not only ask our partners to take new steps towards us. We also take a big step towards them. Our shared goal is to speed up their journey towards the EU". It is not necessary to read much between the lines for the clear message Von der Leyen conveyed to both the leaders and the citizens. This is unquestionably a great opportunity which should be taken advantage of, being also an encouraging sign given the specific background in view of divided opinions about joining the EU.

Due to the several overlapping global economic crises, we faced in the past 3 years, this is good news, and we should undoubtedly make the most thereof. We should begin by seizing the historical moment and take maximum advantage thereof, all to the end of implementing the necessary reforms and to bring "Europe home" even before we join the EU. This should be followed by realizing all the advantages and challenges, as well as by reaching a rational decision, which would bring benefits to our citizens, with a view to enjoying their presence, while willing to build their future in our country rather than outside of it.

The above may be considered as an affirmative reply to why "yes" and why "join" the EU right now. The debate is open, and we hope to contribute to this discussion, all to the end of making the best decision for a better today and even better tomorrow as part of Europe.

The European Union Is Not a Destination but Rather a Journey Democratic society, observance and protection of rights and rule of law, multi-ethnicity, multiculturalism, freedom of movement of goods, capital, and people, peace and security, development and prosperity are the common values that unite 450 million citizens in 27 countries in a single and pacifistic union, single market and economic superpower. However, EU membership is not a trophy at the end of the race, or as the EU Commissioner, Johannes Hahn, pointed out at the Skopje Economic and Financial Forum (SEFF 2023), "The EU is not a cash machine, an ATM, joining the Union is also joining common values". "Bringing Europe home before joining the EU" is the axiom arising therefrom, which remarkably captures the essence of the EU integration process—to take actions, while being guided by true values and goals, all to the end of creating a better future. Membership in the European Union is not our destination, but rather an approach to a "common journey" towards a better future, prosperity, and a higher living standard.

The Path to the EU Is the Only Way Forward Although the sentiment about joining the EU has varied throughout the years, the destination we are aiming for has remained the same over the past 30 years. Policy discussions should be geared towards accelerating the EU integration process, i.e. improving economic performance, the social conditions, providing an efficient legal system, and promoting regional cooperation and connectivity. The 3-year period that followed, i.e., several overlapping crises, was not a challenge that policy makers, companies, and citizens could neglect (Besimi 2024). Commitment to transparent, broad discussion and a holistic approach in the creation of new ideas and instructions about acting thereupon has become a necessity.

7 Development Synergy via European Integration and Regional Connectivity

The very concept of the EU is synergy, i.e. improved economic performance via integration. Although the reader is already familiar with the commitment to connecting the Western Balkan countries with the purpose of enjoying the benefits of the four EU freedoms by the region, we will try to explain hereby further, as vividly as possible, the reason why this is crucial on our road to the EU, i.e. in building a better life for our citizens.

Economic Benefits As per the World Bank assessments, intra-regional trade in the Western Balkans is estimated at around 20% of the total trade in 2019, thus highlighting the room for regional trade growth. Simplifying the cross-border procedures leads to lowering the trade-related costs. The World Bank estimated that the costs for cross-border trade in the Western Balkans are relatively high, whereby approximately 17 h are needed for export. As the World Bank Country Director for the Western Balkans pointed out, by cutting the time period by 3 h, the customs tariff rates are reduced by 2 percentage points. Furthermore, a more integrated regional market may attract more foreign investments, as evident from the example with Europe; a larger market actually attracts more investors.

Infrastructure Development Regional connectivity and ties are the bloodstream of infrastructure development. Efficient transport connections, energy, and digital networks across the region provide for a smooth flow of goods, services, and ideas. The regional corridors exactly provide for adding value to the national economies via investments, trade, transport, tourism and strengthened geostrategic positions of the countries.

Free Movement of People Facilitating the travel of citizens in the region contributes to encouraging tourism and travel in general. Prior to the pandemic, the World Tourism Organization (UNWTO) recorded 18 million tourist arrivals in the Western Balkan countries. Facilitating the free movement provides for an increased number of tourist arrivals. Moreover, the procedures related to study visits and the opportunity to exchange experience, training, and education in the region, are also simplified.

Increased Resilience of the Economies to External Shocks Regional connectivity and ties, infrastructure development, diversification of trade partners, and near-shoring may contribute to strengthening the resilience of certain economies against further potential global shocks, all this being coupled with energy safety.

Regional Stability Regional cooperation is particularly significant in maintaining regional stability, considering that the higher level of cooperation reduces the conflicts, all to the end of protecting the economic activities. In addition, regional cooperation is encouraged by the EU, given that the connectivity and the ties are specifically the primary goal of the EU. The first two of the four pillars of the new EU plan on growth of the Western Balkans pertain to the regional and the EU connectivity and ties. As the European Commission President announced, the Western Balkan countries will be given the possibility to reap, much earlier, the benefits from the main driver of the EU economic growth—the Single Market, most probably through a broader segment thereof, as the means of trade in goods and services via digital channels.

Politicians should always put things in perspective. Thus, the benefits of connecting people, companies, and economies in the region should be at the top of the agenda.

8 Structural Reforms for Accelerating the Convergence Towards the EU

Next process, which will contribute to strengthening the Western Balkan economies, as well as accelerating the convergence towards the EU, covers the implementation of structural reforms in support of boosted economic growth, greater competitiveness, opening new businesses, and job creation (Besimi and Monasitrioits 2010). *Rule of Law, Corruption Prevention, and Public Administration* are part of these reforms, by implementing measures focused on combatting corruption, judiciary reforms, and public administration.

Human capital reforms equally play the pivotal role therein. As per the latest data on the Human Capital Index, calculated by the World Bank, the average in 2021 for the Western Balkan countries is 0.57 (the index ranges from 0 to 1). This means that children who are born now will only exploit 57% of their potential when they reach adulthood, as a result of the education, the health and the social care system their country provides. Although Republic of North Macedonia has the highest HCI in the region (0.59), there is still much room for improvements, considering that the value of this Index in the development economies ranges above 0.7. Our government strives, by allocating substantial budget funds, as well as by implementing qualitative reforms, to contribute to continuous improvement of this Index. In addition to the human capital investments, matching the skills produced by the workforce with the labour market needs is also of crucial importance. Investing in the educational process, training for workers meeting the market needs, while also implementing reforms that will balance job security and market flexibility, will provide significant support for the economy and the business adaptation to changes. Introduction of continuous learning also contributes to improving the quality and relevance of education. Support of science and research, by encouraging the synergy between the science and the private sector, plays a part in strengthening innovation and entrepreneurship in the private sector.

I mentioned the significance of *infrastructure development* above; however, touching upon the structural reforms is also inevitable. Development of transport and energy infrastructure will boost the investment process, improve connectivity and ties and trade, and thus stimulate economic development.

The competitive private sector is of vital significance for economic growth. Investments and entrepreneurship are stimulated through continuous easing of regulations for doing business, their simplification and reduction of bureaucracy. Undertaking activities aimed at increasing access to finance for small- and medium-sized enterprises, via development of financial markets and support mechanisms, is extremely significant.

Environment Sustainability becomes increasingly important for long-term and sustainable development. Structural reforms should be focused on strengthening environmental regulations and sustainability in the field of energy, agriculture, and production. Furthermore, it is necessary to scale up investments in renewable energy sources, all to the end of reducing carbon dioxide emissions and increasing energy safety.

9 Geopolitical Background: Best Timing for the Western Balkans

The current geopolitical background brings both challenges and possibilities for the Western Balkan countries. Outbreak of the armed conflict in Ukraine implied high inflation and increased trade deficit for the open and the energy-dependent Western Balkan economies, whereby, on the other hand, the need to continue the European integration process with Western Balkans as an integral part thereof, became the obvious path. The best timing for EU enlargement has been highlighted in the analyses of all renowned agencies, think tanks, as well as by EU officials. A new European Commission Growth Plan for the Western Balkans is also aimed thereon (European Commission 2023b). The need to consolidate Europe with the Western Balkans as an integral part thereof is evident. Hence, the development processes, as well as the political process should wisely take advantage of the geopolitical background since it is uncertain whether such an opportunity will arise again.

Finally, we must recognize the European path as the road to progress. Boosted competitiveness by exploiting the benefits of digitalization, investing in sustainable, renewable energy sources, investing in human capital are opportunities that have been mapped by the business community to accelerate economic development. Informal economy in Western Balkan countries, as well as the migrations and the needs on the labour market, are the challenges we should still overcome.

References

Badinger H (2005) Growth effects of economic integration: evidence from the EU member states. Rev World Econ 141:50–78

Besimi F (2024) Economy and integration in times of polycrisis. Besimi F, Skopje

Besimi F, Monasitrioits V (2010) The role of EU integration in accelerating structural reforms in the Western Balkans: evidence, theory and policy. In: LEQS Paper No. 140/2019. London School of Economics and Political Science

Campos N, Coricelli F, Moretti L (2014) Economic growth and political integration: estimating the benefits from membership in the European Union using the synthetic counterfactuals method. Econ Papers No. 8162. Available at: https://EconPapers.repec.org/RePEc:hal:wpaper:hal-01267266. Accessed Aug 2024

European Commission (2006) Enlargement, two years after - an economic success. COM.2006:200. Available at: https://eur-lex.europa.eu/EN/legal-content/summary/enlargement-strategy-2006-2007-challenges-and-integration-capacity.html. Accessed Aug 2024

European Commission (2020) A European industrial strategy: a single market that delivers for businesses and consumers. Available at: https://ec.europa.eu/commission/presscorner/api/files/attachment/863068/EU_single_market_strategy_en.pdf. Accessed Aug 2024

European Commission (2023a) Communication on EU Enlargement Policy. Brussels: COM.2023:690. Available at: https://neighbourhood-enlargement.ec.europa.eu/document/download/cc71d42b-6c07-4deb-9069-5ca2082d166d_en?filename=COM_2023_690%20Communication%20on%20EU%20Enlargement%20Policy_and_Annex.pdf. Accessed Aug 2024

European Commission (2023b) New growth plan for the Western Balkans. Brussels: COM.2023:691. Available at: https://neighbourhood-enlargement.ec.europa.eu/document/

download/8f5dbe63-e951-4180-9c32-298cae022d03_en?filename=COM_2023_691_New%20Growth%20Plan%20Western%20Balkans.pdf. Accessed Aug 2024
European Commission (2023c) The Single Market at 30. Brussels: COM.2023:162. Available at: https://eur-lex.europa.eu/legal-content/EN/TXT/?uri=CELEX%3A52023DC0162. Accessed Aug 2024
Eurostat (2024) GDP per capita, consumption per capita and price level indices. Available at: https://ec.europa.eu/eurostat/statistics-explained/index.php?title=GDP_per_capita,_consumption_per_capita_and_price_level_indices#Relative_volumes_of_GDP_per_capita. Accessed Aug 2024
Freeman D, Meijerink G, Teulings R (2022) Trade benefits of the EU and the Internal Market. CPB Netherlands: Bureau for Economic Policy Analysis. Available at: https://www.cpb.nl/sites/default/files/omnidownload/CPB-Communication-Trade-benefits-of-the-EU-and-the-Internal-Market.pdf
In 't Veld J (2009) The economic benefits of the EU Single Market in goods and services. J Policy Model 41(5):803–818
SEFF (2023) European integration and economic prosperity. In: Conference Europe yes, Europe now. Skopje Economic and Finance Forum, Skopje
Stojkov A, Besimi F (2024) Maximizing finance for sustainable development goals. In: The sustainable development goals - how to accelerate their achievement in North Macedonia and leave no one behind. United Nations Development Programme, Skopje, pp 11–20
World Bank (2024a) World development indicators. Available at: https://data.worldbank.org/indicator/NY.GDP.MKTP.CD?locations=EU. Accessed Aug 2024
World Bank (2024b) World governance indicators. Available at: https://www.worldbank.org/en/publication/worldwide-governance-indicators/interactive-data-access. Accessed Aug 2024

Montenegro 2.0: The European Vision of Montenegro

Ivan Jovetić, Ivana Vojinović, Milica Vukotić, and Sandra Tinaj

Abstract

Political stability is inevitable for economic growth and development regardless of the EU accession. It must be followed by the economic freedom concept in order to achieve the full potential. In case of Montenegro, the concepts of micro-state, its hybrid version as well as green transition based on economic freedom are the key pillars. It also enables quite efficient and effective institutional branding if executed properly. Future perspectives of Montenegro-EU relations must include full membership till 2030 (based primarily on the geopolitical changes) the latest, stable state institutions, applied rule of law, full structural funds access, investments' attractiveness, full foreign policy compliance, full environmental protection compliance, positioning itself as the regional economy hub (including down thresholds for any joint interval or decision among member states or divided jurisdiction), SME's access to the market and funding sources, diversification of the economy, and company's ability to cope with the single market pressure. In order to achieve the aforementioned, the following has to be achieved: (1) political stability, (2) economic freedom, (3) secure country, (4) environment friendly design, (5) efficient educational system, (6) effective rule of law, (7) entrepreneurial culture, and (8) Montenegro as the EU member state. Existence of functional and efficient institutions based on market economy principles, functional education system, and implemented EU negotiation process criteria based on the vision of micro and green Montenegro are the (pre)condition for making the respective viable at all.

I. Jovetić (✉) · I. Vojinović · M. Vukotić · S. Tinaj
University of Donja Gorica, Podgorica, Montenegro
e-mail: ivan.jovetic@udg.edu.me

A. Stojkov, T. Warin (eds.), *Western Balkans and the Future of Europe*, The Future of Europe, https://doi.org/10.1007/978-3-031-86465-0_9

Keywords

Political (in)stability · Economic freedom · Development · Micro-state · Green transition · Vision · The EU · Montenegro

1 Introduction

The history of civilizations as well as the history of nations is a history of continuous wars, clashes, and fight against hunger. It can also be said in more modern terms it is a *fight for development and growth, for creation and accumulation of wealth.* This has been claimed by many prominent authors. Benjamin (2009) believes that every feature of civilization has a barbaric side at the same time. Morin (2006) also considers that civilization and barbarism are two parallel and intertwined processes and confirms the initial premise. Bouthoul (1962) claims that "the history of large societies is the history of continuous wars". Following the core idea, Vukotić (2011) believes that history of civilizations is the history of fight against hunger.

The history of Montenegro is precisely described by the respective ideas and quotes even if it is completely unintentional. Organized and internationally recognized "state" system in Montenegro occurs in 1077 in the form of the Kingdom of Doclea, continues with the Zeta in the fourteenth century and Montenegro in the fifteenth century. Regardless of the form and name of the organized system in Montenegro from the eleventh to the twentieth century, its history has been shaped by numerous wars and conflicted interests of the great powers in the Balkan or Adriatic area. Yugoslav era from 1945 to 1991 has been an era of peace and relative growth and development. Post-Yugoslav era has also been defined by UN sanctions, wars, soft borders, different values set, and other forms of preventing the stable society creation. In that period, "fight against hunger" has been also seen in the form of introducing Deutsche mark as the legal tender as well as other consequential forms of economic sovereignty. The process that finally led to the political sovereignty in 2006. The post-independence period has been the period of economic growth in capital market, real estate market, FDI inflow and it seems still as the period of remarkable economic results. In 2012, the EU accession path has been started while in 2017 the country joined the NATO. However, certain and important changes in the institutional setup as well as values setup have either not been undertaken or lacked significantly. Respective—alongside particular interests of great powers and their representatives—has resulted in the period of instability. Luckily, not only the period of peace (even though certain strong civic and political citizens' riots have happened) but also the period of decreased economic development and indeed unstable political institutions. The key question is what is required to be achieved and done in order to reach the European reality of Montenegro (the *why* question) and what it takes to be done in order to indeed get there (the *how* question).

2 The Two Important Questions?

The *why* question has two intertwined angles. First, which is also the core hypothesis of the paper is importance of *existence of the functional and efficient institutions, existence of the free-market economy principles, functional education system, and implemented EU negotiation process criteria in many important areas such as environment protection*. These are the (pre)conditions of creating Montenegro a stable, prosperous, and investment attractive destination. Second, the *why* question is not important because *of* or *for* the state, its institutions and acting political parties. It is mainly related to the sovereign individual(s) which are the core base of any society, any economy, any market exchange as well as any integration process. Later has to be an anthem for each acting individual regardless of his/her political and economic view. The process is indeed for him/her. But the *how* question and consequentially the answer(s) to it are the demanding part of equitation.

Future perspectives of Montenegro-EU relations must include full membership, until 2030 the latest primarily based on geopolitical changes and importance of stability, stable and functional state institutions, applied rule of law, full structural funds access, investments' attractiveness, full foreign policy compliance, full environmental protection compliance, positioning itself as the regional economy hub (including down thresholds for any joint interval or decision among member states or divided jurisdiction), SMEs' access to the market and funding sources, diversification of the economy, and company's ability to cope with the single market pressure.

To achieve the aforementioned, the following has to be achieved: (1) political stability, (2) economic freedom, (3) secure country, (4) environment friendly design, (5) efficient educational system, (6) effective rule of law, (7) entrepreneurial culture, and (8) Montenegro as the EU member state.

Redesign of the system might look feasible and easy. However, one of the paper's points is that such process will be significantly demanding.

2.1 Political (In)stability?

Political stability is one of the two main and necessary preconditions for creation of successful, peaceful, and prosperous society. It goes in line with the security of the state or the system. Political stability is usually interpreted as the ability of government institutions to secure previously described and targeted goals as well as predictable political environment. One of the democracy's prescribed elements is electoral change of the political majority. Montenegro has witnessed political stability since the independence which directly led to the increase of the FDI inflow, increase of GDP and GDP per capita, economic growth, but also NATO membership and the EU candidate country status with started negotiations. In the respective period, there were issues to be (re)solved and many different challenges arose from the transition process. Crucial remark in the democracy and lack of stability context have been dominance of one party or one coalition for three decades. Without any attempt to defend or attack any political party it seems that such an outcome has been the result of the electoral processes. In 2020, the very same process led to new political majority. Political transition in Montenegro has been smooth and stable at first. However, that has led to severe turmoil in this 3-year period. If Montenegro has had the "same" government for three decades while in a bit more than 3 years, it changed three different governments while entering the phase of political instability. This instability and many of its policies impacted the economic instability and induced inflation even regardless of the external shocks related to the supply-chains issues, invasion on Ukraine, energy sector challenges, etc. In this regard, it is inevitable that Montenegro has predictable political environment fully aligned with the foreign and security policy of the EU as well as in line with the EU rule of law and defined standards. Moreover, in the respective period, government signed Basic Treaty with the Serbian Orthodox Church (SPC) by which it probably violated Montenegrin Constitution in numerous aspects and gave to it jurisdictions and prerogatives even above the one it has in Serbia as its country of origin. Transfer of Montenegrin cultural heritage can and should be seen as the potential criminal offence and be part of prosecuting processes in case of justified doubt. The EU did not intervene or objected at all even though: (1) it is probably against the legislation which Montenegro is supposed to adopt in the negotiation process and (2) the European Parliament adoption the resolution regarding the role of SPC in the Western Balkan's political arena.

Political (in)stability can also be measured by different more objective indicators as well as standards' sets and referent sources. According to the Global Economy report which ranks 200 countries worldwide based on the World Bank data, Montenegro has had different positions per annum (Table 1). Observing the data from the independence, i.e., 2006 we can see the following situation for Montenegro.

It can be observed from both the table and the graph that negative rank happened in 2017 for the first time since measuring Montenegro as the independent country (Fig. 1). In the next two consecutive years, Montenegro has improved it rank. However, since 2020 for the two consecutive years it has negative rank which even worsened twice in 2021 compared to 2020 but also its tripled worsened than the 2017. First negative consecutive years' row and rank's significant worsening are the signs of continuous political instability in the country.

Political stability alongside security is the key denominator of potential economic stability and prosperity creation. This has to be especially valid in the region historically known for its instability. Western Balkan has been crossroads of civilizations and clashes. Observing only the twentieth century, it can be seen that the Western Balkan zone has been affected by the 11 armed conflicts in the 1912–1999 period: (1) First Balkan war, (2) Second Balkan war, (3) First World War, (4) guerilla war in Montenegro after its annexation by Serbia in 1918, (5) Second World War, (6) war in Slovenia after dissolution of SFRJ, (7) war and civil war in Croatia, (8) war and civil war in Bosnia and Herzegovina, (9) war in Kosovo, (10) armed conflict and civil war in North Macedonia, and (11) NATO intervention in SRJ in 1999. Jovetić (2021) has shown that security is an economic resource per se. In the past 87 years, the respective region witnessed 11 different armed conflicts, i.e. an armed conflict almost every 9 years. The

Table 1 Ranking of political stability in Montenegro

Year	Score	Rank	Comments
2006	0.05	95	n/a
2007	0.11	97	n/a
2008	0.77	50	Better ranked than Croatia, Estonia, USA, Italy, France, Hungary, Lithuania, and Cyprus
2009	0.82	45	Better ranked than Portugal, Lithuania, Croatia, Estonia, Hungary, France, and USA
2010	0.58	63	Better ranked than Latvia, USA, UK, Italy, Cyprus, Bulgaria, and Romania
2011	0.57	64	Better ranked than the UK, Latvia, Bulgaria, and Spain
2012	0.60	63	Better ranked than France, Italy, Latvia, UK, and Bulgaria
2013	0.50	64	Better ranked than the UK, France, Bulgaria, Romania, Albania, and Spain
2014	0.22	81	Better ranked than Serbia and Bulgaria but worse than N. Macedonia, Albania, and Croatia
2015	0.14	85	Better ranked than France and Bulgaria but worse than Serbia, Albania, Italy, and Romania
2016	0.28	79	Better ranked than Romania, Serbia, and Bulgaria but worse than Albania, Croatia, and Latvia
2017	−0.05	105	First time ever negative score
2018	0.04	92	Better ranked than France, Serbia, and N. Macedonia but worse than Bulgaria, Romania, and Italy
2019	0.07	88	Better ranked than Serbia and N. Macedonia but worse than Albania, Bulgaria, and Romania
2020	−0.06	95	Second negative score behind the whole region except Serbia
2021	−0.15	105	The worst score ever; behind the region except Bosnia as well Moldova and Belarus

Source: World Bank, The Global Economy Report, 2023

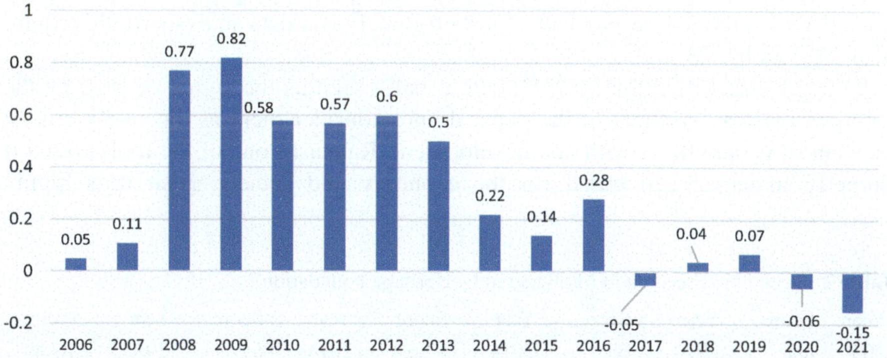

Fig. 1 Overview of political stability in Montenegro, 2006–2021. Source: World Bank, The Global Economy, 2023

question is how to create stable and prosperous society in the realm of armed conflicts. However, the preceding question is whether political instability led to armed conflicts. It seems indeed both theoretically and in practice that terrorism, (un)conventional war, and any armed conflict form are outcomes of political decisions and political instability. Therefore, political stability and security remain the corner elements of economic, social, and every other growth and development.

2.2 Economic Context, Growth, and Freedom

Besides political stability measurement, one of the key indicators refers to the economic freedom. The reason is quite simple—the freer the country economically is the higher is the individual rather than collective is but also overall stability. The two most prominent sources of economic freedom measurement are the Heritage Foundation and the Fraser Institute (Table 2).

According to the Heritage Foundation, Montenegro has been ranked similarly from 2010 to 2018 while the starting 2008 position has been lower and marked the country as less free in the moderately free group of countries. The positive exceptions were 2015, 2016, and 2018 in which Montenegro had the best ever score above 64 and close to 65. In 2019, there has been certain decline which relatively has been better performed in 2020. However, 2022 has been the worst score since the measuring started. The respective result has been slightly improved in 2023. Nevertheless, Montenegro remains 38th economically free country out of 44 European countries. In addition, lowered sub-elements of the overall score which decreased in 2023 were related to the property rights, judicial effectiveness, labour freedom, and monetary freedom. The respective is mainly highly correlated with political instability and lack of reforms. According to the Fraser, Montenegro in 2021 as the last available result per year ranked as 32nd with 7.59 score where the worst sub-results have been size of the government and legal system and property rights in which globally ranked 89th and 62nd, respectively. Furthermore, Fraser data analysis would require also 2022 and 2023.

Foreign direct investments (FDI) are usually seen as the signal of trust by the foreign investors. Authors of the paper do not consider them as the solely crucial element of economic growth and development. Rather as one of the tools which if properly managed can transform the economy and society. Also it is highly

Table 2 Economic Freedom in Montenegro by Heritage Foundation

Year	Score	Year	Score	Year	Score	Year	Score	Year	Score
2006	n/a	2010	63.6	2014	63.6	2018	64.3	2022	57.8
2007	n/a	2011	62.5	2015	64.7	2019	60.5	2023	60.9
2008	n/a	2012	62.5	2016	64.9	2020	61.5		
2009	58.2	2013	62.6	2017	62	2021	63.4		

Source: The Heritage Foundation (2023)

desirable to have a rise of the domestic entrepreneurial class and investments from numerous reasons. Among the most important ones is genuine growth and development of, in particular, small- and medium-sized firms and startups as well as locally established corporations. Their potential impact on country's economy is exceptional. Nevertheless, existence and rise of FDI are beneficial for growth and development but also are signs of political stability. Since its independence, Montenegro has become an interesting destination for FDI but also for portfolio investments. Its success in early days from 2006 to 2009 can prove that especially in the capital market and real estate sectors.

In 2019, net FDI has been almost 4% higher compared to 2018 which has been continuous trend of the net FDI inflow increase according to the Central Bank's data. Overall FDI inflow has had 4.6% decrease compared to 2018 with the total amount of 712.8 million of euros. The reason for such scenario had been decrease of equity investments for almost 21%. This is in particular important, having in mind that equity investments have amounted to 32.4% of total FDI inflow. Real estate investments amounted to 156.7 million euros or 21.9%. In 2020 as the Covid-19-year, overall FDI inflow decreased by 17.1% as the result of equity investments decrease. The later amounted almost 60% of overall inflow while the real estate investments amounted 16.4% of the overall inflow. In 2021, there has been increase of the overall FDI inflow to 764 million euros or 29.2% growth compared to 2020. In the respective year, there has been strong increase in real estate investments of 154%. And in the structure of FDI inflow investments in companies and banks were almost the same with the real estate investments, amounting to 35% and 32.2%, respectively. In 2022, there has been also an increase in overall FDI inflow for 36.69%. In the respective period, real investments supersede the companies and banks investments amounting each 39.29% and 34.43%, respectively. In January–July 2023, overall FDI inflow has decreased for 22% while the net FDI inflow has decreased for 40.6%. In the respective period, investments into the companies and banks failed for almost 47% while the real estate investments increased for a bit above 9%. In the FDI inflow structure, real estate investments significantly overpass the investments into the companies and banks, and each were 50.4% and 32.4%, respectively. The later proves the economic instability argument as the SME/corporate capital reacts on the first signs of (in)stability. Increase in real estate investments is directly positively correlated to the situation in Ukraine and open borders Montenegro induced.

The classical economic theory suggests that minimum wages increase not only leads to unemployment, but also hurts the ones it claims or supposes to help. In addition, it hurts the entire society which for sure happened in Montenegro. One of the key issues is the introduction of the minimum wage without any meaningful resonance with the business community. Such negotiations can be challenging—but have to be done—to achieve a sustainable level. Otherwise, the key outcome must be the rise of inflation which precisely happened in Montenegro. Despite the fact that certain inflation factors have been induced by the global shocks, the researchers identifies that the size and scope of the inflation in Montenegro have some additional causes. The increase of minimum wage for 200% is an internal shock and must result in increased cost prices and therefore an increase of the sales prices. Some of the projections inputs that internal shock as well as external shock have the same value of impact on the overall inflation. The model of such increase has not been technological advancement or productivity increase or any other acceptable form of wage increase. On the contrary, it has been restructuring of the health care contributions, i.e. their demise. They have been replaced by the central government funding which consequentially led to higher government consumption or at least worsening of its already inadequate structure. (Un)employment effects are yet to be seen especially as Montenegro has a shortage of employable individuals in certain sectors at least. However, each arbitrary administrative decision has such (un) intended consequences. Also, it provides economic (un)stable conditions and in certain manner decreases political and economic trust in the system.

Economic instability is still in the progress unfortunately. Potential successor of the minimum wage increase programme labelled "Europe Now 1" is supposed to be labelled as "Europe Now 2". However, this attempt of an additional minimum wage increases for announced almost 156% is even more dangerous. According to the speculations, there are two sources of such process funding: (1) demise of the pension fund contributions and (2) IPO of the EPCG (state owned energy company) at the London Stock Exchange. The later as the form of (second and major) privatization would be seriously welcomed due to significant form of political capitalism and cronyism there. However, privatization for the sake of the government's consumption has always had terrible consequences. The first is perhaps even worse. However, it is more likely to happen. Current pension fund situation is inadequate, as the pay-as-you-go system has a tremendous monthly gap for pensions funding. Calculations of the announced "Europe Now 2" programme are inclining towards the first scenario taking the account level of increase and its ratio with the pension contributions. Demise of respective contributions would make situation even worse. These are (un)intended consequences of never-ended pension system reform and lack of political will.

3 Institutional Branding: Micro & Green

The core meaning of the institutional (country's) branding is to become more attractive, economically, and socially friendly. There are many country branding examples. Personal affective always relates to the Ireland which had labelled itself as the e-heart of Europe as well as the transatlantic gate to the EU. The branding fostered FDI inflow and tremendous economic and social change of Ireland. Estonia, on the other hand, labelled itself as the e-country enabling tremendous e-services to its residents but also foreigners. In both cases, respective labelling has been followed by economic freedoms whose predecessor was political stability as well as security.

What Montenegro did or could have done? First, Montenegrin labelling attempt has been unique, eco-friendly before the eco-friendly and environmental protection concepts and it has been an exceptional "selling" point. In 1991, it became the first-ever proclaimed ecological state in the world. Moreover, in 1992, the respective concept and project have been presented to the UN. In 1991, Montenegro had decided to fight against the ecological challenges of the twentieth and twenty-first centuries. Respective idea has been created and promoted by Professor Dragan Hajdukovic, a well-known scientist. Besides its nobility, respective idea had great practical benefits. Unfortunately, none of them has ever been achieved due to inexistence of concepts' implementation. Today even during our EU negotiations, we are witnessing the importance of the Chap. 27 which is a form of executed Montenegro ecological state concept. It also proves vision professor Hajdukovic had.

Ten years after, the new institutional label arises. Montenegro as the micro-state concept created and presented by Professor Veselin Vukotić, well-known economist and reformist had arisen (Vukotić 2002). It has been aligned to ecological state concept but comprehended more sectors and areas including the change of the political system from Parliamentary to Presidential. It seems that failing to do so has been the biggest Montenegrin obstacle in the twenty-first century either because of the elements of representative democracy or lack of responsibility and courage. Respective issues including economic, social, ecological, and security context also show tremendous vision professor Vukotić had. Moreover, its practical usage has been proven by the result of the official policies based on 2006 Agenda of Economic Reform which has been fundamentally based and leveraged on the micro-state concept. Rejection of its successor (Rejected) Agenda of Economic Reforms 2007–2011 and achievement of less favourable results are also in favour of the respective vision and concept.

An important question is what the opposite of micro-state concept is. It seems it is a kind of a welfare state, state of the so-called social justice, state of large political capitalism, state of large public tender's-based businesses, and state of macro consequences. Political elites are inclining towards higher public employment as it provides (potentially) new and stable votes for consequential elections. High central and local government employment, redistribution management, crony usage of public funds as well as endangered democracy are the opposite of the micro-state concept. Political opposition in case of Montenegro has been accusing the political position for decades. Many intellectuals believed them. They had beliefs they would change and make some changes when they reach the power. And intellectuals were both, right and wrong. Right—as the new political elites are exercising more of political capitalism and cronyism. Wrong—they did not change the system rather their public statements. This can be proven with statistical data regarding new employment in the public companies and institutions but also with drafted idea about the new government—in order to reach the political consensus about government formation it is (probably) necessary to increase the number of ministries and consequently deputy ministers, chief of staff, advisors, etc. The democratic question would be—Did anyone asked the individual(s) regarding it?

3.1 Micro and Hybrid: Is It Possible?

Technological development ever since has been changing the economy, economic relations, society as well as social relations. Current technological changes are no exception at all. One of the new technologies which can have potentially strong impact is distributed ledger technology, i.e. blockchain. In a certain form, blockchain represents intersection between economy, technology, and society. In its essence, blockchain can provide new opportunities for achieving of the more comprehensive economic and social causes. Slightly contradictory, blockchain is in the same time both: (1) continuation of the digitalization process which has begun in the mid of twentieth century and (2) conceptual and contextual renunciation of it. The reason of the latter is its structure as well as almost completely redefined (business) processes design and implementation. Moreover, it also provides completely different ratio towards data and their tracking and recording but also strengthens the position of the user(s) becoming the "global decentralized source of trust". Blockchain positively impacts the transparency, fight against corruption as well as is positively correlated with the responsible public consumption and public finance control concepts. Implemented properly alongside the *smart contracts* concept, it can transform public governance in Montenegro. In addition, it can tackle the European integration's goal, i.e. reform of the public governance, transparency increase, and potential corruption decrease. Moreover, it can help create the new version of the micro-state concept which can be labelled as the *diffused micro-state* concept. The micro-state concept has been based on efficiency, centralization of the individual(s) role, small and limited but powerful governance, institutional trust, positioning of the state solely as the arbiter, decreased political arbitration, increased safety and security of individual(s), and rise of entrepreneurial vs. political capitalism. It seems indeed that blockchain as the distributed ledger technology can precisely enable all of that. The 2003 concept of professor Vukotić was supposed to be a form of Kuhnian structural revolution. Even though it has not been possible to identify potential technological changes of 2019 or 2023, there are some similarities: (1) form and design of the economy has been changing in 2003 but is also changing in 2023; (2) new ideas cannot be implemented on the pillars of former social order (either it is transition or technological development); (3) political (in) stability existed in 2003 while also exists in 2023, and (4) certain instabilities can create fertile ground for new solutions. *Diffused micro-state* can be based on citizens' wallet, i.e. an Internet of Things (IoT) device based on distributed ledger technology.[1] The IoT device would comprehend direct communication and all-owner-related and publicly available ledgers. Respective date would be kept in the cloud and assessed through electronic ID and several authentication levels. The respective can validate each element of the micro-state concept.

The key principles of the micro-state concept are: (1) practicality, i.e. efficiency of services provisions which are result steered; (2) rationality, i.e. price cost of

[1]The idea is a semi-product of severe and indepth discussions with Rob van Kronenburg including his vision of the concept during the Milocer Development 2017.

administration which individual(s) can and should bear; (3) direct access, i.e. transaction costs decrease through direct communication with individual(s); (4) internationalization of business and doing business, i.e. ability to communicate with the surroundings; (5) transparency and openness, i.e. disabling any private relations and discretionary power; (6) anticorruption, i.e. decreasing the possibility of usage of public function in a private context; and (7) professionalism, i.e. creating the more professional attitudes vs. political obedience. Similarity between micro-state concept and blockchain application is tremendous. However, it has to be noted that micro-state concept is wider and more meaningful than blockchain's applications and that it represents philosophical concept while blockchain is its technical application.

3.2 Green Transition Perspectives?

In contrast to previous EU candidate countries, Montenegro conducts part of the negotiation process with the EU in conditions of global disruptions caused by the consequences of Covid-19 pandemic, energy crisis, potential food shortages, geopolitical challenges, and security risks brought about by the war in Ukraine. As far as the implementation of the EU legislation in the field of environment and climate change is concerned, it will bring Montenegro both costs and benefits. This economic aspect is surely the most important factor that should be considered in decision-making process. The costs are enormous (e.g. in wastewater treatment and waste management facilities, remediation of industrial and air pollution, etc.), and, in Montenegro, they still have treatment of "externality", because there is no understanding of the need for their inclusion/internalization into the macroeconomic projections and strategic planning. It is wrongly understood that environmental investments are exclusively a "cost" that Montenegrin taxpayers and businesses should pay. On the contrary, when put into the context of the inevitable environmental and climatic transformation that Montenegro needs to achieve at the latest by 2050, they are seen as investments with long-term potential that can make Montenegrin economy more resilient to future shocks and bring enormous benefits to the society. Put differently, environmental investments, in addition to environmental benefits for ecosystems and resources, should lead Montenegro to reap the benefits that are not directly related to the environment. These are health benefits, such as the improvements in public health and quality of life, and socio-economic benefits that go beyond direct economic exploitation, including local development (e.g. tourism benefits from clean beaches and constructed infrastructure) and attraction of investment, leading to the increased employment, higher productivity of companies as a result of modern technologies with lower emissions, development of new and existing sectors of the economy, as well as effects on the balance of payments and trade (reduced import of raw materials due to reuse and recycling of materials). In addition, by integrating the goals from the European Green Deal (EGD) and the Green Agenda for the Western Balkans (GAWB), the benefits are expected to be maximized and full potential of the green transition in Montenegro

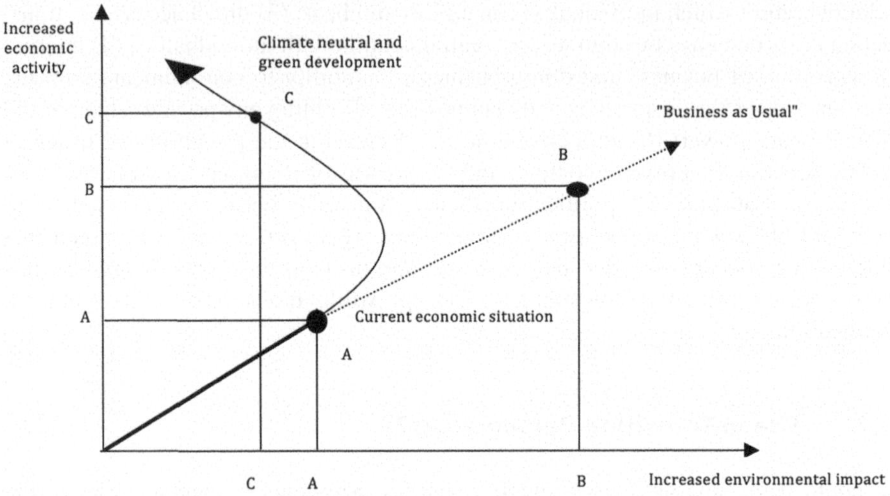

Fig. 2 Alternative models of environmental economic development in Montenegro. Source: ECOTEC (2001)

realized. This represents an argument for the realization of a series of investment activities in this area that could contribute to real GDP growth, as well as an opportunity to reshape the concept of the development of Montenegro as an ecological state in a way that corresponds to the context of the challenging twenty-first century.

The Montenegrin economy currently has invisible costs due to the lower environmental standards as compared to the EU requirements, which leads to a loss of GDP and inefficient production. Montenegro still has to take important steps to fulfil the key economic requirements for EU membership (EC 2020), i.e., to ensure the functioning of the market economy and demonstrate the ability to cope with the competitive pressure within the EU as a territory with 450 million inhabitants, which makes a quarter of the world economy, a half of the world trade, and third of the world capital markets (Baldwin and Wyplosz 2006). This requires reform of the economic governance, implementation of economic structural reforms and especially development of a strong private sector which, among other things, is crucial for the creation of new jobs and stronger regional integration (EC 2020). EU can only benefit from Montenegro's accession if it accepts a more sustainable model of economic development. On the other hand, one of the most important economic benefits that Montenegro will have from the implementation of the environmental *acquis* is the integration of its economy into the EU internal market. As the EU is the "birthplace" of green technology, implementation of EU environmental and climate regulation will bring Montenegro closer to the "green" modernization of enterprises and further development of the thematic innovative ecosystems in Montenegro and their inclusion in European strategic value chains. According to the new methodology of negotiations with the EU based on clusters of negotiating chapters, the progress of Montenegro as a candidate country in terms of economic criteria from

Copenhagen will be one of the crucial in determining the overall pace of negotiations with all its negative and positive consequences (Mrak et al. 2022). Basically, Montenegro has the following environmental based development options (Fig. 2):

1. *"Business as Usual"*. Economic growth that is based on linear economy and that leads to environmental damage, economic, social, and health costs. The implication of this development model in Montenegro, which implements the EU acts transposed to the national legislation at the current level, is that the economy will grow from point *A* to point *B*. Scientific evidence shows that this economic model is not sustainable in the long term.
2. *Climate neutral and green development*. This scenario assumes orientation of Montenegro towards a circular economy as a new development model in which increased economic activity is separated from the use of natural resources (the so-called decoupling), implying continuation of growth with a reduced impact on the environment (position C). Meadows et al. (1972) made it clear that "the development trajectories of resource use, economic activity and social well-being must begin to diverge from each other, and especially all three trajectories must have an inverse divergence in relation to environmental pollution". "Decoupling" occurs when "resource use or pressure on the environment grows more slowly than the activity causing it ('relative decoupling') or declines while economic activity continues to grow ('absolute decoupling')" (Fischer-Kowalski et al. 2011). The globalized nature of the world economy means that this divergence should be discussed in an international context, and not in relation to individual states (Everett et al. 2010). In this scenario, the impact on the environment is reduced compared to the current scenario (C compared to A), because circular economy and principle of climate neutrality are applied. Greening of the Montenegrin economy should be considered as a long-term project for which in the EU pre-accession period all market participants (investors and consumers) should get the message that in the future investments with low CO_2 emissions will bring the highest return and be the only ones possible on the market.

Initiating green transition in all sectors of the Montenegrin economy, in accordance with EGD and GAWB, requires the role of the state that better informs, supports, and motivates business community in Montenegro to go through comprehensive environmental transformation and decarbonization. More understanding about potentials that changed paradigm of sustainable production and consumption brings about is crucial, because otherwise process can bring certain threats to those who will delay accepting the new reality, risking losing their market share and revenues. In fact, economic reform lies at the heart of the transition (Mrak et al. 2002). Small and medium size enterprises (SMEs) make up the majority of the Montenegrin economy. Given the lack of funding and capacity, they need support that will enable them to participate in effective collaboration with larger companies in research and innovation partnerships. SMEs should be informed about the commercial and economic opportunities of the circular economy, especially the potential savings from resource-efficient production processes, increased security of supply chains resulting from the procurement of recycled/sustainably produced raw materials, improved reputation, etc. The implementation of regulations in the field of environment and climate change in Montenegro will increase the responsibility and corporate awareness of companies about the impact of their operations on the environment. As a consequence of understanding environmental risks and the need to minimize them, the corporate culture will also improve. At the same time, consumers should receive reliable information and data about products and be empowered to make a wise decision about consumption, consumerism, and maintenance of resources in the economy.

However, the dilemma is how to solve the gap between the purchasing power of taxpayers, on the one hand, and the real costs of green transition reform, on the other. It is a question of "affordability" of reaching a high level of environmental protection and the fight against climate change as defined by EU regulations in relation to the real possibilities of Montenegrin taxpayers. In the context of the limited financial and economic capacities of Montenegro, this issue is one of the prerogatives in the EU accession process. Thus, the centre of attention should be strengthening of the financial potential of the economy to absorb significant investments that should be realized. Stimulating growth through the investment in low CO_2 technologies ("supply-side impact") is more sustainable from an environmental and macroeconomic perspective compared to the growth model based on consumption and public debt ("demand-side impact"), although there are views that financing the transition to the economy with lower CO_2 emissions with the public debt could bring greater social consensus for the final acceptance of CO_2 taxation (Bolton et al. 2020, p. 58). Properly designed tax reform (shifting the tax burden from labour to the pollution of environment) can strengthen economic growth, resilience to climate shocks and encourage sustainable behaviour of both producers and consumers. In this regard, tax reform together with issuing of green bonds (if budget space allows for the latter) should be seriously considered in order to have real prices reflecting environmental costs.

The membership in the EU is a fundamental decision, with many consequences, and the policy direction Montenegro will opt for will determine whether positives or negatives ones will outweigh. Considering the structure of the Montenegrin economy and the requirements of EGD and GAWB, the model of green economic development, which sets the ultimate goal of achieving climate neutrality in Montenegro by 2050, as required by EU integration process, is not possible without the simultaneous and synchronized development of the following processes in the economic pillars that need to go through the transition. The later refers to the following sectors especially: (1) agriculture, (2) energy, (3) construction, (4) tourism, and (5) industry.

The Carbon Border Adjustment Mechanism (CBAM), adopted in 2023, should be considered not to lose the competitiveness of Montenegro on the EU market, which is a huge risk if its companies remain trapped in conventional and outdated technologies that intensively emit CO_2. Barriers to the use of climate-neutral and circular materials and products should be removed by stimulating demand and developing markets for such products, improving the necessary infrastructure, and applying modern technologies. The ultimate goal should be reaching economies of scale and consequently price reduction, making circular products available and affordable. This should pave the way to improving the sustainability of primary production of raw materials so that sustainable production and the use of recycled materials and products become a norm in Montenegro. Of particular importance is the creation of necessary new Science, Technology, Engineering, and Mathematics (STEM) jobs in new green industries, services, and infrastructure, which could compensate for jobs that are very likely to be significantly constrained by technological advances in the new digital economy (Bolton et al. 2020).

The transition to a climate-neutral and green economy will certainly change market preferences in Montenegro in the short term, i.e. increase market and financial risks (e.g. increase of costs of capital or terms of borrowing, insurance claims and premiums, and losses of insured value). The lack of predictability of the green investments policy can affect investor confidence and may lead to reduced financing of green projects. In accordance with the EU Sustainable Finance Strategy, Montenegro will have to introduce the practice of green budgeting (annual budgets and medium-term fiscal plans). The future of the financial system of Montenegro must be directed towards its "greening", principles of sustainable finance and commitment to the management of climate and environmental risks. Banks should become more ambitious in supporting innovation in investments that facilitate the transition to low CO_2 emissions. Achieving the banks' net zero goals, however, will not depend only on the lending policy. The decarbonization pathways of bank clients in exposed sectors, consumer preferences that will determine the demand for green products and services, and incentives (especially the price of CO_2), play an important role. Although individual banks can accelerate the reduction of their exposure to climate change, the financial system as a whole can only do so in line with the low-carbon transition in the real sector. If banks in Montenegro in the pre-accession period, i.e., commit to a climate outcome that reflects the goals of the Paris Agreement within their portfolio over the current decade, this would represent a significant additional step forward. There is a potential for this, because there is "stability, satisfactory quality of assets and capital adequacy of the banking sector of Montenegro" (Government of Montenegro 2022). However, all financial institutions need to reorient capital flows towards sustainable investments in order to contribute to the green and climate-neutral development and manage financial risks arising from biodiversity loss and climate change.

4 Vision 2.0 or Instead of Conclusion?

The vision is the road map from the future as professor Vukotić usually points out. It refers to the imagined view from the future and such position and mapping the activities necessary to be done today to achieve such future position. Precisely, micro and green Montenegro are such road map's elements to be a successfull EU member state.

The existence of functional and efficient institutions based on market economy principles, functional education system, and implemented EU negotiation process criteria based on the vision of micro and green Montenegro are the (pre)condition for making it the stable, prosperous, and investment attractive destination. The idea behind is to create an entrepreneurial society based on education, development, and individual(s) and their freedom of choice. As each idea has its own moment in time, it is strongly believed that respective ones have it right now. If passed, probably respective idea cannot be implemented even though there are potential exceptions.

The EU has been created to prevent wars and enable economic cooperation leading towards growth and development. Montenegro's fight for independence as well as its European journey has the same *raison d'etre*. However, are we doing anything to achieve it? If we failed to execute ecology-state concept and its successor micro-state concept, the answer seems obvious. Both concepts were steered into the higher quality of living, higher standards, rule of law, private property protection, environmental protection, usage of natural resources in sustainable manner, usage of natural and cultural heritage in the manner of overall development and protection, creation of more sustainable jobs, creation of more SMEs, higher quality education of all levels, sparking the entrepreneurial spirit, efficient social justice, meritocracy, less governmental related jobs and networks, more entrepreneurial capitalism, and less political capitalism. Aforementioned in the majority belongs to the set of the so-called European values and standards. It is strongly believed that respective values are the values of humanism, renaissance, and enlightenment as well as classical liberalism ideas. However, respective values are shared among the pillars of the European unity. They have also been elements of both proposed concepts, ecological-state and micro-state.

In the Vision Montenegro 2.0 must be seen as the EU member state which promotes respective ideas even when some EU officials do not understand it. Montenegro has to be a country of well-educated, highly entrepreneurial, and ecologically cautious individuals. It has to be a country with a well-protected nature and cultural heritage. Also, it must be a country with efficiently executed rule of law, standards of chances not outcomes equality, standards of proper social justice, and a country of openness.

Aforementioned refers more to the philosophical "why". However, there is also a practical "how". The latter is the most demanding element of the equation. It is highly believed that respective answer is related to, indeed, a higher-quality educational system. The system oriented towards unexpected events and future of twenty-first and twenty-second centuries rather than oriented towards job posts and such skills. The current situation in general in the first two levels of the Montenegrin education system is indicated by the Programme for International Student Assessment (PISA) results. According to this date, Montenegro ranks relatively low at the 51st position with the overall score 422. Sub-results in PISA math are slightly above the overall score at 430 or 49th globally while the Science score and Reading score are below overall with 415 and 421 are 57th and 49th globally, respectively. It is the starting point. Second, tertiary education must open itself to the very same issues and challenges as well as to the world. Reaching a university tenure just by writing papers is something like becoming the CEO just by getting a college degree. Yes, it is possible to happen but is unsustainable without proper experience. Quoting the Institutional Evaluation Programme (IEP) by the European University Association, it seems there are already good examples in the country in the area of educational reform. Authors have indicated UDG—University of Donja Gorica as one of the good examples for others whose approach, modules, openness but also its global reached network should be executed indeed. The core reason why education is important relates to the change of mindset of the population and each (well-educated) individual(s). In this regard, UDG is also contributing significantly to the development of the entrepreneurial culture itself. In spite of being one of the biggest entrepreneurial projects in Montenegro, UDG fosters entrepreneurship and company's creation as an important part of the curriculum. It has created the Entrepreneurial Nest as the student's factory of ideas enabling students to create and manage their companies from it alongside the mentoring and trainings. In addition, it is creating and managing several different projects such are DigNest, Start1Up, and many more European projects.

Moreover, Montenegro is challenged how to transform EU integration process in the area of environment and climate change and consequently green transition that it brings about, into the unique opportunity that will encourage the efficient use of resources (decoupling their use from economic growth), ensure the long-term competitiveness of the Montenegrin economy by moving towards low-carbon and circular economy, along with the necessary digital transformation and especially sustainable financial system that will protect Montenegro from the systemic risks. To achieve all these by 2030 or 2035, the philosophy of environmental policy in Montenegro shaped in accordance with the EU standards should be the following one:

1. Environmental investments should be perceived as investments in the quality of life and health of citizens, as well as in competitiveness and economic performance of companies from Montenegro.
2. Implementation of EU legislation in the field of environment and climate change is nor a simple neither cheap process, so it is more important to be done adequately and not quickly.
3. Failure to invest into the environmental and climate change policy will deteriorate the environmental system and make it financially unsustainable, not allowing Montenegro to take decisive move in greening model of its economic development.
4. Transformation of the Montenegrin economy (as well as the European and global one) towards a sustainable, climate-resistant, and competitive economy in which economic growth and development are separated from the use of resources, has no alternative.
5. Supporting orientation of private companies that are active in the green and circular economy (whether in energy, transport, or agriculture) towards sustainability. This will raise quality of standards of Montenegrin companies and the availability of export-oriented investments, as well as the increased benefits of the private sector from the integration of trade with increasingly green and carbon-neutral common EU market. Montenegro should effectively use the process

of EU integration in the field of environment and climate change and, in parallel, facilitate the process of integrating the goals of EGD and GAWB into its political and legal framework with the aim of maximizing the intensity and exploiting the full potential of the foreseen green transition. It should be borne in mind that the implementation of reforms is becoming more and more difficult, because they will take place in a dynamically changing regulation. Montenegro will not only have to improve implementation of its current obligations, but also to continuously adapt to the changes taking place in the EU in all areas, be it the environment, climate actions, energy, or transport, in order to ensure the achievement of climate neutrality by 2050. As already mentioned, green transition requires a huge financial effort and preparation of public and the economy, and therefore must not be ignored or postponed, especially since it goes beyond the short-term or even medium-term capacities of the economy of Montenegro.

In the future relation's perspective, the EU must undertake more active and more serious approach. Up to now, the EU has been neglecting the real situation and their representatives seem not to be aware of certain processes. This could undermine the security and stability of the country. It is consequentially important also as with each enlargement the security borderline is being distracted from the Brussels, i.e. it keeps the security in the EU's heart viable.

Montenegro might have not been an excellent student in the integration process even though has been quite well and capable one. However, in the same process, the EU has been quite inactive student and failed to understand the process and to think out of the box, i.e. have so important and the so-called critical thinking.

It may seem indeed that micro and green are the recipe for Montenegro. Finally and experience based it seems that such *recipe* is indeed adequate for creation of sustainably prosperous Balkan economic "tiger". It appears to be potential competitive advantage of Montenegro at the highly competitive European market. Finally, the key important questions are (1) *How* the European *aristocracy* will accept it and (2) do *we have enough strength and vision to execute it.* It is also highly important to understand that relations must be mutually respectful including the Member States representatives but also that Montenegro should not accept any semi-colonial approach and behaviour. And precisely this is the cornerstone of the future relation's perspective of the EU and Montenegro as the almost *equal* partners. Finally, the micro-state concept alongside the green pillar of development is currently as Professor Vukotić said one "expensive avoidance of inevitable" (Vukotić 2002).

References

Baldwin R, Wyplosz C (2006) The economics of European integration, 2nd edn. McGraw-Hill Education, Berkshire

Benjamin W (2009) On the concept of history. CreateSpace Independent Publishing Platform

Bolton P, Després M, Pereira da Silva LA, Samama F, Svartzman R (2020) The Green Swan: central banking and financial stability in the age of climate change. Bank for International Settlements (BIS)

Bouthoul G (1962) War, psychology and sociology. In: Sun Book SB3. Walker
ECOTEC (2001) The benefits of compliance with the environmental acquis for the candidate countries: sub-study assignment request No. 3, DGENV Contract: environmental policy in the applicant countries and their preparations for accession. Final Report. ECOTEC Research & Consulting Limited (Adopted to the Case of Montenegro)
European Commission (EC) (2020) Economic and investment plan for the Western Balkans
Everett T, Ishwaran M, Ansaloni GP, Rubin A (2010) Economic growth and the environment. Defra Evidence and Analysis Series Paper 2
Fischer-Kowalski M, Swilling M, von Weizsäcker EU, Ren Y, Moriguchi Y, Crane W (2011) Decoupling natural resource use and environmental impacts from economic growth. A Report of the Working Group on Decoupling to the International Resource Panel
Government of Montenegro (2022) Program ekonomskih reformi za Crnu Goru 2022–2024. Available at: https://www.gov.me/dokumenta/e75a225c-375c-47bb-af21-5b595523b305. Accessed 18 July 2024
Jovetić I (2021) Economics and security: the paradigm (r)evolution. J Int Bus Econ
Meadows D, Meadows D, Randers J, Behrens WW (1972) The limits to growth. A report for the club of Rome's project on the predicament of mankind. Universe Books, New York
Morin E (2006) Evropska civilizacija i evropsko barbarstvo. AGM, Zagreb
Mrak M, Rojec M, Potočnik J (2002) The transition process in Slovenia: Transformation to an EU-compatible economy. J Int Relat Dev 5(1):37–62
Mrak M, Đukanović N, Redžepagić S, Jaćimović D, Rogić S (2022) Global competition challenges facing the single market and its implications for the Western Balkans. J Int Relat Dev 26(1):111–130
Index of Economic Freedom (2023) The Heritage Foundation. https://www.heritage.org/index/
Vukotić V (2002) Mikro država—skupo odložena neodložnost. Available at: www.vukotic.net. Accessed 18 July 2024
Vukotić V (2011) Istorija budućnosti. CID, Podgorica

The Future of Serbia's Relations with the European Union

Stevan Gajić

Abstract

The prolonged EU accession process faced by Serbia has been primarily hindered by a significant misunderstanding of the European Union's nature by the Serbian political elite. Many leaders failed to grasp that the EU project has always been a geopolitical extension of the United States, aimed at maintaining dominance over Europe. This misperception has influenced the EU's political stance towards Serbia, mirroring Washington's approach. The breakup of Yugoslavia, influenced heavily by Western intervention, left Serbia, seen as a geopolitical obstacle due to its Orthodox Christian identity and historical ties to Slavic and Byzantine civilizations, in a complex political position. This paper explores the historical context, the dynamics of Serbia's EU relations post-Yugoslavia, and the future of Serbia–EU interactions, considering the changing geopolitical landscape. The analysis spans from the end of the Cold War to the present, highlighting the impact of EU policies, the influence of US geopolitics, and Serbia's evolving stance towards European integration.

Keywords

EU accession · Geopolitical extension · Orthodox Christian identity · Breakup of Yugoslavia · Western intervention · Changing geopolitical landscape

S. Gajić (✉)
Institute of European Studies, Belgrade, Serbia

A. Stojkov, T. Warin (eds.), *Western Balkans and the Future of Europe*, The Future of Europe, https://doi.org/10.1007/978-3-031-86465-0_10

1 Introduction

The primary challenge faced by Serbs, and to a significant degree by the Serbian state, throughout the extended process known as accession, stemmed from a profound miscomprehension regarding the essence of the European Union project. The Serbian political elite, for a very long time, did not understand (or intentionally ignored, which is still the case for a significant part of it) that this project was, from the very beginning, essentially a geopolitical extension of the United States, or the "peaceful" wing of the occupation in service of its political, economic, military, cultural—in a word, complete domination over Western Europe, expanding across almost the entire European continent after the fall of the Berlin Wall.

In reality, it was not understood that, with all the differences among EU countries, the political approach towards Serbian state(s) in the Balkans could not be different from Washington's stance towards the Serbs as a people. Unfortunately, Washington fundamentally saw Yugoslavia—which had balanced between East and West since, from a worldview perspective of Samuel Huntington, it was a place where civilizations and major religions came together and separated during the country's dissolution—as an unnecessary state when the bipolar world era ended. It was no longer needed as the pillar of the non-aligned world, which served to prevent the spread of Soviet communist internationalism and block the influence of the Soviet Union in third-world countries or in the so-called developing countries of the capitalist periphery, often referred to as the global South nowadays. After the initial destabilising push from Germany and The Vatican which supported the secessionist movements in Slovenia and Croatia, the outcome was as one could expect. Soon enough, other actors from around the world were drawn into the Yugoslav conflict in one way or the other. "Tribal wars and ethnic conflicts will occur within civilisations. Violence between states and groups from different civilisations, however, carries with it the potential of escalation as other states and groups from these civilisations rally to the support of their 'kin countries' or 'kin groups' (Huntington, 1996, p. 28).

Given that the West's need for such a Yugoslavia ended, it was broken up with the most direct participation of Western countries led by the United States. Since the Serbian people were recognized in the eyes of the West as the most constitutive and at the same time the most dangerous among the Yugoslav peoples, as the originally state-forming people, this determined their political position in the places where in the then unipolar world decisions were made about the fate of Yugoslavia, and therefore of the Serbs. This predestined their political position and the overall dynamics of the relationships the Serbs had established with the European Union and its predecessor, the European Community.

Additionally, Serbs turned out to be a significant obstacle due to their Orthodox Christian religion, even when a considerable part of Serbs, having been secularized by communism, did not even know that they were Orthodox. Yugoslavia was indeed a very secular society, with an extremely low number of believers, especially

Orthodox ones, but this, in the eyes of the West, and for the EU as a party geopolitically subordinate to the US, represented a problem.[1]

In other words, the Serbs, as Orthodox Christians and as a nation has throughout history, especially since the beginning of the creation of modern Serbia, that is, since the Serbian revolution in 1804, seen as a factor that could potentially hinder the West. Later, the Serbs were seen more and more openly as the most western nation, representing a combination of Slavic and Byzantine civilizations, that is—as Konstantin Leontiev would say—a combination of Orthodoxy and Slavism. Moreover, he sees in the strong connection with Byzantism not only a necessary condition for the power of Russia, but also the only hope for the preservation of Slavism: "For the survival of the Slavs, the power of Russia is necessary. Byzantism is necessary for the power of Russia... He who wages war against Byzantism, without even knowing it, wages war indirectly against the entire Slavdom... Whether we like that Byzantine principle or not, whether it is good or bad, it is the only sure hope of our not only Russian, but all-Slavic preservation..." (Леонтјев 1994, 54).

The West saw and still sees Serbs as the most western Russians in civilizational terms. Since the Serbian people were recognized by the West as the most Western part of Slavs that form a junction of Slavic and Byzantine civilizations, a unique mix of Orthodoxy and Slavic culture, they were seen as a problem. The most paradoxical thing is that after the end of the communist era, the Russians were, one would say, even less Orthodox than the Serbs. However, understanding the Orthodox civilizational basis of the Serbs, and its implications in the eyes of the West was crucial. This is especially important because the Huntingtonian worldview was prevalent in places where decisions about the fate of Yugoslavia, and thus, Serbs, were made. Only when all this is understood can the events of that time, their logic, causes, and the prospects of this relationship for the future be understood.

In response to the question posed in the title of this essay, whether there is a common future for Serbia and the European Union, and what it looks like, a simple answer might be an agonizing cry: "No future", the exclamation of the punk-rock band Sex Pistols in their song "Anarchy in the UK". However, it is not entirely like that because the relationship between the European Union and Serbs does not deviate from the tradition of the relationship between Serbs and various Western actors in general.

Serbs are a contact civilization. They are, as it is already mentioned, located at the westernmost junction of Orthodoxy and Slavdom. Nonetheless, as if during the years in Yugoslavia, when they submerged their statehood into a broader Yugoslav nation, they somehow forgot this simple fact. However, the transitional period of

[1] This applies not only to the Serbs but also to Orthodox Christianity as a whole, which is systematically under attack by the West. This is evident in the persecution of the Serbian Orthodox Church in Montenegro, intensified in the last years of Milo Đukanović's rule, and now, in Ukraine, where the canonical Church is subjected to repressions not seen anywhere in the world for decades. All of this is happening with complete silence from the West, which can only be interpreted as approval. The persecution and the introduction of schism are being supported from within, with the most significant responsibility falling on the Ecumenical Patriarch Bartholomew, who is often accused of being under the direct influence of the United States.

30 years, that followed the breakup of Yugoslavia, simply served as a reminder. Since Serbs are where they are, both the Serbs and the Serbian people, as a contact civilization, will continue to cooperate with their surroundings.

To see exactly where we start and what positions today's cooperation can be observed from, given the tectonic geopolitical changes in Europe, and the world, a deeper understanding is necessary. This work will be divided into several parts: First, between the dissolution of Yugoslavia and the so-called October fifth political changes, from 1989 to 2000, then from 2000 to 2008, when most Western countries recognized the secession of Kosovo and Metohija from Serbia, and finally from 2008 until today. In the final part, I will try to provide a projection of future developments in political, security, and economic relations with Brussels and various actors within the European Union, and even broader in the European space, considering that the United Kingdom, which left the EU based on the 2016 referendum, also represents a Western actor.

2 From the End of the Cold War to October 5th, 2000

Towards the end of the 1980s, Europe experienced significant turbulence, especially Yugoslavia, due to its unique position. As the leader of the Non-Aligned Movement but plagued with numerous internal structural problems, including a quasi-federal system established by the 1974 constitution, Yugoslavia was not equipped to survive the changing world order. In these circumstances, the European order was also shifting with the fall of the Berlin Wall and the withdrawal of the Soviet Union from Eastern Germany, and later from all of Eastern Europe, where socialist regimes were collapsing one after another.

Yugoslavia embarked on the path of dissolution. This brings us to the core subject of this article. Serbs found themselves on the losing side, which they were not aware of at the time. A telling illustration of how Serbs perceived the world at that time is an episode from a football match between Belgrade's "Red Star" and Zagreb's "Dinamo", played in Zagreb 6 months after the fall of the Berlin Wall, where one of the leaders of the Serbian club's fans, Sima "Zulu", stated in front of a TV camera that England was our (Serbian) friend. The wrongness of such a view of the state of affairs became clear to every Serb not long after that match.

Considering the atmosphere of the fall of communist regimes, many Serbs believed that the West saw them as a part of the future democratic or Western world. This way of thinking was expected especially because of the fact that many Serbs had emigrated to Western countries, after World War II, due to ideological reasons. However, this illusion quickly collided with reality: one by one, Western European countries, and later the United States, began to act unfriendly towards Serbs during the process of Yugoslavia's disintegration and a series of civil wars.

Germany and Austria, working in synergy with the Vatican, were the first to show their unfriendly faces, recognizing the secession of Croatia and Slovenia, thus dictating the future approach of Western states towards the Serbian people. France, to some extent, was an exception while François Mitterrand was its president, as he remembered the time of Serbian-French friendship or at least the echo of that time, which made him somewhat reserved towards the strict German stance against Serbs. However, with the arrival of the new French President Jacques Chirac, the policy shifted, although it is worth noting that even Chirac's France was somewhat more favourable to Serbs, though it did not change France's fundamental policy position. The essence was that the civil war, especially in Bosnia and Herzegovina, and the image created by the West about Serbs, particularly after 1995, determined the entire West's attitude towards the Serbian people and the Serbian question.

Very quickly, the policies of Western countries became uniform. They only differed in style; Germans led openly anti-Serbian rhetoric and imposed humiliating conditions, which were communicated by well-known figures at the time, such as the German Foreign Minister Hans-Dietrich Genscher and Chancellor Helmut Kohl. However, other European countries began to adopt an increasingly unified policy towards the Serbian issue. It was a policy steeped in realism, which, in practical terms, meant that, since Serbian forces dominated on the battlefield, the West needed to find a way, through various deceptions and tricks, to end the conflict at the expense of Serbs.

At that time, essentially the most prudent approach came from the United Kingdom, which balanced things best, using its image as a fair player. This was translated into a plan presented by former U.S. Secretary of State Cyrus Vance and British Lord David Owen for ending the war in Bosnia and Herzegovina. According to this plan, the Serbian position would dramatically worsen, as the political "clock" would be turned back to 1992 when Serbs were put in a completely subordinate position being outvoted by the other two nations, depriving them of their right to political subjectivity. However, the humiliating plan was not accepted, despite even the strong pressure from the President of the Federal Republic of Yugoslavia (FRY), Slobodan Milošević, who succumbed to the demands of the West, as evidenced by the rigorous sanctions imposed by the FRY on the Republic of Srpska (Serbian part of Bosnia and Herzegovina) in the summer of 1994.

In an effort to break the Republic of Srpska and subsequently implement their own ideas, the West quickly played its strongest repressive card, commencing a heavy bombardment of Serbian positions. NATO's warplanes, under the code names Operation Deliberate Force and Operation Deadeye, bombed the positions of the Army of the Republic of Srpska from August 30 to September 20, 1995, targeting both military and civilian objectives, using depleted uranium munitions without restraint. NATO aviation had previously acted on targets in the Republic of Srpska Krajina[2] in early August 1995, prior to and during the Croatian "Operation Storm", significantly contributing to the ethnic cleansing of Serbian territories within

[2]The Republic of Serbian Krajina consisted of parts of today's Croatia where the majority population was Serbian. It was created as a reaction of the Serbs to the fact that after Croatia's separation from Yugoslavia, the Serbs were excluded from the constitution. The right that the Serbs had to be a nation-building people on that territory was not given by Croatia or Yugoslavia, but rather it was an inherited collective right from the time of the Habsburg Monarchy. This country existed from 1991 to 1995, when the Croatian army, with decisive assistance from the United States, expelled the Serbian people in Operation Storm.

Croatia, in collaboration with the Croatian army and the active participation of American private military contractor services, Military Professional Resources Inc., with various governmental and commercial clients.

This political-diplomatic-military action was supported by the Western academic community to some extent, even artistic productions, especially documentaries imbued with objectivism but promoting an anti-Serbian narrative, like the scandalous "Serbian Epics" directed by Pawel Pawlikowski, which suggested that Serbs were a genocidal people due to the nature of their culture, an "argument" not seen since the time of Hitler's Nazi propaganda. Similarly, several Hollywood feature films were produced with notably low artistic quality, most of them subsequently commercially failing. In this orchestrated campaign, Western media played a particularly significant role, consistently spreading anti-Serbian sentiments. From the current perspective, it is recognized as pure propaganda in the service of geopolitical interests rather than the informative content of "independent" media, as many perceived it at that time.

Again, the scope of perspectives is wide, from a softer approach, in the French case to the objectivist view of the British. BBC's documentary series "Death of Yugoslavia" is objectivist in tone but ultimately leads the viewer to the conclusion that in the competition among actors in the civil war, Serbs are the biggest culprits. This is common to all documentary films of the kind because the West constantly positions itself as an undisputed arbitrator—never as an extremely active player in the events, which was undoubtedly the case during the tragic disintegration of country of the South Slavs, as evidenced by a multitude of evidence presented even in such a biased judicial body as the Hague Tribunal. It is sad, but it would be funny if it were not: as if NATO did not participate in the war! Or as if it were an organization with which the West has no connection.

The same applies to the International Criminal Tribunal for the Former Yugoslavia, known as the Hague Tribunal, which was essentially a racist court, given that its mandate for war crimes in the former Yugoslavia excluded Western actors, as some kind of higher arbitrators, a superior race that cannot commit any crimes because it does not belong to the same category of species as the Yugoslav peoples. Moreover, in the Hague Tribunal, these peoples were treated according to different standards, and Serbs were proportionally the most punished. However, their status in the eyes of undisputed arbitrators did not differ essentially from the status of Croats, Bosnian Muslims, or Albanians because they were all treated as primitives, while the Western actor was not only exempt but was also appointed as the judge. This court was nominally international, but in reality, it was under the exclusive control of the West, as seen in the composition of judges and prosecutors and their biographies, especially in the judgments that have been delivered.

Returning to the media or propaganda field, it should be noted that Germans were the most adamant, with openly racist comments, led by Frankfurter Allgemeine Zeitung. Americans were not far behind; their reports, highlighting CNN editor Christiane Amanpour, were scandalous. Much more space was given to non-Serbian actors, and crimes against Serbs were ignored, even shameless forgeries occurred. Serbian victims were presented as victims of Serbs, and such "mistakes" even happened, where reporters reported from cemeteries with clear Orthodox Christian crosses, as places of burial of Muslims killed by Serbs! During the war, foreign TV stations sent reports from areas controlled by Serbs without any Serbian control, which was a mistake on the Serb part, according to the chief and responsible editor of Serbian Radio and Television, Maritza Lalovic (Радовановић Шаренац 2019, 117)[3] Among many distortions of facts, there is also the CNN report (to which, ironically, engineering-technical teams of Serbian Radio and Television provided a connection with the headquarters in Atlanta and the studio in London) from 4 July 1992, in which Serbian victims were depicted as Muslims (Јевтовић 2000, p. 158).[4]

German historian Marie-Janine Calic points out the assessment of the Hague Tribunal that the extent and nature of the war horrors, especially in Bosnia and Herzegovina, cannot be fully understood without determining the responsibility of journalists (Чалић 2013, p. 133). The problem, however, is that this tribunal "in this case only speaks of the responsibility of domestic journalists and media, not considering at all the involvement of global media houses... The crisis in the former Yugoslavia and the wars, especially the civil war in BiH, attracted a large number of foreign journalistic teams, which from the very beginning were inclined towards the Muslim-Croat side. Globally influential and expensive media (AP, Reuters, AFP, CNN, BBC, CBC, WTN, etc.) interpreted the causes and course of events on the fronts in B&H in accordance with the will and interests of their governments, creating a distorted and biased image of the war in B&H. With a pronounced negative approach and media bias towards the Serbian people, its political leadership, the army, Western media broadcasted reports every day based on half-truths, forgeries, selective information, creating an image of 'Greater Serbian aggression', 'crimes', 'genocides'." (Радовановић Шаренац 2019, p. 117).

After the end of the Yugoslav civil wars, until the NATO aggression against the Federal Republic of Yugoslavia (FRY) in 1999, which lasted for 79 days, following which President Milošević was ousted from power in October 2000, there was a brief calm. Simply put, the West was satisfied with the outcome of the peace process, and Milošević went from being a "Balkan butcher" to a "factor of peace and

[3] "This was a mistake because it gave us a completely distorted picture of what was happening in Bosnia and Herzegovina. After the massacre committed by Muslim soldiers in Žepa on June 4, 1992, the funeral and burial in Pale of 45 killed Serbian soldiers, coffins covered with Serbian flags, the French television broadcast a report and an image of that event, stating that it was about Muslim soldiers killed by Serbs".

[4] "So, on July 4, 1992, CNN broadcasts an image of a destroyed city with text claiming it to be Sarajevo, as a result of Serbian bombing. It was not mentioned that the image represented the remains of Trebinje, a Serbian city that had been devastated by Croats. The same house was often shown in reporting on the war in Bosnia as scenes of street battles in Tbilisi, Georgia, because they were more terrifying... Serbian victims' funerals were portrayed as Muslim or Croatian, even though a cross, an Orthodox priest, or people wearing Serbian traditional caps (šajkača) were visible. Immediately after the United States ordered the bombing of Serbian positions in the Republika Srpska, in May 1993, a picture of a 'Serb' shooting a wounded person in Brčko appeared on the front page of Newsweek. It was later proven that the photograph came from Slovenia, from the Reuters agency, and was taken a year earlier. The man in the photo was not Serbian at all, but this was never reported".

stability" because he had yielded in negotiations at the American military base in Dayton (Ohio), and because the Yugoslav army had refrained from assisting the Army of the Republic of Serbian Krajina, which prevented the escalation of the war, and thus NATO and the entire West had fewer headaches, especially the European Community at the time, which was preparing to become the European Union and establish its currency, the euro.

Economically, at that time, Germany dominated overwhelmingly, united and self-assured, as evidenced by the fact that the main alternative currency throughout the Yugoslav space was the German Deutsche Mark. This dominance has continued to this day through the euro, while in Bosnia and Herzegovina, there is a local currency called the convertible mark, which has had a fixed exchange rate to the euro all along. Similarly, in Serbia, the exchange rate of the dinar to the euro has hardly changed for about a decade. This domination is characteristic of other Balkan countries too, not only for Greece, which is in the eurozone, but also for Bulgaria, which nominally has its own currency, the lev, but it has also had a fixed exchange rate for about 20 years. The same applies to the denar in North Macedonia, while in Montenegro, the issue is resolved radically: its currency is the euro, although the country is not in the eurozone, nor is such a thing in sight.

Anti-Serbian propaganda, diplomatic and military activities against Serbs, a war on a cultural level—all of this had already been to a large extent standardized, carefully planned, and orchestrated, as evidenced as soon as the first signs of Albanian rebellion in Kosovo and Metohija appeared in 1997. The image of Milošević and Serbia as a constructive factor began to change systematically in Western media and Western diplomacy. Anti-regime protests in Serbia, caught up in political turmoil after disputed elections, influenced this to some extent. It turned out that Milošević's regime had stolen local elections, but in a critical moment, the West threw him a "lifeline" in the form of the OSCE mission led by the former Spanish Prime Minister, Felipe Gonzalez. He proposed the adoption of *lex specialis*, which would resolve the election crisis, allowing the opposition to take control of some cities, which Milošević accepted.

At that time, there was a possibility of toppling the regime, but the West essentially helped Milošević. It is possible that this happened, which is a very popular thesis, because it was easier to "brand" Milošević as a "war criminal" for future wars, which was already evident by the end of 1997 and culminated in the NATO aggression against the FRY from March 24 to June 10, 1999, when Serbia was demonized once again in the West.

This turbulent period ended with the NATO occupation of Kosovo and Metohija, which occurred after the Kumanovo Agreement and UN Security Council Resolution 1244, where Russia helped Serbia by guaranteeing its territorial integrity and the possibility of returning a limited contingent of Serbian army and police to the province of Kosovo and Metohija at some point in time. With the fall of Milošević in October 2000, a brief period began in which Serbia could somewhat approach the European Union and the West as a whole. Nonetheless, the West permanently missed that opportunity in 2008.

3 From Post-Milošević Honeymoon to 2008

What Klaus Schwab would call the "Great Reset" happened in Serbia, or the FR Yugoslavia (at the time), in the year 2000. A significant change occurred after the NATO bombing and occupation of Kosovo and Metohija. Political life resumed, and Milosevic lost the elections on 24 September 2000. Then something happened that some say was the defence of election results, but for some time, there has been a strong belief in Serbia, and not only there, that a coup had actually taken place involving the very Western countries that had bombed Serbia in the previous years. It is essential to mention that such a thing would not have been possible in Serbian society if there had not been a growing discontent with Milosevic's rule and fatigue from constant confrontation with the West.

The belief of many Serbian citizens that there would be a rapprochement with the West after Milosevic's fall unfortunately fell apart. Instead of significant investments in Serbia, a plunderous privatization began, and the West continued the process of disintegrating Serbian lands. Javier Solana, NATO's Secretary-General during the aggression against FR Yugoslavia, quickly became a mediator in the so-called Belgrade Agreement that preceded and was essential precondition for the future separation of Montenegro from Serbia. Montenegro's leadership had made a fundamental deal with the West a few years earlier to avoid ending up in history with Milošević. A coup occurred within the ruling party in Montenegro, from which Milo Đukanović emerged as the winner, and continued to rule over Montenegro for more than 20 years.

The essence is that the first serious blow to the joint state of Serbia and Montenegro was dealt in 2001 during the Albanian rebellion in the Vranje Valley, which was suppressed thanks to the ability of the new Serbian authorities. They skillfully used the *honeymoon* with the West, which was at its end, to achieve victory through a combination of military means and diplomacy, as described by one of the main actors in this episode of Serbian history, Nebojša Čović.

The next blow happened shortly thereafter—the assassination of the Prime Minister of Serbia, Zoran Đinđić, on 12 March 2003. To this day, it is not clear how the assassination actually happened, but strong suspicions about the official version of this event exist within Serbian society. These suspicions have been elaborately expressed in a book "The Third Bullet" by Đinđić's bodyguard Milan Veruović and investigative journalist Nikola Vrzić. The book suggests that the West was dissatisfied with Đinđić's shift towards solving political issues and opening the Kosovo and Metohija question. This shift happened when Đinđić realized the promised foreign direct investments from the West will never reach Serbia. The book Treći metak (The Third Bullet) by Zoran Đinđić's long-time personal bodyguard, Milan Veruović (who was seriously wounded during the assassination the Serbian Prime Minister), and Nikola Vrzić, exposes a series of lies and fabrications underlying the official version of the assassination. it delves into the role of Western, particularly Anglo-American, intelligence agencies and their governments, their involvement in the murder and the covering up of traces, as well as the role of their Serbian collaborators, including key figures in the political and judicial spheres. "...the existence of the fact that British and American security structures were involved in practically every segment of the story surrounding Đinđić's assassination and the subsequent establishment of the false official truth about his murder, coupled with the fact that the assassination of the Serbian Prime Minister brought them political benefit, gives no one the right to dismiss as mere conspiracy theory the possibility that the role of these services and their states in the assassination of the Serbian Prime Minister was far more sinister than the opportunistic exploitation of the fact that Zoran Đinđić was no longer alive to disturb and disrupt their plans." (Veruović and Vrzić, 2014, p. 444). The book also exposes the political background of the assassination, primarily the immense dissatisfaction of Washington and Brussels with Đinđić's insistence on resolving the issue of Kosovo and Metohija before any potential legalisation of what he called the "illegal construction," and his adherence and his strict adherence to UN Resolution 1244, which upholds the sovereignty and territorial integrity of the Republic of Serbia. The book concludes with two key points: the undeniable involvement of Anglo-American intelligence services and the fact that the truth about the assassination has not been established. "The only way for Serbia to survive that shot was to establish the complete and irrefutable truth about the assassination of Zoran Đinđić, about his killers and motives. Only then could the goal they sought to achieve by the assassinating the Serbian Prime Minister be thwarted. Unfortunately... there are too many indications and pieces of evidence that the complete and irrefutable truth has not been revealed. And that would mean that the victim of March 12, 2003, was not Zoran Đinđić but that we are all victims." (Veruović and Vrzić, 2014, p. 444).

Đinđić's assassination was the cause of the next major crisis and the moment when the West did something that produced consequences it least desired. Almost all Western countries, including EU member states (except for five of them), quickly recognized the unilaterally declared independence of Kosovo on 17th February 2008. This was preceded by the events of 2004 and the 3-day massive March pogrom of Kosovo's ethnic Albanians against the Serbian population of the province. This certainly did not improve Serbs' attitude towards the West since the NATO (KFOR) forces present in Kosovo and Metohija did not protect the Serbs from ethnic violence they were exposed to.

It might sound paradoxical, but in the early years after the NATO bombing, the West had the best opportunity to peacefully integrate Serbs. Even if their idea was malicious to begin with, it could have been implemented, through a quick and full integration of Serbia into the Western political and economic realm. Recently, a pro-western Serbian politician Čedomir Jovanović testified that German Chancellor Gerhard Schroeder told Đinđić in 2002 that there was no chance of Serbia entering the European Union (S.M.L. 2021),[5] which was confirmed by Chancellor Angela

[5] "Schröder was furious because we insisted on Kosovo, as Iraq was the topic at the time. Zoran told him then: 'What Iraq is to you, Kosovo is to me. I want to know where the borders of my country are'. Schröder asked him why that was even important, and Đinđić said it's because they (the West) want Serbia in Europe. To this, Schröder replied, 'Well, you are already more European than me, look at how you look, how you speak. But Serbia will never be a part of the European

Merkel in 2013 after Croatia joined the EU, stating that the door for new member states was closed for an extended period.

All of Serbia's concessions, including the humiliating surrender of military and political leaders to the Hague Tribunal, were justified by the prospect of someday entering the "paradise" of the European Union. In any case, it turned out that 2008 was the year when the EU closed its window of opportunity to integrate Serbia and therefore silently and softly subjugate the Serbs in that way. The frustration that built up among Serbs at that time and their resistance to the EU and its "values" only grew in the years that followed, especially among the younger generation, as confirmed by all the serious sociological research. In fact, from that time onwards, each subsequent generation of Serbian youth is more anti-Western oriented then the previous one.

That year was not just a turning point for humanity due to the global economic crisis, NATO's decision at the Bucharest summit to expand into Ukraine and Georgia, which directly provoked Russia. The short August war in which Georgia suffered defeat was the first result of the summit. It was also the year when the West, by recognizing Kosovo, essentially closed the door through which it had the opportunity to pass in order to win the hearts and minds of Serbs, especially the younger generation. That battle was permanently lost for the West in 2008.

This is the foundation on which the West must now rely on in considering any future relations between the Serbian people and Western countries or the collective West, as it is now called. No matter how strange it may seem, 2008 proved to be more critical for future relations than even the NATO aggression itself. It is the turning point and the moment when Serbs, as victims, became aware of the trauma they experienced and are perfectly aware that they have no friends in the West, that no reconciliation will occur, and that they are now in a state of semi-occupation. Something that European nations still do not fully understand, even though they themselves are in a similar position in relation to the United States.

4 The Failure of Euro-Integrations and the Resurrection of Realpolitik

After 2008, it seemed that even in the West, the model of winning the hearts and minds of Serbs had come to an end. Therefore, they had to resort to a trick because it was clear that the pro-EU-oriented parties had exhausted that ideological matrix. That's why the West welcomed the division in the strongest opposition party, the Serbian Radical Party, from which the majority formed a new party, the Serbian Progressive Party that was forged to serve the western geopolitical interests.

Many circumstances and pieces of evidence point to the connection between the West and this party, and the first one came to light immediately: a congratulatory message for the Serbian Progressive Party's presidential candidate, Tomislav

Union. The EU borders are the borders of the Austro-Hungarian monarchy, plus the front towards Russia".

Nikolić, from the European Union arrived 3 h before the closing of polling stations!? This initially appeared entirely illogical because the then-President of Serbia and the Democratic Party, a pro-Western politician, Boris Tadić, seemed like a natural ally of Brussels (and Washington) in Serbia. However, the Serbian public was mostly unaware that the Serbian Progressive Party was in full agreement with the West, which became evident very quickly.

Nikolić's victory paved the way for Aleksandar Vučić to take power. In the years that followed, Vučić did everything, primarily through the Brussels agreements of 2013 and 2015, to dismantle what remained of the Serbian state in Kosovo and Metohija. These agreements were opened by the former British diplomat Robert Cooper, the famous author of the book "The Breaking of Nations: Order and Chaos in the Twenty-first Century", which is, in fact, a kind of manual for Western diplomats on how to use deception to achieve British and Western interests. For the postmodern state there is, therefore, a difficulty. It needs to get used to the idea of double standards. Among themselves, the postmodern states operate on the basis of laws and open co-operative security. But when dealing with more old-fashioned kinds of state outside of the postmodern limits, Europeans need to revert to the rough methods of an earlier era - force, pre-emptive attack, deception, whatever is necessary for those who still live in the nineteenth-century world of every state for itself. In the jungle, one must use the laws of the jungle. (Cooper 2004, pp. 61,62). Later, EU "mediators" in negotiations between Belgrade and the illegally separated southern Serbian province were Catherine Ashton and Federica Mogherini, but the essence remained unchanged.

The new Serbian authorities, elected by the people due to their disillusionment with the so-called pro-European parties, former nationalists, accelerated the erosion of Serbian statehood, orchestrated by the West. However, these events at that time contributed to an awareness that the Serbs possess today, but a kind of awareness that doesn't exist in most European countries. It is clear that after World War II, all Western EU countries, except for the UK, which has left the organization, to a greater or lesser extent, became vassals of the United States, which has military bases throughout Europe, especially in Germany and Italy, countries that were part of Hitler's pact. However, in these countries, there is barely any awareness about the true status in which the exist. On the other hand, in Serbia, the awareness about its colonial or vassal status matured during the rule of Aleksandar Vučić.

Meanwhile, the war in Ukraine escalated, and the enlightened Serbian people, who had permanently ceased to believe in any rapprochement with the West, undoubtedly supported Russia in the West's proxy war against it. Such an atmosphere is evident at every step, and it is confirmed by all public opinion polls, in which more than 80% of Serbian citizens are categorically against imposing sanctions on Russia, making Serbia an exception in Europe. The phrase "hyper-Westernized Kurds" is close to me when talking about Serbian youth, especially those for whom the key event was the year 2008, the declaration of the secession of Kosovo and Metohija, supported by 22 out of 27 EU member states. The norms of international law were only upheld by Spain, Slovakia, Greece, Cyprus, and

Romania, whom never recognized NATO orchestrated illegal secession of Kosovo and Metohija from Serbia.

The current state of affairs is one in which the European Union, due to its completely subservient and compliant position towards the United States (this essay was written one year prior to Donald Trump's victory in 2024 US presidential election), seems to disregard its own vital interests. Regarding the war in Ukraine, the EU's strongest countries—Germany and France—unquestionably accepted every request from Washington to send weapons to the regime in Kiev. As a result, the European Union has ceased to be even a politically relevant player and has become an entirely irrelevant factor in global politics. Its status as an occupied territory has been further confirmed, and the United States has completely disregarded it. This is particularly evident in the humiliating fact that no one in Germany dared to protest when a terrorist attack on the Baltic Sea gas pipelines, Nord Stream 1 and Nord Stream 2, occurred. The German officials completely ignored reports of American journalist Seymour Hersh, a Pulitzer Prize winner, who provided evidence that the attack was carried out by the United States.

Essentially, Serbia finds itself in a position of open hostility towards the West, a situation comparable to Japanese kabuki theatre, where male actors disguise themselves with makeup, voices, and gestures to pretend to be women. In this "kabuki theatre" on European soil, Serbian authorities pretend that Serbia wants to join the European Union, even though relevant research shows that the majority of the Serbian population is against it. Meanwhile, in the European Union, they pretend to want Serbia amongst its ranks, but both sides continue to discuss Serbia's European integration. This "kabuki" actually serves to de-sovereignize Serbia as a whole, primarily through the Kosovo and Metohija issue.

The fate of the Serbian people will be determined, as always, from within and as a result of their relations with European countries, with global events being crucial for their future. One thing is certain: the European Union in the emerging new world order will not exist in its current form. It is already incomplete without the United Kingdom. While Serbia is in a partially vassal position to the EU, its population is fully aware of this relationship's unsustainability, which will also affect Serbia's international position and its future relations. Serbia, as an avant-garde in building of global relations, might establish relationships with European countries on new, completely realpolitik-based foundations, devoid of any ideological aspirations for European integration in its current form. In all this, geography is immutable: Serbia borders the countries of the West. But the relations will be quite different. Perhaps the relationships will resemble those of Yugoslavia with Austria or West Germany after the end of World War II.

In late October, the President of the European Commission, Ursula von der Leyen, visited Belgrade, which was part of a series of such visits characterized by constant western ultimatums to Serbia. The first item on the list is the so-called Franco-German plan, which practically calls for Serbia to capitulate and hand over Kosovo and Metohija, thereby initiating the process of its complete disintegration. However, this model of western demeanour will undoubtedly come to an end due to the high awareness of the Serbian people regarding the vassal or even occupation character of the country and the Western hostility towards Serbia. In a way, it is almost tragically comical, as European officials use this to compensate for their powerlessness and strong frustration towards the United States.

The world is rapidly changing during the global conflict we are witnessing, and in this new emerging world, the dialogue between the Serbian state and individual European countries or the EU for that matter as a whole, if anything remains of it, will have an entirely different tone.

References

Cooper R (2004) The breaking of nations: order and chaos in the twenty-first century. Atlantic Books, London

Huntington SP (1996) The clash of civilizations and the remaking of world order. Simon & Schuster, New York

S.M.L. (2021) Šreder je rekao Đinđiću: Vi nikada nećete biti deo EU! Granice EU su granice austrougarske monarhije, plus front ka Rusiji. Blic. https://www.blic.rs/vesti/politika/ceda-jovanovic-sreder-je-rekao-djindicu-vi-nikada-necete-biti-deo-eu-granice-eu-su/3hj6148

Јевтовић З (2000) Тоталитаризам и масмедији. Студио РАС, Неготин-Београд

Леонтјев К (1994) Византизам и словенство. Логос, Ортодос, Београд

Радовановић Шаренац ДД (2019) Настанак и развој телевизије Републике Српске и њена улога у медијском систему (докторска дисертација)

Чалић МЖ (2013) Историја Југославије у 20. веку. Clio, Београд

Veruović, M. & Vrzić, N. (2014). Treći Metak. Pirot: Moja knjiga, 3rd edition

European Integration Prospects for Western Balkans

Thierry Warin and Aleksandar Stojkov

Abstract

The further integration of the EU stands at a crossroads, characterized by increasing geopolitical complexity and internal challenges. While Western Balkan countries suffer from slow accession processes, the accelerated candidacy of Ukraine after 2022 shows how political priorities vary. Frustration mounts as leaders such as Vučić of Serbia express their frustration over delays across issues, including the resolution of Serbia-Kosovo relations. Meanwhile, the EU's target enlargement date of 2030, advanced by the European Council President Charles Michel, reflects new impetus. The Growth Plan, based on four pillars, points out economic integration, fundamental reforms, and financial aid, thus offering a strategic opportunity to the region. On the other hand, geopolitical fragmentation—epitomized by the invasion of Ukraine by Russia—makes things difficult. The integration of the Western Balkans is vital for regional stability, a decrease in emigration, and socioeconomic disparities. While EU membership offers mutual benefits, its realization requires bold reforms, enhanced governance, and adherence to democratic values. Ultimately, EU enlargement is a means and not an end—a journey to prosperity and unity.

Keywords

Geopolitical landscape · EU integration · Populism · NATO · External influences

T. Warin
HEC Montréal, Montréal, QC, Canada

A. Stojkov (✉)
Ss. Cyril and Methodius University in Skopje, Skopje, North Macedonia
e-mail: a.stojkov@pf.ukim.edu.mk

A. Stojkov, T. Warin (eds.), *Western Balkans and the Future of Europe*, The Future of Europe, https://doi.org/10.1007/978-3-031-86465-0_11

1 The European Integration at Crossroads?

As one of the founding fathers of the European Union and the French Minister of Foreign Affairs, Robert Schumann, underscored, "Europe will not be made all at once, or according to a single plan. It will be built through concrete achievements, which first create a de facto solidarity" (Strasbourg Europe n.d.).

Western Balkan leaders are increasingly frustrated as Ukraine seems to be advancing faster in the EU accession process, further delaying their long-standing efforts to join the bloc. Serbian President Aleksandar Vučić expressed his sentiments to the Financial Times, stating that while he has no ill will toward Ukrainians, the EU's rapid support for Ukraine—granting candidate status within a year of its application and possibly starting membership talks soon—highlights a lack of similar political support for the Western Balkans. Ukraine applied for EU membership in February 2022, shortly after Russia's full-scale invasion, and was granted candidate status 4 months later. In contrast, Serbia waited over 4 years after its application to start membership talks in 2014, and its negotiations have since stalled, primarily due to its unresolved relations with Kosovo and its refusal to adopt EU sanctions against Russia.

The EU has promised to speed up the membership process for six Western Balkan countries—Serbia, Kosovo, Montenegro, Albania, North Macedonia, and Bosnia and Herzegovina—with the European Council President Charles Michel suggesting the first accessions could happen by 2030. However, at a recent event in Slovenia, Albanian Prime Minister Edi Rama questioned this new target, sarcastically suggesting that war seems to accelerate membership. He joked about hypothetical conflicts among the Balkan countries to expedite their EU accession, reflecting the frustration felt by many in the region.

North Macedonia, a NATO member that waited 18 years to start EU membership talks, views Ukraine's situation differently. Its Foreign Minister, Bujar Osmani, emphasized that Ukraine's struggle is not just for itself but for the future of Europe. The 1990s breakup of Yugoslavia led to wars and significant loss of life and displacement in the region, and unresolved issues, particularly involving Bosnia and Kosovo, continue to hinder EU integration.

EU foreign policy chief Josep Borrell reiterated that without normalization of relations, there would be no European future for either Kosovo or Serbia. Kosovo, which applied for EU membership last December, is still awaiting candidate status. Vučić argued that Serbia is in better shape than Romania and Bulgaria were in 2007 when they joined the EU and blamed the EU's diminishing capacity to absorb new members for the delays.

At the Slovenian conference, Michel stated that Russia's invasion of Ukraine had reignited the push for Balkan enlargement after two decades of stagnation, calling the 2030 pledge ambitious but necessary. However, analysts remain skeptical, pointing to persistent rule of law and corruption issues that have hindered progress. The current geopolitical climate, influenced by Ukraine, is challenging, and compared it to 2003 when EU membership for the Western Balkans was first considered amid a sense of urgency following recent conflicts (Mujanović 2023). He highlighted the

EU's broken promises and the resurgence of nationalist politics in the region as significant obstacles to credible improvement.

2 Reshaped Global Context

The global economy today is characterized by rapid geopolitical fragmentation and growing trade restrictions. There are numerous signs of technological decoupling, evidence of reduced capital flows, cross-border migration restrictions, and heightened risk of fragmentation of the international payment system (Aiyar et al. 2023). Additionally, a number of ongoing geopolitical conflicts and tensions are fueling uncertainty: the Russian invasion of Ukraine, the Israeli-Hamas military conflict in Gaza, the dispute between People's Republic of China and Taiwan as well as Serbia-Kosovo tensions.

The world is also witnessing "slowbalization" (or slow globalization). After the 2008 Global Financial Crisis, there has been a slower expansion of cross-border lending and international trade. Slowbalization involves a shift away from the rapid pace of globalization that characterized much of the late twentieth and early twenty-first centuries. It suggests that various factors such as rising protectionism, trade tensions between major economies, nationalist policies, and the localization of production and supply chains are contributing to a slowdown in global economic integration.

The world also witnesses politically supported re-orientation of the net international capital flows and the global supply chains. Reshoring, friend-shoring, and near-shoring are recent phenomena related to shifting business operations away from authoritarian or politically unfriendly states: (1) back to the country of origin; (2) toward geopolitical allies; or (3) toward neighboring countries.

Even though it might be too soon to declare a deglobalization, what we are observing is a policy-driven Geoeconomic Fragmentation. This fragmentation can lead to the formation of distinct economic blocs or spheres of influence, with countries aligning themselves based on shared geopolitical interests rather than purely economic considerations. As elaborated by Aiyar et al. (2023), the cost to global output from trade fragmentation could range from 0.2% (in a limited fragmentation scenario) to up to 7% of GDP (in a severe fragmentation scenario).

3 The New Momentum

In May 2023, the President of the European Commission, Ursula Von der Leyen, announced the new plan for getting Western Balkans closer to the European Union, as well as the economic support therefor. This plan may be perceived as a helping hand lent to the Western Balkans. She pointed out at the Global Security Forum in Bratislava that, "[...] we do not only ask our partners to take new steps towards us. We also take a big step towards them. Our shared goal is to speed up their journey towards the EU" (von der Leyen 2023). It is not necessary to read much between the lines for the clear message Von der Leyen conveyed to both the leaders and the citizens. This is unquestionably a great opportunity which should be taken advantage of, being also an encouraging sign given the specific background in view of divided opinions about joining the EU.

The new four-pillar Growth Plan for Western Balkans already sent a very powerful message that the enlargement is back on the agenda (European Commission 2023). It comes at a difficult time of radical uncertainty and geopolitical complexities. This Growth Plan for Western Balkans envisages to: (1) boost economic integration within the Western Balkans through the Common Regional Market, which could add 10% to their economies; (2) to enhance economic integration with the European Union's Single Market; (3) to accelerate fundamental reforms, aimed at accelerating accession, improving economic growth, and strengthening regional stability; and (4) to provide increased financial assistance. For illustration, the Reform and Growth Facility for the Western Balkans for the period 2024–2027 pledges an amount of EUR 6 billion in grants and concessional loans.

The Western Balkans must seize the unique geopolitical momentum and the renewed enthusiasm for a next round of EU enlargement around 2030. One of the biggest proponents for the next EU enlargement, the European Council President Charles Michel, distinctly elaborated this enthusiasm on 28 August 2023, at the Bled Strategic Forum in Slovenia:

> To be stronger and safer, the EU needs to reinforce our bonds and become more powerful. That's why it is now time to tackle the challenge of enlargement. Both for us in the EU and for our future member states. Yes, I believe this is how we should now call the countries with confirmed EU perspective, future member states. […] To be credible, I believe we must talk about timing and homework. And I have a proposal. As we prepare the EU's next strategic agenda, we must set ourselves a clear goal. I believe we must be ready - on both sides - to enlarge by 2030 (Michel 2023).

Fortunately, there is a very strong support in Western Balkans for joining the EU. The EU integration is considered an issue of highest strategic priority, which enjoys broad consensus among political parties and citizens. The prospective EU membership is perceived as a strong impetus for structural and institutional reforms that would contribute to country's prosperity and sustainable development (e.g., Besimi and Monastiriotis 2019).

The development model of the EU candidate countries must be geared toward accelerated, inclusive, and sustainable development through a considerable progress in the priority areas such as human capital formation, digitalization, social inclusion, infrastructure investment, etc. As presented in Fig. 1, the third dimension—that will reinforce these processes—is the degree of European integration of the society and the economy.

The European Union membership is not a destination but rather a journey! Democratic consolidation, high observance and protection of rights and rule of law, respect for multi-ethnicity and multiculturalism, freedom of movement of goods, capital, and people, peace and security, development and prosperity are the common values that unite 450 million citizens in 27 countries in a single and pacifistic union,

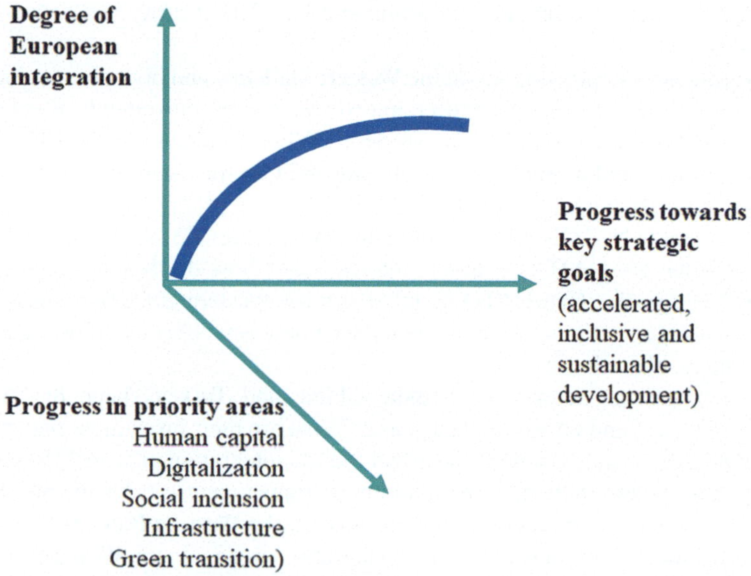

Fig. 1 Illustration of a Three-Dimensional Development Model for an EU candidate country. Source: Stojkov and Besimi (2024)

single market, and economic superpower. However, the EU membership is not a trophy at the end of the race, or as the EU Commissioner, Johannes Hahn, pointed out at the Skopje Economic and Financial Forum (SEFF) in 2023, "The EU is not a cash machine, an ATM. Joining the Union is also joining common values." "Bringing Europe home before joining the EU" is the axiom arising therefrom, which remarkably captures the essence of the EU integration process—to take actions, while being guided by true values and goals, all to the end of creating a better future. Membership in the European Union is not our destination, but rather an approach to a "common journey" toward a better future, prosperity, and a higher living standard.

4 Geopolitical Dynamics and EU Integration in the Western Balkans

How do recent global events shape the Western Balkans' path to EU integration? This chapter invites readers to explore how the Russian invasion of Ukraine, the resurgence of populist movements, and NATO's influence impact the political and economic stability of the Western Balkans. Can the EU effectively navigate these geopolitical complexities to support the region's integration?

The Russian invasion of Ukraine has significant implications for the Western Balkans, but what are the direct and indirect effects on the region? How does this conflict influence the foreign policies of Western Balkan countries, and what security concerns arise? How should the EU strengthen its position and support the region? Is the increased urgency for alignment with EU security and defense policies achievable?

What role does populism play in the Western Balkans, and how does it challenge the EU integration process? How do populist leaders and movements affect governance and public opinion on EU membership? What strategies can the EU adopt to counter populism and promote democratic norms? Can the rise of populism be mitigated, or is it an inevitable challenge?

How crucial is NATO's presence in maintaining regional stability in the Western Balkans? What are NATO's strategic interests, and how do they align or conflict with the EU's goals? Can NATO membership for Western Balkan countries reinforce their EU aspirations? What is the balance between NATO's influence and the EU's strategic objectives?

How do external actors like Russia, China, and Turkey shape the Western Balkans' political and economic landscape? What are their investment patterns and political alliances, and how do these affect the EU integration process? How should the EU counter these influences to maintain its strategic interests? Is the presence of these external actors a threat or an opportunity for the Western Balkans?

What are the key obstacles to the EU integration process in the Western Balkans? How do political instability, democratic backsliding, and economic vulnerabilities hinder progress? Is the EU's conditionality and pre-accession assistance effective in promoting necessary reforms? How can the EU address these challenges to support the Western Balkans more effectively?

Why is the Western Balkans strategically important for the EU? How does the region serve as a bridge between Europe and Asia, and what potential does it hold for economic growth? What role does the region play in the EU's broader geopolitical strategy? How does the integration of the Western Balkans influence the EU's global standing and regional stability?

Through specific case studies of Western Balkan countries, what can we learn about their unique geopolitical challenges and progress toward EU integration? How do these case studies illustrate the diverse experiences and the interplay of internal and external factors? What lessons can be drawn from these examples?

The geopolitical landscape presents both challenges and opportunities for the Western Balkans' EU integration journey. How can the region navigate the complexities of the Russian invasion of Ukraine, rising populism, and external influences? What policy recommendations can be made to enhance stability, foster democratic governance, and accelerate the integration process? Is the current approach sufficient, or does it require a significant shift?

The overarching question remains: Can the European Union maintain its commitment to enlargement while ensuring that its strategic interests are safeguarded in a rapidly changing geopolitical environment? This chapter seeks to engage readers in a critical examination of these pressing issues, encouraging a deeper understanding and stimulating ongoing dialogue about the future of the Western Balkans and its integration into the European Union.

Dennis Gabor, a Nobel Prize Laureate in Physics, is often quoted as saying "the future cannot be predicted, but futures can be invented" (Gabor 1963). In this spirit,

European leadership must invest more energy in formulating a strategic vision and inventing a brighter future for the European continent. The deepening and the enlargement of the Union do not necessarily have to be competitive processes. On the contrary, these processes can complement each other, as the inclusion of new EU members can bring fresh perspectives and dynamics that enrich the Union's political, economic, and cultural fabric. The current strategy of European integration, which predominantly relies on work permits and subsequent citizenship, contributes to significant demographic devastation of the Western Balkans. Such intra-European migration patterns undermine the socio-economic stability and long-term development prospects of the Western Balkan countries, exacerbating issues related to aging populations and labor shortages. Although this approach benefits European labor markets in the short term, it ultimately risks creating a super-periphery of the European economy that lacks viable development prospects. This super-periphery would be characterized by economic stagnation and limited opportunities for growth, exacerbating disparities between the core and peripheral regions of the European economy. Such a scenario could lead to long-term socio-economic imbalances. It could ultimately undermine the overall stability and cohesion of the European economy.

Europe needs leaders capable of transcending the historical southern confines of the nineteenth-century Austro-Hungarian monarchy and fully integrating the Western Balkans into the European fold. Such politicians must possess the vision and political will to address the historical and cultural divisions and embrace the Western Balkans as integral to Europe's future development and stability.

One must fully acknowledge the argument that the present European Union with 27 members is difficult to manage, let alone a future Union with 33 members (incorporating the WB-6) or with 36 members (also including the Association trio—Ukraine, Georgia, and Moldova). The Union could also contemplate establishing constituencies of countries akin to the operational structures of the International Monetary Fund and the World Bank Group. These constituencies could feature a rotating presidency to ensure balanced representation and prevent any single nation from dominating the leadership. Of course, such a reform requires bold political decisions.

5 Conclusions

Western Balkans must seize the unique geopolitical momentum and the renewed enthusiasm for the next round of EU enlargement around 2030. Opening the EU accession negotiating chapters would be seen as the first important step to create a level of certainty that can guide the country's short- and medium-term development strategy and have a positive impact on the political and socio-economic situation. The EU accession talks would focus the minds and resources of political elites on the specific conditions that the country needs to fulfill for the successful completion of individual chapters in the negotiation process.

A transformational development pathway (from a middle-income to a high-income economy) requires thinking beyond political cycles and designing coherent, integrated, and coordinated policies for accelerated, inclusive, and sustainable growth. The reforms that are beneficial for a country's prosperity are highly complementary with the EU integration agenda and the United Nations 2030 Agenda for Sustainable Development. Since these two agendas serve as powerful incentives for reforms, the authorities must strive to capitalize on their transformative power. A failure to implement the much-needed reforms—with or without the EU accession—may easily result in disappointment, resentment, and large-scale emigration, particularly of young people.

The approach to EU accession reforms and EU-related policies should include (but not be limited to) designing a clear roadmap, planning the accession dynamics, and focusing on implementation.

Clear roadmap. It is of critical importance for the country to have a clear reform roadmap well before the early stage of the EU accession. This roadmap must include a comprehensive estimation of the implications (benefits, costs, and trade-offs) of a wide set of coordinated policy measures with emphasis on their sequencing and optimal pace. The availability of such estimates will equip the policy makers and economic agents with tools for well-informed decisions. This roadmap will also facilitate building a culture of transparency and evidence-based policies, for ex ante planning of the adjustment costs, by both the public and business sector. The timely and well-organized preparations should also increase the absorptive capacity and preparedness of society for the upcoming reforms.

Accession dynamics matters. The accession dynamics specific to each chapter plays a crucial role. The space for maneuvering is more significant in those chapters that are more difficult to close. Even before the European Commission completes the clustering of EU negotiating chapters, action plans must be designed.

Implementation is extremely important. Any results in achieving sustainable development rely not only on adopting a legal framework such as the acquis, but also on dedicated implementation. The institutional capabilities and resources for implementation continue to be a major obstacle that must be carefully addressed if the Western Balkans are to reap the rewards of European integration.

Although the sentiment about joining the EU has varied throughout the years, the destination has remained the same over the past 30 years. Policy discussions are becoming increasingly geared toward accelerating the EU integration process, i.e. improving the economic performance, the social conditions, providing an efficient legal system, and promoting regional cooperation and connectivity. The 3-year period that followed, i.e., multiple and overlapping crises, was not a challenge that policy makers, companies, and citizens could neglect. Commitment to transparent, broad discussion and a holistic approach in the creation of new ideas and instructions about acting thereupon have become a necessity.

The EU integration of Western Balkans is a "win-win" game for both parties. On one hand, the EU would fulfill the dream of a truly united Europe, ensure prosperity on the continent, strengthen security and peace, and become a truly borderless union. On the other hand, the Western Balkans would improve the rule of law and good governance, increase trade and financial integration, speed up income convergence, and strengthen democratic consolidation.

From an EU's perspective, a closed-club strategy is not an optimal one. Even countries that were not strongly supportive of enlargement—such as Finland and Sweden—have markedly changed their sentiment. The citizens of the EU member states understand the new realities and the need for political and economic unity. Enlargement of the EU strengthens security and stability in Europe by promoting democratic governance, rule of law, and respect for human rights among member states. By offering membership prospects to countries in Eastern Europe, the EU signals its commitment to supporting their sovereignty, territorial integrity, and democratic development.

In foreseeable future, there is no viable alternative to the EU integration for the Western Balkans. A prolonged EU integration would only result in a widening income gap between the EU member states and the aspiring countries. This would fuel large-scale emigration of both skilled and non-skilled individuals and their entire families. Net emigration would continue even in the scenario of an EU expansion, but it is expected to be of a smaller magnitude, as living standards would rise faster.

Opening access to conditional pre-accession funds and expertise will enable, and require, elites to tackle a number of persistent problems. There is a strong expectation that international trade integration and net inflows of Foreign Direct Investment (friend-shoring, in particular) would increase with the expectation of significantly reduced political risk, easier access to the common market, and an improved regulatory framework.

The resulting consolidation of democracy and accelerated economic development over time would contribute to a reduction in socio-economic and regional inequalities. In a mirror image of dynamics expected in a pessimistic scenario of no integration, there is a widespread view that the EU integration would contribute to accelerated economic growth, inclusive prosperity, and sustainable development of the Western Balkans.

Obtaining a date for the opening of EU accession negotiations is seen as the first important step to create a level of certainty that can guide countries' short- and mid-term development strategy and have a positive impact on the political and socio-economic situation. Despite the lack of strong commitment on the next EU enlargement wave, the Western Balkans must continue to implement development-friendly institutional and structural reforms.

The new European Commission's four-pillar growth plan already sent a very powerful message to Western Balkans that the enlargement is back on the agenda. It comes at a difficult time of radical uncertainty and geopolitical complexities. On one hand, multiple actors have different preferences for this region and there are reform-opposing coalitions. But the citizens of Western Balkans overwhelmingly support the EU integration and the European future.

Despite numerous disappointments and hardships, EU integration remains *the* main strategic goal for all Western Balkan countries.

References

Aiyar, S, Chen J, Ebeke C, Garcia-Saltos R, Gudmundsson T, Ilyina A, Kangur A, Kunaratskul T, Rodriguez S, Ruta M, Schulze T, Soderberg G, Trevino J (2023) "Geoeconomic Fragmentation and the Future of Multilateralism", Staff Discussion Notes No. 2023/001, International Monetary Fund, Washington D.C. https://www.imf.org/en/Publications/Staff-Discussion-Notes/Issues/2023/01/11/Geo-Economic-Fragmentation-and-the-Future-of-Multilateralism-527266

Besimi F, Monastiriotis V (2019) The EU integration process of Western Balkan countries: challenges and prospects. J Balkan Near East Stud 21(5):603–620

European Commission (2023) Growth plan for the Western Balkans. https://enlargement.ec.europa.eu/enlargementpolicy/growth-plan-western-balkans_en

Gabor D (1963) Inventing the future. Secker and Warburg, London

Michel C (2023) Speech at the Bled Strategic Forum, Slovenia. https://www.consilium.europa.eu/en/press/pressreleases/2023/08/28/speech-by-president-charles-michel-at-the-bled-strategic-forum/. Accessed 18 July 2024

Mujanović J (2023) Western Balkan leaders are increasingly frustrated as Ukraine seems to be advancing faster in the EU accession process. Financial Times. https://www.ft.com/content/b654fe14-25b0-44f3-bea6-96a8596d6cde. Accessed 18 July 2024

Stojkov A, Besimi F (2024) Seizing the European Integration in a New Geopolitical Era. Iustinianus Primus Law Review 15(1):1–13. https://journals.ukim.mk/index.php/iplr/article/view/2590/2160

Strasbourg Europe (n.d.) The Schuman Declaration. Available at: https://www.strasbourg-europe.eu/the-schuman-declaration/. Accessed 18 July 2024

von der Leyen U (2023) The New Momentum for EU Enlargement. Speech at the Global Security Forum, Bratislava. https://enlargement.ec.europa.eu/news/keynote-speech-president-von-der-leyen-globsec-2023-bratislava-forum-2023-05-31_en [Accessed 18 Jul. 2024]

The manufacturer's authorised representative in the EU is Springer Nature Customer Service Centre GmbH, Europaplatz 3, 69115 Heidelberg, Germany. If you have any concerns regarding our products, please contact ProductSafety@springernature.com

Printed and bound by CPI Group (UK) Ltd, Croydon, CR0 4YY
01/10/2026
02225949-0005